The Greek Fire

A VOLUME IN THE SERIES

THE UNITED STATES IN THE WORLD

Founded by Mark Philip Bradley and Paul A. Kramer. Edited by Benjamin Coates, Emily Conroy-Krutz, Paul A. Kramer, and Judy Tzu-Chun Wu.

A list of titles in this series is available at www.cornellpress.cornell.edu.

The Greek Fire

American-Ottoman Relations and Democratic
Fervor in the Age of Revolutions

Maureen Connors Santelli

Cornell University Press
Ithaca and London

First published 2020 by Cornell University Press

Library of Congress Cataloging-in-Publication Data

Names: Santelli, Maureen Connors, 1982– author.
Title: The Greek fire : American-Ottoman relations and democratic
    fervor in the age of revolutions / Maureen Connors Santelli.
Description: Ithaca [New York] : Cornell University Press, 2020. |
    Series: The United States in the world | Includes bibliographical
references and index.
Identifiers: LCCN 2020011144 (print) | LCCN 2020011145 (ebook) |
    ISBN 9781501715785 (cloth) | ISBN 9781501715792 (epub) |
    ISBN 9781501715808 (pdf)
Subjects: LCSH: Philhellenism—United States. | United States—
    Relations—Greece. | Greece—Relations—United States. |
    Greece—History—War of Independence, 1821–1829—Foreign
    public opinion, American. | United States—Foreign relations—
    19th century. | United States—Relations—Turkey. | Turkey—
    Relations—United States.
Classification: LCC E183.8.G8 S26 2020 (print) | LCC E183.8.G8
    (ebook) | DDC 327.730495—dc23
LC record available at https://lccn.loc.gov/2020011144
LC ebook record available at https://lccn.loc.gov/2020011145

Contents

Acknowledgments

The completion of this book was made possible through the support of countless individuals. First, I would like to thank my mentors. Harry Fritz, David Emmons, and Anya Jabour of the University of Montana (UM) history department inspired me to choose nineteenth-century American history as my field of study. Their enthusiasm for the discipline and devotion to student success provided my early foundation as a historian. I also want to thank Hayden Ausland and Linda Gillison of the UM Department of Classics. Their respective zeal for Greece and Rome made it difficult for me to choose history over classics as my focus in graduate school. When I arrived at George Mason University, I soon realized that I could have the best of both worlds. At George Mason, Mack Holt, Randolph Lytton, Cynthia Kierner, and Rosemarie Zagarri helped me to bring together my interests in the classics and early America. Each of these historians inspired me in different ways, and my work has benefited from their unique historical perspectives. I owe one of the biggest debts of gratitude to my adviser, Rosie. She has inspired my growth as a scholar by providing encouragement when I most needed it while continuing to offer guidance and support. Both as a mentor and friend, she has helped make this book possible.

I was fortunate to be introduced to the United States in the World series editor Amy Greenberg, who encouraged me to submit the first draft of the manuscript to Cornell University Press. She has been enthusiastic about this project from the beginning, and that has helped me persevere through the revision process. Through Amy I met Michael McGandy, who has been an encouraging and patient editor to this first-time author. I would also like to thank those who served as readers for Cornell University Press: Emily Conroy-Krutz, Caleb McDaniel, and an anonymous historian of the Ottoman Empire. In their own ways, all pushed me to think about how different historiographies, voices, and ideas could best come together in this book.

Several friends have also played a part in the long journey toward completion of this book: Ashley and Brian Luskey provided much-needed encouragement and support during the work and challenges we all faced in simultaneously writing and raising small children. I am also indebted to my dear friends Jenny Reeder and Gwen White, who read portions of the manuscript and offered invaluable advice as to how it could be improved. These two amazing women have provided me with scholarly insight as well as friendship. Jenny was one of the first friends I made when we worked together at George Mason's Center for History and New Media. Her positive attitude is inspiring. I often think of her mantra: "Don't be bitter, be better!" I aspire to live up to that advice whenever I face a setback. Gwen was my constant companion when we served as the first George Mason University fellows at George Washington's Mount Vernon. She read one of the final versions of this book and provided invaluable feedback. I greatly appreciate all her hard work.

In addition to mentors and friends, I am also grateful for institutional and financial assistance. George Mason University awarded me a number of research, academic, and travel grants that made possible the early stages of research for this project. I would also like to thank the Library Company of Philadelphia and the Historical Society of Pennsylvania for awarding me a short-term fellowship and providing me with invaluable research assistance. The librarians helped my research expand beyond the scope of my original project, and it was at their suggestion that I first considered the influence of the Greek Revolution on American reform movements. I would also like to thank the librarians at the American Antiquarian Society, New York Historical Society, Massachusetts Historical Society, Special Collections at the College of William and Mary, and Harvard University Archives for helping me locate the writings and records of the important players and organizations in my story. Finally, I would like to thank Northern Virginia Community College for recognizing me for scholarly engagement in my field. This award helped me complete the final phase of research and writing.

Portions of chapters 2, 3, and 5 were published in "'Depart from That Retired Circle': Women's Support of the Greek War for Independence and Antebellum Reform," *Early American Studies: An Interdisciplinary Journal* 15, no. 1 (Winter 2017): 194–223; copyright 2017 by The McNeil Center for Early

American Studies, all rights reserved. Much of the material in this book was initially presented at conferences of the Society for Historians of the Early American Republic and the Society for Historians of American Foreign Relations. Each panel session generated helpful feedback from panelists and audience alike.

Last and certainly not least, I thank my family for helping me see this book to completion. My parents, Ed and Mary Connors, have been supportive the whole way. I especially thank my mother, who flew on an airplane for the first time in fifty years to come live with me and my family for two months so I could manage taking care of my toddler as well as completing the initial revision process. My sister Maggie and sister-in-law Beth have also spent many hours babysitting as I worked on this book and my husband wrote his dissertation. Maggie and Beth also provided support, friendship, and distraction when I needed it most. I want to thank my father-in-law, Jim Santelli, who with his expertise as a former historian for the Marine Corps read an early version of the book and provided helpful feedback. A special thanks to my husband, Steve, who has lived with early Americans, Greeks, and Turks for more than ten years. I have prevailed upon him to read and listen to portions of the manuscript, often late at night as we both tried to accomplish work while our toddler slept. The triumph of finishing this book belongs not just to me but also to him. Finally, a big thanks goes to the littlest person in my life, my daughter Gabrielle. For her whole life her mother has been working on this book as she quietly (and often not so quietly) played in the same room. Gabrielle has kept me grounded in the present and has helped me keep in perspective what really matters in life.

The Greek Fire

Introduction

The Spark of the Greek Fire

As James Monroe put together his seventh annual message to Congress in 1823, he was reluctant to address one issue. An ardent supporter of republics, Monroe had lately been, like much of the public, swept up in popular enthusiasm for a particular revolution then taking place: the Greek Revolution. Since 1453, when the Turks conquered Constantinople, Greece had been under the rule of the Ottoman Empire.[1] Early American public servants and intellectuals had long entertained the hope that Greece would one day gain independence, and now it seemed the moment had come at last.[2] Monroe, however, accepted the guidance of his advisers, particularly his secretary of state, John Quincy Adams, who argued that the interests of the United States did not lie in providing official government support to the Greeks. In early December, President Monroe issued his message to Congress wherein he publicly declared the United States would not provide official aid for the Greeks, even though popular opinion supported it. The public reaction to Monroe's message was instantaneous and sweeping.

From mid-December 1823 to Washington's Birthday in 1824, American communities large and small planned public events designed to financially support the Greek War of Independence. A carnival-like atmosphere energized the city of New York the week before Christmas as "a most noble and patriotic spirit" prevailed on the subject of the Greek cause. "Every body seems disposed to do something," observed the *New-York Commercial Advertiser*, "the Theatre, the Circus, the Forum and the Lions and Tigers, all give the Greeks a benefit." Philadelphia planned a "fancy dress ball" with "about one hundred

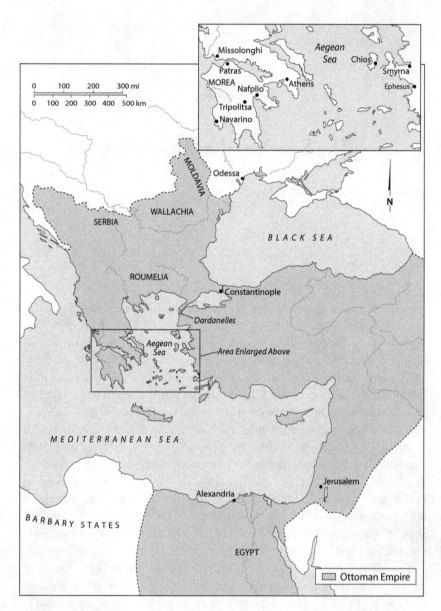

Map 1. Map of the Ottoman Empire in the eastern Mediterranean. The enlarged area is of Greece and the western coast of modern-day Turkey. The cities and ports marked on the map denote places visited by the philhellenes, merchants, missionaries, and reformers introduced in this story. Courtesy of William L. Nelson.

ladies and gentlemen" expected to attend from New York. Boston planned a similar event. Churches held special services that included sermons addressing the worthiness of the Greek cause; "Ladies, as well as gentlemen," were "respectfully solicited to attend." Citizens of Alexandria, in the District of Columbia, and Petersburg, Virginia, organized local celebrations of Washington's Birthday while also devoting special attention to raising funds for the Greeks.[3]

The sentiments that informed this fund-raising were not new. By the 1820s, Americans related their political identity to that of the ancient Greeks and expressed the hope that modern Greece might one day achieve independence. Popular American and European literature of the time portrayed the Muslim Ottoman Turks as the enemy of liberty and a font of pernicious despotism. Early Americans viewed the Ottoman subjugation of the Greeks as the equivalent to slavery, and once the revolution began there were indeed examples of Greek enslavement.[4] The Greeks, on the other hand, were seen as the heirs of an ancient political tradition of liberty and self-government. As the revolution began in 1821, the American romantic poet James G. Percival captured these sentiments: "Greeks! arise, be free, /Arm for liberty; / Men of Sparta! hear the call, / Who could never bear the thrall / Of coward Frank, or savage Turk; / From those mountains, where you lurk, / Send the voice of freedom forth."[5] Percival's poem illustrates the popular fervor for Greek nationhood that existed throughout the United States.

Percival's poem, like so many other similar pieces of popular literature printed in the early 1820s, drew on rhetoric Americans would have associated with their own revolution and urged the public to come to the Greeks' aid. The comparison resonated with American audiences throughout the country. When President Monroe made it clear that his administration would not openly support the Greek cause, the American public acted on these existing philhellenic sentiments.

Early American newspapers labeled the national outpouring of sympathy and support for the Greek cause as "The Greek Fire," a reference to a secret weapon, believed to be an early form of napalm, used by the Byzantine Empire (a medieval Greek empire) against Muslim forces.[6] Though the components of the Byzantine weapon have been lost to history, the elements of the American Greek Fire consisted of enthusiasm for the Greek cause, driven by the belief that democratic ideals bound early Americans to Greece's ancient past. One newspaper described the "Greek Fire" as "the zeal in the cause of the Greeks" that was "spreading like wild-fire throughout this country."[7] Supporters of the Greek cause defined the Greek Revolution in terms of politics, religion, race, and reform, generating such heated discussion that the Greek cause became associated with these topics throughout the antebellum era.

When the Greek Revolution began, American merchants, missionaries, and reformers had a presence in the Ottoman Empire and desired to increase their influence in the region. These American nonstate actors, or individuals who operated partly or wholly independent from the U.S. government, transmitted news of the Greek Revolution to Americans. Nonstate actors both indirectly and directly steered the early course of American foreign affairs in the eastern Mediterranean, or the Levant as it was often called. At times, these different nonstate actors worked at cross-purposes and jeopardized one another's goals in the region.

Defining the extent to which the U.S. government of the 1820s exerted or wished to exert power in the Mediterranean is a complex task. The historiography of the United States in a larger world has traditionally focused on the latter half of the nineteenth century, though historians of the early American republic have more recently challenged this paradigm. Because the U.S. government did not have an official presence in the Ottoman Empire and did not express the same kind of imperial interest in the Balkans that some of its European counterparts did, the United States was usually placed on the periphery of foreign relations in the early nineteenth century. Early Americans, both regular citizens at home and nonstate actors abroad, not only exerted influence in a larger world but also worked to increase their presence in the eastern Mediterranean. This influence complicated European, Ottoman, and American foreign and domestic affairs. The Greek Fire was a movement that pushed the borders of the early American republic into the eastern Mediterranean, infusing a global perspective into a larger conversation concerning freedom and reform that would have international as well as domestic consequences.

American Philhellenism and the Classical Tradition

The philhellenic movement originated as a transatlantic phenomenon that gained momentum from the poetry and activism of Lord Byron. Before the Greek Revolution many people in Europe as well as in the United States supported the prospect not only of a Greek nation but of all things Greek, including Greek architecture, literature, philosophy, and fashion. Supporters of an independent Greek nation embraced their cause with such fervor that they were designated "philhellenes," or lovers of Greece and Greek culture. In addition to supporting the prospect of a Greek nation in theory, some Europeans and Americans went so far as to travel to Greece, taking up arms against the Turks. Samuel Gridley Howe was one such American who joined the Greek army, forever associating his future reform and charity work with his earlier efforts in Greece. Over the course of the 1820s, relief societies began to shift their focus from military aid to assistance for Greek civilians—men, women, and children—who were the victims of war. The Greek Revolution proved to be a cause with mass appeal among political and reformist circles alike.[8]

Americans concerned themselves with the Greek cause because they felt a strong, sympathetic tie with the Greeks. American philhellenes believed the Greek Revolution would be successful if the Greeks followed the United States' example in regard to the course of the revolution and the type of government they should eventually establish. American philhellenes, both those who went to Greece to directly aid in the war effort and those who helped organize aid at the local level in the United States, hoped to influence Greek revolutionaries to create a republic. Although they were not interested in nation-building in the modern sense, American philhellenes did imagine they were engaging in a civic duty by aiding the Greeks to create a free nation in the image of the United States. From the late 1820s to at least the late 1830s, philhellenes and education reformers continued to take an interest in an independent Greece through creating new schools and sending teachers and missionaries to the region. American philhellenism became an intellectual and political avenue by which early Americans could extend their influence into the eastern Mediterranean.

Early Americans articulated their philhellenism in terms of a perceived cultural, intellectual, religious, and even racial connection to Greece.[9] Imagining the Greeks as white, or at least the Ottoman Turks as anything but, philhellenes managed to mobilize support on the basis that the Turks had historically oppressed and enslaved white Christian Greeks.[10] For early Americans this was especially poignant given that American sailors had been captured and imprisoned during the Barbary Wars. The Greek cause attracted widespread interest partly because by participating in the movement American philhellenes could assist in freeing from the Muslim Turks not only the descendants of the ancient Greeks but also modern Christian Greeks.

Long before the Greek Revolution, early Americans made distinctions between races, casting the ancient Greeks as white and part of a superior line through which white Americans were connected. Thomas Jefferson made this comparison, for example, in his *Notes on the State of Virginia*. In Query XIV Jefferson argued for the superiority of white intelligence over black. Noting that Roman families held Greek intellectuals such as Diogenes, Terence, and Phaedrus in bondage, Jefferson observed, "But they were of the race of whites. It is not their [black slaves'] condition then, but nature, which has produced the distinction." Jefferson had concluded from his own observations and experience that blacks were "inferior to the whites in the endowments of both body and mind."[11]

Classical Greek statuary was also frequently associated with ideal human beauty and reflective of white intelligence. The physicians Josiah C. Nott and George R. Gliddon, for example, published *Types of Mankind* in 1854, wherein they compared Africans' facial and skeletal features to the Apollo Belvedere, a classical statue they argued was the representation of "the perfect type of manly beauty."[12] That the Greeks were seen as white may also explain how Southerners were able to denounce the alleged enslavement of the Greeks while still advocating for the persistence of slavery in the United States. It is perhaps because of the assumed whiteness of the Greeks and the admiration felt for Greek classicism that, despite sectional tensions that flared during the Missouri Crisis, the Greek cause would at least briefly unite North and South.

The classical tradition in American politics and popular culture had a long history of its own. It was an integral part of the Enlightenment's understanding of civic duty, virtue, and defense of liberty against tyranny, and it would come to play an important role in American revolutionary rhetoric.[13] Americans imagined their society as part of the legacy of the ancient world. The ideals of classical authors were especially influential to the founding generation and served as a cornerstone for revolutionary literature and later for the foundation of a new American society and government.

After the American Revolution, the classical tradition persisted but became more democratized. Although highly educated scholars were expected to know Greek and Latin, ordinary people would learn about the classical tradition in other ways. Both Latin and Greek texts were available in English translation, and by 1820 there was growing interest in educating not only boys but girls as well. Americans of the early nineteenth century would also have encountered the classical tradition in what was known as the Grecian style, which exerted a profound influence on American art, architecture, fashion, literature, and government.[14] Thus, even nonelite American men and women would have encountered the classical tradition on a regular basis.

The United States' relationship with the Ottoman Empire also played an influential and complicated role in early American support for Greece. For most early Americans, Ottoman politics and governance were synonymous with despotism and oppression. During the process of ratification of the U.S.

Constitution, some Anti-Federalists argued that Islam was so corruptive that no Muslim could serve in political office and be completely dedicated to upholding the Constitution. In their belief that any Muslim public servant would almost certainly prove to be despotic, these Anti-Federalists favored a religious test for officeholders, although such a test was never included in the U.S. Constitution.[15] Early Americans expressed dislike for the Muslim world on the basis of religion, but by the beginning of the nineteenth century the Barbary Wars had intensified the antagonism. Contrasting their Western classical tradition with the Muslim origins of the Ottoman Empire, Americans imagined their nation as the freest country in the world and the Ottoman Empire as the most despotic. Based on intellectual, religious, and racial connections to the Greeks, early Americans devoted themselves to the Greek cause, hoping to weaken Ottoman power in the eastern Mediterranean.[16]

The rise of American philhellenism paralleled support for other revolutions of the period. Early Americans had supported the French Revolution, but they did not advocate a similar level of fund-raising for French independence. Some early Americans had, however, adopted French revolutionary styles of dress, manners of speaking, and political values.[17] Contemporaneous to the Greek Revolution, revolutions in Latin America, most notably in Venezuela led by Simón Bolívar, were also supported by a significant number of Americans. News reports kept the public informed about the progress of events in South America, and some evidence suggests that ordinary people supported these revolutions—for example, South American patriotic songs were popular, and some American children were even named "Simón Bolívar."[18] Early Americans also demonstrated interest in the Serbian Revolution, although to a lesser extent, and expressed their desire for a Serbian Christian victory over the Muslim Turks.[19] Early Americans' support for these revolutions stemmed from a deeply felt political attachment and pride in their own revolution. They believed that a republic was the best form of government and that it afforded the most freedom and liberty to individual citizens, at least insofar as a citizen was defined at the time. Moreover, there was general national enthusiasm that the idea of republicanism was spreading throughout the world.

Both Northerners and Southerners expressed a romantic idealization of Greece and articulated a perceived link between ancient Greece and the United States. These sentiments were prevalent, even though sectional tensions over slavery had solidified in national debates during the Missouri Crisis. The issue of defending the modern Greeks from Turkish slavery and oppression, however, was agreed on by both Northerners and Southerners. Philhellenes in the South seemed to have little trouble denouncing slavery in a foreign land while promoting it within their own borders. For Southerners there was no contradiction in opposing Greek slavery abroad and supporting African slavery at home. The Greeks were perceived as white, and they were also thought to be historically the victims of nonwhite oppression. In supporting the modern Greeks, Southerners not only hoped to right historical wrongs, but also aid in restoring the independence the Greeks had lost centuries before.[20] Not until after the philhellenic movement had united Americans throughout the country in a mutual effort to aid the Greeks did abolitionists point out the inherent hypocrisy in supporting the end of slavery abroad. In supporting the Greek Revolution, Americans believed they were participating in the ultimate battle for virtue and truth, which meant helping the Christian Greeks overthrow the Muslim Turks and reclaim an independence not seen since before Alexander the Great.

Source material from the period suggests that the Greek Revolution was particularly special to early Americans. This is not just a story about the extent to which early Americans supported the Greeks, however. The movement to support Greek independence provides a unique vehicle for exploring early American interests in Greece and the Ottoman Empire, the ways in which Americans believed bestowing an American identity on the Greeks would assist them in securing independence, and how these efforts influenced nineteenth-century domestic reform movements. American support for the Greek Revolution had social implications and political meanings in the United States and was not simply a nostalgic dream or a romantic indulgence. Rather, the Greek War of Independence helped early Americans to define themselves as a people and interpret the legacy of the American Revolution on an international stage.

Reformers and Merchants

Philhellenes joined efforts with benevolence and missionary groups, and together they promoted humanitarianism, education reform, and evangelism. The redemption of the Greeks by various pro-Greek organizations assumed a "secularized missionary spirit," which endeavored to spread an American understanding of freedom, liberty, and Christianity to all parts of the world.[21] By appealing to a range of social reform groups, the Greek cause enjoyed widespread support beyond the conclusion of the Greek Revolution. The classical scholar Edward Everett and the philanthropist Mathew Carey, who helped pro-

mote the Greek cause to philhellenes and social reformers, led local and national Greek relief efforts.

The effects of the Greek Revolution had domestic as well as international
ramifications. Besides inspiring a popular movement, American support for
the Greek Revolution also influenced the social reform movements of antebellum America. That the Greeks were Christian and the Turks were Muslim
was an obvious reason for Christian organizations to take an interest in the
region. Invoking their perceptions of Muslim tyranny over the Greeks, American missionaries, led by the American Board of Commissioners for Foreign
Missions, began to evangelize in Greece and the surrounding regions, spreading both their Protestant beliefs and educational reforms. As support for the
Greek cause reached its height in the late 1820s, the domestic abolitionist and
women's rights movements also began to gain momentum. The popularity of
the Greek cause as well as the rhetoric used by philhellenes to condemn Turkish oppression against the Greeks helped cultivate interest in these reforms.

Reformers who had also supported the Greek cause began to realize that
philhellenic language could potentially be useful in drawing attention to domestic reform. How could Americans, as champions of liberty in the world,
support the liberation of the Greeks when slavery persisted in the United
States? These realizations heightened the popular influence of reformist rhetoric and added impetus to these movements. Moreover, increased participation in local pro-Greek organizations was easily translated into participation
in other kinds of social reform groups. Ultimately, American popular interest
in the Greek War of Independence developed into something more than a
transient movement. By the end of the 1820s, philhellenism had become a
practical school for political action, playing a part in the rise of the abolitionist
movement and generating support for female education and women's rights.

Women's participation in the Greek Revolution provides an insight into the
evolution of antebellum social reform movements. Historians have discussed
the reasons that women became involved in abolitionist and women's rights
activism, but few have examined female involvement in the Greek war effort
and its connections to these subsequent reform activities. Women who involved
themselves in charitable societies, benevolent groups, abolitionism, and women's
rights organizations argued that participation in such activities did not represent an intervention in the male realm of politics but was simply an extension
of their feminine role in preserving the moral integrity and virtue of their
families and communities.[22] As were many men, women were sympathetic to
the Greek cause, especially after the focus shifted from military aid to civilian

assistance and educational outreach. More than other domestic reform activities, however, the Greek Revolution became a way in which female social reform could be extended abroad. Through their involvement with the Greek cause, women increasingly came to recognize the shortcomings in their own country, particularly with respect to the plight of enslaved people and the oppression of their own sex.[23]

American reformers in the eastern Mediterranean complicated the interests of yet another group present in the region. Rather than aid a rebellion against the Ottomans, American merchants advocated for a navigational treaty with the Sublime Porte, a term that refers to the central ruling authority of the Ottoman Empire. Until 1832, the United States had no official trade alliance with the Sublime Porte. Before the first commercial treaty between the United States and the Ottoman Empire, American merchants frequently acted in unofficial roles as diplomats. Ottoman officials, however, often favored the diplomatic and commercial interests of European diplomats, who were present in the region in an official capacity, over those of the United States. As a result, American merchants had to cultivate unofficial alliances with European powers, especially Great Britain, in order to make a living. David Offley, one of the first successful American merchants in the Levant, effectively acted in this capacity to protect his business interests. Offley and other American merchants sought trade agreements without the official consent of the United States, essentially acting in unofficial roles as diplomats. Consequently, these merchants helped blaze the first diplomatic and commercial trails for the United States in the region.

American merchants naturally saw their approach to both commercial trade and diplomacy through a republican lens. American merchants sought trade and commerce on "equal terms" with other countries.[24] In addition, American merchants did not see themselves as engaging in the same kind of foreign policy as their European counterparts. Devoted to commerce and navigation in the eastern Mediterranean rather than empire, American merchants struggled against other European powers that already had treaties with the Sublime Porte.[25] This strengthened the desire to conduct business based on diplomacy, not on the payment of tributes. Attempting to achieve this objective and negotiate a treaty with Ottoman officials proved to be difficult, however, given the well-known popular sentiment in favor of Greek independence.

Although the United States did not have a treaty with the Ottomans, it did have a military presence in the Mediterranean. The purpose of the U.S. Mediterranean Squadron was to protect American merchants and commercial interests from foreign powers and marauding pirates.[26] In addition, the

Mediterranean Squadron also delivered members of the philhellenic movement to the shores of Greece. For the duration of the Greek Revolution, the squadron played an intermediary role relative to the U.S. government, merchants, and philhellenes. Directly involved in the negotiations for a treaty, the squadron's association with American philhellenes complicated their official government business and jeopardized the interests of American merchants.

The sentimental bond with ancient Greece and the desire to engage in business with the Ottoman Empire played dual roles in producing the Greek Fire. Popular enthusiasm for Greece led American citizens as well as some elected officials not only to rhapsodize in favor of the Greek cause but also to send substantial amounts of material assistance to the country's beleaguered people. Muddying the waters, however, was the American government's desire to maintain official neutrality in the struggle. Merchants, in particular, pressured the U.S. government to pursue commercial ties with the Ottomans. Yet continuing calls for American intervention in the war complicated the diplomatic goal of obtaining a commercial treaty and thus created continual tension between the government's official policies and popular political sentiment.

Extending the Borders of the Early American Republic

Inspired by Rosemarie Zagarri's "global turn," I place early American support for the Greek War of Independence into a global context.[27] Historians of the early American republic have recently sought to expand their studies beyond the borders of the United States to encompass much broader frames of reference. They emphasize that the United States did not develop in isolation. The country both influenced and was influenced by other peoples and places in the world. People, goods, and ideas circulated throughout the globe. Americans imagined their society as being very much a part of a global as well as an ancient tradition.[28] Nevertheless, early Americans saw themselves as unique compared to other global powers and endeavored to project and protect that identity in the world. The Greek Fire was a movement that aided early Americans in extending their ideas into the eastern Mediterranean, but their efforts also inadvertently helped to define Americans and their flaws in the antebellum era.

This book also aims to join the growing body of scholarship contending that American foreign relations with a wider world began much earlier than has traditionally been claimed by historians. Edward Said's *Orientalism*, for example, argued that American interaction with the East was not significant until after the United States rose to global power following World War II.[29] Within American historical circles, the United States is traditionally described as developing foreign relations in the late nineteenth century.

Some historians have investigated how Americans perceived the far-off and distant Muslim world, especially through the lens of the Barbary Wars. At a moment when Americans planned to chart their own course in the Atlantic World and beyond, sailors and merchants were confronted with conflict surrounding trade routes. Many American sailors found themselves imprisoned by Barbary pirates and held for ransom. Through this conflict and subsequent literature on the subject many early Americans came to know the East and, in particular, the Ottoman Empire. These studies endeavor to expand the traditional borders of the United States and suggest that maritime contact not only aids in contextualizing the way Americans viewed the larger world but also provides another manner of thinking about early American influence in the eastern Mediterranean.[30]

Defining the nature of early American presence and interest in the eastern Mediterranean is a challenge. Early Americans were not pursuing traditional empire building on the Balkan Peninsula as other European powers were at the time. Early Americans were, however, drawn to the Ottoman Empire for commerce and reform, and they desired to impart to the region an American perspective on these subjects.

The historian Nancy Shoemaker has observed that "there is no handy label" to use when describing Americans abroad and their efforts to expand the global presence of the United States in the early nineteenth century.[31] American merchants thought of themselves as Americans abroad, merely conducting business in a foreign land while attempting to navigate, and at times influence, the local and international commercial laws and customs. Reformers and missionaries also worked to effect change while operating under the laws of a foreign land. Americans abroad endeavored to persuade peoples of these foreign lands to adopt American ideas concerning commerce and reform. Though it cannot be said that these early Americans were imperialists in the traditional sense, they were, nevertheless, attempting to build an empire of American ideas, where free trade, republicanism, and Protestant reform would have a transformative influence over foreign peoples.

In this book I address the role of early American missionaries and merchants who sought to make an impression on the peoples of the eastern Mediterranean. Historians more recently have taken up the subject of early American missionaries and diplomats, contextualizing the interest these groups had in

the East and the Ottoman Empire in particular. Some of this scholarship addresses the period of the Greek Revolution and the perceptions early Americans had toward both the Greeks and the Ottoman Turks. The American
philhellenic movement offers a lens through which we can view the early
American understanding of the East, but the book also reconstructs the influence this contact had on the development of American identity, politics, and
reform at home.[32]

In placing the American philhellenic movement in a global context, I incorporate Ottoman and European historical frameworks. The complicated political circumstances of European and Ottoman affairs in the early nineteenth
century must be taken into account to better understand the larger complica-
tions faced by early Americans as they tried to build a presence in the region.
American merchants, philhellenes, and missionaries all had their own separate
interests and goals in mind when they traveled to Ottoman shores. These goals,
however, could be easily snuffed out if they conflicted with the interests of
more powerful European players or with the political and commercial interests of the Ottoman Empire itself. European and Ottoman perspectives are
therefore an important aspect of this study.

Although this book is about American involvement in the Greek Revolution and its aftermath, it does not intend to offer new material on the Greek
Revolution itself. I have incorporated European and Ottoman historical frameworks to better illustrate the global world of which early Americans were a
part. The historical frameworks of modern Greece and Turkey are complex
and have traditionally disagreed, especially on the subject of the Greek War of
Independence. Language also presents a challenge to understanding how Greek
revolutionaries defined themselves, how they wanted to be seen by American
philhellenes, and how Ottoman officials classified them during the revolution.
Modern scholars of Greece and the Ottoman Empire have navigated these
challenges and written nuanced studies on the Greek Revolution and Ottoman reaction to it. To contrast American perspectives with Greek and Ottoman
ones, I have drawn from these secondary scholarly studies.[33]

Locating American ideas and practices in a global context provides useful
perspectives on domestic issues. The transnational nature of the philhellenic
movement brings an additional kind of insight. American attitudes toward the
persistence of the classical tradition and perceptions of the Muslim world had
a discernible influence on the growth of community-based social reform activities, the involvement of women in social reform movements, and the increasing awareness of the injustice of slavery and the oppression of women at

home and abroad. Ironically, by identifying the injustice of Turkish slavery and subordination of women it became easier for some Americans to identify the existence of similar injustices in their own country.

Organization

In the chapters that follow, I trace the origins of Americans' support for Greece, their distrust of the Ottoman Empire, the influence of this dynamic on early American identity and reform, and how these concepts evolved through the antebellum era. The chapters are organized chronologically as well as thematically, outlining conflict within the Ottoman Empire, Ottoman interaction with European actors, and how Americans attempted to fit into this already complex scene. American, European, and Ottoman characters play important roles throughout the book. I present the influence of the American philhellenic movement at the national level and also take individual regions into account. Although the role of national organizational leaders was obviously important, the movement was successful because it was sustained at the local level. When possible, I have tried to give voice to the ordinary people who donated money, supplies, and time to the Greek cause. Newspapers, committee records and receipts, and philhellenic literature have provided the primary bases for putting these stories together. The account of the origins and development of the Greek Fire describes an international event that helped early Americans articulate their differing perceptions of who they were to the rest of the world. The movement was not static, however, but rather evolved and matured with time.

Chapter 1 provides context for the years leading up to the Greek War of Independence. It traces how early Americans came to know Greece and the Ottoman Empire through popular European and American literary sources of the time. The chapter also illustrates how the Greek Revolution brought together different groups of people with very different interests. American engagement in commerce and charity on a global scale is introduced through nonstate actors such as Edward Everett, David Offley, George Bethune English, Levi Parsons, and Pliny Fisk. I discuss their respective interests in the Ottoman Empire and lay the groundwork for the later response of Americans to the Greek War of Independence. Greek as well as Ottoman perspectives are introduced, including those of the members of the revolutionary secret society Filiki Etaireia and members of the Ottoman government. Already existing conflict within the Ottoman Empire combined with European and

American interest in the region played an important role in the outbreak of the Greek Revolution and influenced how an American audience came to perceive the war.

Chapter 2 describes how Americans embraced European philhellenism and how it first evolved as a movement in the United States. Lord Byron's philhellenism and his subsequent pledge to join the Greek army particularly energized interest in the Greek cause on both sides of the Atlantic. Chapter 3 explores the evolution of the American philhellenic movement and its emergence as distinct from the European movement. An important aspect of this transition concerns the way the American philhellenic movement became an extension of benevolent organizations directed toward assisting Greek women and children instead of Greek soldiers. The chapter traces popular support for the Greek cause and illustrates how this support became more solidified through the activism of Lord Byron and the lack of official support from the U.S. government.

Chapter 4 examines the internal conflict that emerged over popular support for the Greek cause. In 1815 after the War of 1812 and the Barbary Wars ended, American merchants hoped they had finally secured the ability to freely conduct business abroad. Trade with the Ottoman Empire was especially attractive. Widespread support for Greek independence in the United States, however, caused a heated debate. Philhellenes were joined by missionaries and education reformers, each hoping to help mold the foundation of a new Greek nation-state. With the American government communicating one message to the Ottomans, and the actions of the American public communicating another, the interests of all sides came into question.

A discussion of the masterpiece of the American sculptor Hiram Powers, *The Greek Slave*, opens chapter 5, which addresses the way popular support for the Greeks changed political rhetoric in America, specifically in antislavery and women's rights circles. Even though Americans characterized Ottoman slavery as a mark of despotism, before 1821 few Americans connected Ottoman slavery with American slavery. Slavery inflicted on Americans taken captive by North African states, which were loosely connected with the Ottoman Empire, dominated anti-Ottoman discussion throughout the Barbary Wars and was an important way the American public identified the Turks as tyrannical and despotic. By the close of the Greek Revolution, abolitionist authors, however, began to read philhellenic rhetoric against the grain, calling upon antebellum American audiences to do the same. Many Americans came to realize the contradiction in supporting reform on the other side of the world while similar problems existed at home, particularly with regard to slavery and women's rights.

*   *   *

By understanding popular American support for the Greek War of Independence in a global context, it is possible to gain a new perspective on several domestic issues. Much of what early Americans knew about the Ottoman Empire was understood through existing stereotypes. Americans also had strong opinions concerning their view of their own country in comparison. Familiarity with the classics gave Americans a strong visceral connection to Greece. While the Greek cause did not begin as an effort to reflect on American society's shortcomings, as time passed, antebellum reformers began to use these existing perspectives to turn domestic issues on their head. American debate about the Greek Revolution was more than just a disagreement about what happened on the other side of the world: it influenced early Americans' view of themselves. Examining American support for the war in this light, the abolitionist Franklin Benjamin Sanborn reflected on the significance of the Greek War of Independence in the United States. He concluded that the eventual abolition of slavery in the United States had "begun in Greece" and culminated "in our American Civil War."[34] In rejecting Ottoman slavery and oppression of women, abolitionists and women's rights activists called on Americans to reaffirm their commitment to liberty as a fundamental value shared as much by their own country as by ancient Greece.

Chapter 1

Americans, Greeks, and Ottomans before 1821

American merchant David Offley first established a commercial house in the bustling Turkish city of Smyrna in 1811.[1] Though Offley had expected building his new business in the Ottoman Empire to be a challenge, he was surprised by the friendships he had cultivated within the local community. Forming such friendships, however, sometimes gave family at home cause for concern. "Turned Turk" or "taken the turban" were contemporary phrases used by Western Christians to describe those who had abandoned their faith and converted to Islam.[2] Early Americans and Western Europeans expressed fear of such a transformation in those who encountered Muslims or immersed themselves in lands dominated by the faith. Writing to his sister in 1818, Offley teased that his enthusiasm for the company of the locals had led her to "believe me to be a Turk." He acknowledged to his sister, "With my Turks and Turkish principles, I am like to fill up my letter, & perhaps to a good Christian, so much praise of Infidels may look too much like Infidelity."[3] Offley's enthusiasm for local customs was not just born out of a cultural interest, however. An understanding of local culture and business practices, Offley believed, would assist him in the success of his commercial house.

Despite his sister's concerns, Offley continued to relate to her that he had developed a respect and admiration for many Muslim locals he had encountered, referencing several occasions of hospitality "that astonished even me." Offley also explained that he had begun to earn the respect of Ottoman officials, whose favor he required in order to continue to build his business connections in the region. While at Constantinople, he had received unusual and flattering attention from several Turkish high officials, which led him to conclude that his hard work had begun to pay off. "The name of American is becoming a title of respectability," he explained to his sister, and "ere long, to be a Citizen of the Republic of America will excite as much attention as ever was received by a Roman." Though Offley did not intend to draw a comparison between the imperial successes of ancient Rome, he did envision the United States as one day holding a globally significant place among other major commercial powers of his time.

American interest in the Ottoman Empire and its domains was in part inspired by global efforts to intervene in a declining Ottoman state. By the beginning of the nineteenth century, the Ottoman Empire increasingly had become a pawn in a much larger European struggle for dominance and power. This was both in terms of potential territorial expansion into the Balkan Peninsula, as well as access to trade with the Sublime Porte, the central ruling authority of the Ottoman Empire. Russia, Britain, and France were among the more dominant European nations with interests in the Ottoman Empire. To their consternation, the United States began to make official efforts in the early nineteenth century to gain access to trade with the Sublime Porte. Ottoman officials frequently felt pressure from these European powers, but if an alliance with the United States would benefit its own interests, the Sublime Porte was willing to entertain such a relationship. Merchants such as David Offley played a pivotal role in these negotiations.

David Offley's reference to ancient Rome in his letter to his sister would have been considered random neither to his sister nor to his contemporaries. In the early years of the United States, the patriots of the American Revolution and the framers who wrote the U.S. Constitution looked to a classical past rooted in the ancient Roman Republic rather than in ancient Greece. The founding generation preferred republics to democracies, believing that a republican form of government best preserved the public good through the representation of a virtuous citizenry. Democracies, on the other hand, were thought of as unpredictable and susceptible to mob rule. References to the Roman Republic would have still been in the ascendancy when Offley wrote home to his sister, and she would have understood that her brother meant that he desired to achieve the same kind of success as associated with the Romans.

Yet the classical tradition in America was not static. The development of a republican tradition inspired at first by Rome eventually gave way to a Grecian influence in the early nineteenth century. The infusion of Greece into the American classical tradition expanded the appeal of the classical world beyond educated elites and made the ancient world more accessible to the masses. Where the founding generation drew a distinction between Roman and Greek political thought in the eighteenth century, Americans of the nineteenth century increasingly viewed the classical tradition as a melding of both Greek and Roman traditions. After around 1800, Americans moved away from exclusive interest in the Roman Republic and came to a larger, albeit sentimental, appreciation of ancient Greece. In fact, a demand for Greek fashions, architecture, and literature swept through popular culture in both Europe and the United States. This change influenced how the American public viewed civic duty and political activism by the 1820s.[4]

For many Americans in the 1820s, the Greeks were the descendants of an ancient people who had provided the cornerstone of American government and society but had come to be oppressed by the Ottoman Turks, a group of people that represented the antithesis of everything the United States was not. In addition, early Americans frequently described the Greeks as being white or claimed that the Turks were of a separate race, referencing their nonwhite as well as non-Christian status in American society. This contrast was frequently reaffirmed through contemporary literature and travel narratives.

American philhellenism was at first derived from European origins but became a separate creature by the 1820s. More than just an intellectual movement, American philhellenism was inspired in part by American contact with the Ottoman Empire and the Barbary States, not only through military conflict but also from early missionary interests and commercial trade. As American merchants initially struggled to find autonomy in commercial markets dominated by European powers, they discovered a love for the East as well as a dread of Muslim pirates.

American philhellenism also influenced some of the early interest in expanding into the eastern Mediterranean as well. American missionaries saw Western Asia, as it was frequently called, as a prime location to spread the gospel not only because of the presence of Islam but also because they perceived the Greeks as being especially deserving of salvation from the Turks. At about the same time David Offley wrote his sister optimistically about the expansion of American commerce in the Levant, the American Board of Commissioners for Foreign Missions (ABCFM) had raised funds and organized its first mission to that part of the world. Ironically, such a mission was made possible by the religiously tolerant Ottoman government. As long as Christian missionaries did not interfere with the operations of the Ottoman government, they were able to move freely within the Levant, distributing Bibles and other religiously educational literature.[5] Armed with Bibles and commercial ledgers, early Americans entered Western Asia in the early nineteenth century.

The Global Political Circumstances of the Ottoman Empire

By the late eighteenth century, the Ottoman Empire's expansive empire had been contracting for more than one hundred years. The Ottoman Empire first emerged under the rule of Turkish leader Osman I, who became sultan in 1300. Early Americans often referred to Muslims living within the Ottoman Empire as "Turks." By the eighteenth century, however, the original Ottoman family who founded the empire had intermarried with neighboring groups of people for centuries and was thus no longer the same Turkic group that had founded the empire. The word "Turk" came to be synonymous with "Muslim" by the sixteenth and seventeenth centuries and was used by eastern and western Europeans alike. In reality, the Ottoman Empire was multiethnic. While the government was an Islamic theocracy, it was also multireligious.[6] In 1453 after the Ottomans overthrew the Byzantine capital, Constantinople, the sultan's palace was also placed in this location. As the empire expanded over time, territorial governors, or pashas, residing in places such as Egypt and Algiers managed the power and influence of the Ottoman Empire as regencies.[7]

The Ottoman military defeat at Vienna in 1683 marked the beginning of the initial decline in Ottoman power.[8] The rise of European powers during the seventeenth and eighteenth centuries, especially Russia, threatened the stability and strength of the Ottoman Empire.[9] After a century of problems, the Ottomans suffered yet another setback when Napoleon Bonaparte invaded Egypt in 1798, beginning a period of struggle to keep this territory under Ottoman control.

By the time of the Greek Revolution, the Ottoman Empire's ability to assert itself against European powers had declined not just commercially and politically but intellectually as well. Sultan Mahmud II (r. 1808–1839), who ascended to the throne in the midst of internal political conflict and rebellion, had a difficult situation on his hands. For example, Ottoman officials increasingly felt pressure from European powers to submit to unequal commercial agreements. In addition, the influence of the Enlightenment and ideals of the French Revolution had mobilized a desire for reform throughout the multiethnic Ottoman Empire. While Mahmud II desired to exercise more influence and power over his court, he and his government simultaneously had to deal with several groups of subjects in rebellion in addition to the European and American actors with interests in the Levant. The Greek Revolution, in many ways, became the moment when the Ottoman Empire was forced to grapple with European concepts of nationalism and modernization.[10]

There were also internal conflicts within the Ottoman Empire. The janissaries, which had once been a formidable fighting force, became a liability by the eighteenth century, threatening the sultan's ability to rule effectively.[11] Traditionally, sultans looked to the past for guidance when faced with internal conflict and corruption, but the late eighteenth century marked a transitional moment when sultans looked for reformist ideas in the West. Interest in Westernization first stemmed from the obviously superior technology in the militaries of Europe, especially in France. In addition, France was the traditional ally of the Ottoman Empire, dating back to the sixteenth century under King Francis I and Sulieman the Magnificent. This traditional alliance, combined with the desire to reform, made French military advancements obvious ones to emulate. The janissaries viewed military reform as a threat to their interests and power, frequently overthrowing sultans who tried to implement such reforms. Sultan Ahmet III (r. 1703–1730), for example, risked angering his janissaries for the sake of incorporating elements of Western military reform. Though Ahmet III's efforts at Westernization ultimately failed, subsequent wars with Russia in the late eighteenth century convinced future sultans that European-style military reform was a necessity.[12]

Another problem the sultan increasingly faced was the loss of political supremacy within his empire as regional governors, pashas or deys, threatened his authority. Beginning in 1721, Ahmet III and his grand vizier, Ibrahim Pasha, negotiated power with the sultan's pashas in a manner similar to what Louis XIV had done at Versailles with his subordinate officials. During what became known as the Tulip Period, Ahmet III tried to negotiate power over his pashas through a display of mass consumption, which included not only the cultivation of tulips but also art, cooking, luxury goods, clothing, and the building of large palaces.[13] Ahmet III positioned himself at the center of a consumptive performance, attempting to dominate the social center of the Ottoman Empire as a model to emulate. This method of soliciting allegiance worked, at least for the time being, as the sultan and his pashas sought to both enhance and legitimize their political statuses.[14] The sumptuous consumption and extravagance in the Ottoman court also influenced European aesthetic taste in the eighteenth and nineteenth centuries. For Ahmet III, however, this approach proved ineffective, eventually costing him the throne at the hands of the janissaries.

Western ideas of nationhood and revolution also threatened the sultan's authority. Greece had long been a part of the Ottoman Empire. Prior to the revolution, Greek subjects, or *reaya*, were classified as *zimmis* (protected minorities) within the Islamic state. Under this status, it should be noted that the

Greeks could not be enslaved. Only through rebellion or support of a belligerent power against the Islamic state could the Greeks be put to death or enslaved. In return for their accepted subordinate status they were granted freedom of worship and of property.[15]

Clergy within the Orthodox Church, headed by the patriarch in Constantinople, aided the sultan in his exercise of power over Christian reaya within the empire. Through administering the power of the sultan, church clergy also ensured their own ideological and political interests, making them collaborators in the administration of the empire and the sultan's power within it.[16] While some members of the clergy supported the revolution, as a whole they supported the authority of the sultan and condemned the actions of the Greek revolutionaries. Even the patriarch, who was executed after the initial Greek uprising, had not supported the rebels.

Rhetoric showing a transition from reaya to Hellenes, a term that came to be associated with Greek identity and nationalism, began to emerge at the end of the eighteenth century and was largely promulgated by Greek intellectuals and merchants. Many of these individuals hailed from elite Greek families, or the Phanariotes, who traditionally had served in Ottoman administrative positions. The Enlightenment in Europe, especially in France, inspired ideas concerning Greek nationalism and a secular sense of Greece's historical origins.[17] There are numerous examples of both European and American intellectuals opining that it was especially unfortunate that the modern Greeks lived under the rule of the Ottomans, given that ancient Greece had imparted such a large influence over the Western world. For example, while in France Thomas Jefferson met a Greek Enlightenment figure named Adamantios Korais (Jefferson referred to him as "Coray"). Though Korais's aspirations for an independent Greek nation were inspired by Europe's new nationalism, he looked to Greece's ancient past in order to build a foundation for his nationalist rhetoric.[18] Inspired by Korais's views, Jefferson wrote several times to friends at home in the United States on the subject of ancient Greek history and the possibility of Greek independence.[19] Many more Europeans supported the transition from subjects to Hellenes, perhaps most famously Lord Byron, who joined the Greek revolutionaries at the start of the war.

The spread of Enlightenment ideals did not take place on a widespread scale in Greece as it had in Europe and the United States due to a lack of access to printing and education. Nevertheless, after the start of the French Revolution, Greek intellectuals began to articulate a desire for citizenship status within a Greek nation-state rather than Christian subject status under the sultan. Liberty as a secular idea steeped in modernism and the Enlightenment became the radical political ideology that inspired not only Greek revolutionaries to take up arms against the Turks but also Europeans and Americans with similar ideas on liberty.[20]

Though the origins of the Greek Revolution have been discussed traditionally in terms of religious conflict, Greek Enlighteners cultivated European support for the uprising on an intellectual as well as geopolitical level. The European philhellenic movement was largely spurred on by secular ideas concerning freedom as well as European interest in a declining Ottoman Empire. While Greek Enlighteners desired independence for Greece, the conflict became a focal point of European anxiety as well as ambition. European concern over French revolutionary ideology eventually brought the more conservative European powers of Austria, Prussia, Russia, and Britain together. These European powers, though agreed on the need to limit revolution in Europe, also were in competition with one another, each concerned over who might benefit in the Balkans as the Ottoman Empire contracted.[21] For these reasons, European powers, led especially by Klemens von Metternich of Austria, desired to keep the sultan as the legitimate sovereign in power and discourage revolution within the Ottoman Empire. To some extent, Greek Enlighteners directed popular European interest in Greek independence for their own purposes, cultivating existing philhellenic sentiments in order to garner European support for the Greek cause.[22]

In 1814, Greek Enlighteners founded the Filiki Etaireia (Society of Friends) and effectively set into motion the revolution that broke out against the Turks six years later.[23] Founded as a secret society for the purpose of overthrowing the rule of the Ottoman Empire within the Balkans, this group introduced the Greek population to the concept of liberty as defined by nineteenth-century nationalism. Greek identity before this time was more closely associated with one's family and village, where Greeks understood themselves in a larger sense to be Christian reaya of the Ottoman Empire. The Filiki Etaireia provided the bridge from the Greek identity as Christian reaya to that of Greek citizen.

The members of this secret society were largely from the Greek merchant and aristocratic classes living within Greece and throughout the Ottoman Empire. These Greek aristocratic families, or the Phanariotes, had traditionally exercised influence and power within the Ottoman political system. This began to change as the power of the Ottoman state deteriorated. The sultan's loss of power over regional governors such as Ali Pasha of Ioannina and Mohammad Ali of Egypt, as well as the earlier rebellion in Serbia, contributed to the declining influence of *reaya* within the Ottoman state. Many of the Phanariotes, especially merchants, believed their social status as reaya within the

Ottoman Empire affected how far they could advance themselves socially and financially. The internal conflict of the Ottoman state combined with nationalist ideology helped spark the initial momentum for revolution in Greece.[24]

The organization of the Filiki Etaireia was influenced by British Freemason secret societies and like-minded Greek independence societies throughout Europe. These earlier groups were founded by Greek expatriates and European enthusiasts who were focused on preserving Greek antiquities and promoting Greek education. Several of these groups were initially established outside of Greece, including the Hellenophone Hotel in Paris in 1809, the Society of Friends of the Muses of Athens in 1813, and the Society of Friends of the Muses in Vienna in 1814.

Interestingly, Ioannis Capodistrias, a Greek by birth and a member of the Russian foreign service, helped to establish the Vienna society with the approval of Tsar Alexander I himself as the Congress of Vienna convened. Though the Congress of Vienna was intended to prevent the spread of revolution in Europe, Russia's interest in a declining Ottoman Empire was strong enough that the tsar at least fleetingly supported the idea of Greek independence. The tsar supported a pro-Russian influence over the Greek diaspora in favor of countering the already existing British influence within Athens. Capodistrias later joined the Filiki Etaireia and toured Europe to generate support for Greek independence.[25]

The three founders of the Filiki Etaireia were not part of the Greek aristocracy but rather of the merchant class, a point that shows the influence of Greek nationalism and European Enlightenment ideas outside of elite intellectual circles in Greece.[26] Nikoalos Skoufas, Athanasios Tsakaloff, and Emmanuel Xanthos met in the Russian city of Odessa in 1814 and formed the Society of Friends as an organization inspired by Greek nationalism with the view of advancing Greek independence from the Ottomans. Membership within the society grew over the following years, attracting Greeks from within Greece itself as well as from the Greek diaspora within nearby Ottoman provinces.[27] Capodistrias later joined the organization but refused to assume its leadership. Alexandros Ypsilantis, a member of a prominent Phanariot family with Russian imperial connections, assumed the leadership role instead. Ypsilantis's leadership of the Filiki Etaireia and his role in the early phase of the Greek Revolution caught the attention of American and European philhellenes alike.

Greece became a center of both European and American interest due not only to the declining power of the Ottoman Empire but also to the growing Enlightenment sentiments inspired by the French Revolution. A British philhellenic presence was already established in Greece with the organization of the Society of Friends of the Muses of Athens in 1813. The purposes of the society were to preserve antiquities, support schools for Greeks in Athens, and provide scholarships for Greeks to study at European universities. The society also provided a means for infiltration of English policy within Greece against a French cultural presence.[28] European powers including the British, French, Austrians, and Russians all shared commercial and political interests in the Ottoman Empire, a fact that dominated European affairs throughout the nineteenth century. Greece, in part because it was a subject region within the Ottoman Empire but also because it was viewed as the ancestral origin of Western civilization, attracted cultural as well as economic interest from among the major European powers. The United States, desiring a place within the international political and commercial stage, also shared similar interests in Greece and the Ottoman Empire. These interests translated not only into heated international competition but also internal debate.

The Classical Tradition in Early America

The origins of the American philhellenic movement can be traced to the revolutionary era when an interest in the Roman Republic prevailed over that of ancient Greece. The classical tradition in revolutionary America saturated the political language of the time and was an integral part of the popular culture. Early American public discourse reflected an expectation of classical knowledge through copious references to ancient history and literature, with repetitive calls for republican virtue as a safeguard against tyranny. Men and women of the middle class would have gained a familiarity with the classics either by reading them in translation or through popular references.[29]

Though not all early Americans were literate, a large percentage of Americans, especially men, were literate and had access to printed materials. Literacy for both men and women increased over the course of the eighteenth century. This phenomenon was especially pronounced in New England, but there is also evidence of improved literacy rates in locations with less population density and few schools, such as North Carolina. Scholars define the literate in the eighteenth century as those who could sign their will rather than make a mark. The literacy rate for New England men in the postrevolutionary period was approximately 90 percent, whereas one study conducted on Perquimans County, North Carolina, indicates a literacy rate for men of 79 percent. Literacy for women was lower, but it increased steadily over the course of the eighteenth century. Some studies suggest female literacy in New England at the time of the revolution was as low as 45 percent, while others believe it was as high as 90 percent.[30]

Early Americans could become active participants in the public discourse merely by reading or even hearing about political current events.[31] This was largely made possible through the availability of printed materials. In 1760 there were fewer than twenty newspapers published in colonial America, but by 1820 there were more than 575.[32] The increasing number of printing presses meant that people were able to obtain printed materials more easily and cheaply than previous generations were. Political writers addressed their writing "to an elite, middling, or plebeian audience. Once their texts entered the public sphere, however, authors no longer controlled how they were read."[33]

The use of the classical tradition was prevalent in political writing for all levels of literate society and became an integral part of the vocabulary of the revolutionary and postrevolutionary period. Most public opinion articles of the postrevolutionary period were signed with classically inspired pseudonyms, such as Brutus, Cassius, or Publius. The use of these pseudonyms reflects the obsession early Americans had for "spotting the early warning signs of impending tyranny," which their classical heroes had failed to avoid. These pseudonyms also served as a rhetorical tool that aided the authors in advancing their arguments.[34] It is also likely, given the prevalence of the classical tradition in political literature of the period, that even illiterate individuals could gather at least some cursory understanding of the classics by interacting with literate individuals at public meeting places.

In addition to political identity, the classical tradition also inspired the naming of new towns in the early American republic. By 1820, at least eighty-two towns in New York were given classically inspired names, including Cicero, Tully, and Cato. Ohio already had at least thirty-six classically named towns, and by midcentury there were at least ninety more. Cincinnati, Ohio, named for a Roman farmer who turned down the chance to become king, is perhaps the most well-known of these classically named cities.[35] The use of classically inspired town names was a national phenomenon. In 1820 there were over 170 towns across the United States that used classical nomenclature, and by midcentury there were at least 830 more.[36] The use of such names reveals that many Americans had a familiarity with the ancient classics of Greece and Rome and were eager to appropriate this legacy for their new society.

The importance of the classical tradition to Americans of the early nineteenth century can also be found in both formal and informal early American education. At the close of the eighteenth century, the classics became more accessible for students with the advent of classical sources translated into English.[37] By the 1820s, education in America had changed significantly. The expanded access to printed materials transformed American curriculum and made education obtainable for children outside of elite circles.[38] Not only were more young American boys learning about the classics through a formal education, but young girls were also. Found throughout the United States, academies for girls advertised the teaching of both Greek and Latin. Elites were especially interested in their daughters obtaining at least some knowledge of the classics for personal reasons, not because the girls were preparing for college. By the early nineteenth century, classical texts were even more accessible through new English translations, which were read by both male and female students.[39]

The presence of the classical tradition in popular culture and politics indicates that to contemporaries the classics were integral aspects of what it meant to be an American citizen. Americans of the early republic saw themselves as part of an ancient tradition of freedom and liberty as found within a self-governing community. At the same time, Americans saw themselves as different from other nations of the world: they were citizens of a thriving republic. This American identity rooted in a classical heritage made the European philhellenic movement palatable for early Americans.

Despite the predominance of ancient Rome in the founding era, many American men and women became increasingly interested in Greece in an intellectual as well as popular sense by the beginning of the nineteenth century. The classical tradition took on a more exotic flair due in part to archaeological discoveries in the Mediterranean. Most notably, Napoleon's conquest of the Mediterranean at the turn of the nineteenth century and Thomas Bruce, Earl of Elgin's acquisition in 1812 of the Parthenon Marbles from Ottoman officials in Athens captivated the imaginations of Europeans and Americans alike. Archaeological discoveries were brought back to Europe and put on display in museums and private homes and relayed to Americans through printed materials.

One of the most noticeable shifts from a preference for things Roman to Greek can be discerned through the rising popularity of the "Grecian" style.[40] Popularized by Napoleon's regime, the Grecian style had distinctive aesthetic qualities that combined classical Greece and Rome with an exotic, Oriental flair due to the inclusion of modern Greece under Ottoman rule.[41] The exoticism of the East with its supposed incredible wealth captured the imaginations of merchants and rural farmers alike.[42] Even though the Grecian style often reflected an opulent, exotic flair, it also was defined as possessing simplicity with "moneyed minimalism" and "opulent austerity" intended to illustrate the permanence and majesty of ancient Greece.[43] Classically inspired architecture, painting, sculpture, costume and furniture design, as well as popular literature, reflected both European and American interest in the ancient Mediterranean.[44] In the midst of a rising middle class in the early nineteenth century, Americans sought to obtain classically inspired items in order to acquire the refinement of the upper classes.[45]

The rising interest in Greece coincided with the rise of romanticism, ideals that placed ancient Greece as the origin of political liberty and democracy, thereby emphasizing a desire to revive that tradition. The popularity of the Grecian style increased in the nineteenth century because its greater ornateness was emblematic of refinement and status. With the emergence of the middling class in the United States in the early nineteenth century, classically inspired items in homes expanded beyond the stark republican model of the eighteenth century to encompass a more elaborate and luxurious tradition. By the beginning of the nineteenth century, Americans increasingly were beginning to see their own country as a new Greece. As a result of these sentiments, popular interest in the United States began to shift away from the exclusively Roman Republican tradition and to include a heavy dose of ancient Greece.[46]

Aside from a romanticized view of ancient Greece, modern Greece also entered the popular consciousness. American literature from the 1790s indicates that Americans favored Greek independence. It was well known to literate Americans even by the 1790s that the power of the Ottoman Empire was faltering in some of its territories, and therefore they could not fathom why the Greek people had not yet initiated a revolution against the Turks.[47]

Examples of sympathy for the Greeks can be found in popular literature as early as the late eighteenth century. Hugh Henry Brackenridge wrote in his 1793 novel *Modern Chivalry*, through his character Captain Farrago, "O Poetic and philosophic country, where my mind ranges every day; whence I draw my best thoughts; where I converse with the schools of wise men, and solace myself with the company of heroes, thou art lost in servitude, and great must be the revolution which can extricate thee thence."[48] Brackenridge summed up the romantic vision early Americans had of ancient Greece, contrasting references to Homeric heroes with the supposed servitude the modern Greeks were subjected to under Ottoman rule. Brackenridge's language is also suggestive of the superiority many early Americans felt toward the modern Greeks. Either the modern Greeks would have to be roused to independence, or a people with revolutionary experience would have to assist them. This novel was widely read in the United States and illustrates the philhellenic sentiment already in place in the late eighteenth century.

Public opinion toward Greece was also shaped in part by a new pedagogy in the classics. German classicists were increasingly moving away from the old, memorization approach and instead embracing a new philological approach, which consisted of studying not only language but also classical literature, philosophy, and art as a means for more fully appreciating the Greek and Roman civilizations. The German school of thought was so popular at the beginning of the nineteenth century that Harvard hired a young scholar of Greek literature in 1815 to a newly endowed post using a $20,000 donation from a Boston merchant. This position not only included teaching duties but also required the professor to give lectures to both students and the public on "the genius, structure, characteristics, and excellence of the Greek language." He was also required to "cultivate and promote the knowledge of the Greek language and of Greek literature" so that "the University may send out alumni who possess a discriminating knowledge of the renowned productions of Grecian authors, and the powers of the Grecian language."[49] This young scholar was Edward Everett, a man who went on to make a name for himself as a great orator and politician as well as an active supporter of the Greek War of Independence.

While American taste for the classics followed similar popular European trends, the fervor for Greek independence among Americans took on even greater significance due to the recentness of their own revolution.[50] Americans admired many of the famous European philhellenes such as Lord Elgin and Lord Byron. However, Americans believed they possessed a special bond with the Greeks because of the connections they saw between American liberty and Greece as the ancient source of liberty in the Western world. With Edward Everett in a national leadership role of the American philhellenic movement, along with other philanthropists such as Philadelphia printer Mathew Carey, humanitarian and doctor Samuel Gridley Howe, and American volunteers in the Greek army Jonathan Peckham Miller and George Jarvis, popular support for the Greeks in the United States evolved into a distinctive form during the 1820s.

Muslims in the American Imagination

Early American attitudes toward the Ottoman Empire and Islam evolved over several decades leading up to the Greek Revolution. Some of the earliest conversations concerning whether Muslims could become full American citizens first took place in a hypothetical sense during the debates over the ratification of the Constitution. The new Constitution did not require a religious test, allowing for the possibility that future officeholders could be Catholic, Jewish, or "infidel," a point that drew objections from New England to the lower south.[51] For many Americans, Muslims were incapable of giving full allegiance to the American republic, not just because they were not Christians but because they were thought to be primarily subservient to Mohammed. Catholics were considered to be no better than Muslims because of their allegiance to the pope. Those in favor of ratifying the Constitution without a religious test, however, dissented. In North Carolina, for example, the lack of a religious test generated lively debate wherein those in favor of ratification observed that to include a religious test would damage the principle of religious freedom and open the door to persecution.[52] The states eventually ratified the Constitution despite the fact that Anti-Federalists had fears about the future inclusion of Muslims, Catholics, Jews, and Pagans into American society and government.[53]

Early American contact with the Muslim world became less abstract during the Barbary Wars. The Barbary States of North Africa, composed of Morocco, Algiers, Tunis, and Tripoli, dated to the sixteenth century. Algiers, Tunis, and Tripoli paid loose allegiance to the Ottoman Empire, while Morocco was an independent kingdom. The name "Barbary States" was given by Europeans to these North African provinces. Early Americans primarily associated the Barbary States with conflict between American sailors and Barbary pirates.

The Barbary States did not initially set out to make piracy and tribute the center of their economy; this practice developed over time. The contracting power of the Ottoman Empire meant that its regencies also increasingly lost influence in world trade, making piracy an attractive method of accumulating wealth.[54] Leaders of the Barbary States also were required to pay tribute to the sultan. By demanding tribute from Europeans to pass safely through the Mediterranean, these leaders could fulfill obligations to the sultan while also strengthening their own power base at home. The young United States also found itself vulnerable to pirate attacks, which ultimately influenced future commercial and diplomatic contact in the Mediterranean.

Prior to independence, American merchants had benefited from British protection in the Mediterranean. After independence, because the United States was no longer part of the imperial system, the British were less willing to protect American commerce, especially when tensions rose over international trade. American merchants were forced to pay fees to the British in order to receive this protection—fees that were of course set by the British themselves. Operating under a mercantilist understanding of economics, the British viewed trade competition as a potential threat to their balance of power.

Therefore, Great Britain hoped to continue to regulate and even diminish American trade by refusing to protect it.[55]

The conflict between the United States and the Ottoman Empire began in 1784 when Barbary pirates seized the first of many American ships. By the mid-1790s there were more than a hundred American sailors who had been captured and sold into slavery by Algiers.[56] Like European powers seeking access to the lucrative Mediterranean trade system, Americans were expected to pay tribute to the Barbary States in exchange for safe passage. The United States held that it was against its principles to pay tribute in order to establish commercial trade in the Mediterranean. Instead, American leaders believed that trade should be open to all nations on an equal basis.[57]

George Washington viewed the Barbary pirates as "barbarians." While he would have preferred to punish the Barbary States for imprisoning American sailors, he observed that the new nation lacked the means for inflicting such punishment. In a letter to Marquis de Lafayette, Washington admitted he did not understand "the policy by which the Maritime powers" had acted, and he thought it reflected the "highest disgrace on them to become tributary to such a banditti who might for half the sum that is paid them be exterminated from the Earth."[58] In 1796, the United States finally was able to pay the required ransom of $800,000 to free its citizens from Algiers while also negotiating peace with Tunis and Tripoli. Conflict, however, continued during the Adams administration, with Adams paying tribute in order to avoid war.[59]

Thomas Jefferson proposed a different approach to foreign relations in the Mediterranean. Jefferson had been vocal as early as 1784 in his views that the United States should not pay tribute to the Barbary States. He was convinced that paying tribute would not "render the pirates of Barbary more docile to receive propositions for Peace."[60] In 1801 the pasha of Tripoli, Yusuf Qaramanli, demanded a greater price to maintain the peace established in the 1796 treaty. After negotiations failed, Yusuf ordered that the flagstaff bearing the American flag at the consulate in Tripoli be cut down, and he declared war on the United States.[61]

While the pasha requested payment of several hundred thousand dollars to reestablish peace, Jefferson believed that a naval deployment against Tripoli would be less expensive than continuing to pay tribute and run the risk of only perpetuating conflict in the Mediterranean.[62] The third president strategized that the United States would ultimately avoid warfare by demonstrating its naval power through an occupation of the Tripoli harbor. Jefferson sent Yusaf a letter on May 21, 1801, informing him that while the United States desired "to cultivate peace & commerce with your subjects," Jefferson "found it expedient to detach a squadron of observation into the Mediterranean sea, to superintend the safety of our commerce there & to exercise our seamen in nautical duties."[63]

Even though the United States successfully negotiated peace with Tripoli in 1805, conflict with the Barbary States did not end. Just one month after the War of 1812 began, Algiers refused to accept the annual tribute paid by the United States and demanded a cash payment instead. With British cooperation, Algiers was able to extract this additional sum and subsequently blocked American trade in the Mediterranean for the duration of its war with England.[64] By 1815, England's wars with the United States and Napoleon eventually meant a decreased ability to provide the support promised to Algiers. Algiers itself faced internal political turmoil due to a series of coups and assassinations. Peace was negotiated, and Algiers paid restitution to the United States on July 4, 1815.[65]

The American public did not overlook the fact that the peace with Algiers was signed on July 4. Americans celebrated the triumph of American trade in both the Mediterranean and the Atlantic. This confirmed for many Americans that their own republican views would overcome tyranny wherever it was encountered. One Albany paper wrote that the American navy was "now proud to display that insignia of American glory and freedom in every part of the world." Although small, the navy had "in one week relieved us from the degradation of paying tribute to barbarian Algiers."[66] Another New York paper observed that the Americans concluded the war with Algiers in a "manner as honourable to themselves, as it must be disgraceful, by comparison, to those mighty European powers, who have so long remained tributary to the pirates of Africa. Millions for defence, not a cent for tribute." This motto will be "engraved on the tomb of Algerine pride."[67] This patriotic fervor originating against the Barbary States would remain vital into the 1820s.

In addition to trade, many American merchants and missionaries feared that the rise of Islam posed a threat to Anglo-American Protestant Christianity. The religion of their Eastern adversaries, in the minds of early Americans, became synonymous with state-coerced religious observance. Americans also came to view Muslim societies as violent and prone to corruption, ostentation, and idleness, which among other consequences of these vices yielded economic stagnation.[68] In addition, the memory of the Barbary Wars and the imprisonment of American sailors in Barbary prisons helped shape the public's perspective. In contrast, the United States had established religious freedom while also guaranteeing other Enlightenment ideals for some. Thus at the core, Islam was viewed as indicative of an established tradition of tyranny and therefore the antithesis of the United States.[69]

A larger portion of American society came to know the Ottoman Empire through Middle Eastern–inspired literature called Oriental tales. By the beginning of the nineteenth century the United States had the highest literacy rate in the world, with a growing economy that led to an expanding publishing industry.[70] Oriental stories as a genre were so popular that one in ten stories printed in America prior to 1800 could be classified as an Oriental tale, exceeding any other genre.[71] In 1817 a book called *Lalla Rookh*, an Oriental romance novel, sold more copies than any other book published in the United States that year.[72] The subjects of plays printed and performed in the United States between the 1780s and the 1820s, as well as children's readers and grammars, also reflect the popularity of the Oriental tale.[73]

One of the most popular and influential Oriental stories in America from the late eighteenth into the nineteenth century was *The Arabian Nights Entertainments* or *The Book of One-Thousand-and-One Nights*. *The Arabian Nights* is a collection of stories told by Scheherazade, the daughter of the vizier, and includes such stories as "Aladdin" and "Ali Baba and the Forty Thieves." Scheherazade has been betrothed to the tyrannical sultan, and she tells him a new story every night to postpone the fate he has in store for her. The vizier's daughter is the next in a long line of virgins the sultan has vowed to take every night as a new wife. As he did with his previous wives, the sultan plans to have his way with Scheherazade and then kill her the following morning as revenge for his first wife's infidelity.

Copies of *The Arabian Nights* were imported into the United States from Europe throughout the eighteenth century. The first edition printed in the United States was published by a Philadelphia printer in 1794 and sold over forty thousand copies. Children and adults alike read this book.[74] The stories played on popular themes that revolve around violence, adventure, opulence, and the supernatural—elements that were often associated with Islamic culture.

By the 1820s, *The Arabian Nights* was available in illustrated editions, bringing exotic Western Asia to life and adding incentive for readers to purchase the new editions. Some editions intentionally noted whether the translation was faithful to the original Arabian manuscript, suggesting an interest in authenticity of the translated text. One edition printed in 1822, the sixth American edition from the eighteenth English edition, "translated from the Arabian MSS," included a number of illustrations. The frontispiece illustration, for example, depicted a scene from the story of Zayn Al-asnam, who is gazing at the mysterious and powerful genie that has just appeared before him.[75]

The opulent clothing and furnishings in the image indicate how American readers might have thought of the East: as being a place of mystery, excitement,

Figure 1.1. This illustration is indicative of the orientalized perspective of the East presented in many British and American works of Eastern history and literature of the late eighteenth and early nineteenth centuries. "Zuyn Alasnam and the King of the Genii," *The Arabian Nights Entertainments*, frontispiece (Hartford, CT: Bowles and Francis, 1822). Courtesy of the American Antiquarian Society.

and magic, as well as a place inherently "un–American."[76] Such ideas thus promoted continued interest in Eastern culture while also clearly denoting the East as foreign both literarily as well as culturally.

Thanks in part to the popularity of *The Arabian Nights*, similar stories set in Western Asia became increasingly popular and were published in American grammars and readers for school-aged children.[77] Perhaps the most well-known American educational writer in the early republic was Noah Webster, who first published his reader, *An American Selection of Lessons in Reading and Speaking*, in 1785. In the midst of carefully chosen stories, references to the Orient can be found. The final portion of the reader provided children with lessons on a number of subjects including cleanliness, which Webster stated is especially important in the East, "where the warmth of the climate makes cleanliness more immediately necessary than in colder countries." Webster concluded with a story he claimed was from "an account of Mahometan superstition." The story describes how a dervish, a member of a Muslim religious order, was denied blessings on several occasions, even receiving bodily harm from a "holy camel" that was part of a caravan on its way to Mecca, because he had forgotten to wash his hands that morning.[78] This moral lesson simultaneously taught children that Islam employed superstitious tales while also teaching that there are elements of the East that were useful.

Many children's histories instilled a knowledge of the East through a lens of American or European superiority. English historian Oliver Goldsmith wrote in 1800 that the history of the Greeks must be understood as being "under the influence of foreign councils, and the controul of foreign arms." As a result, the modern Greeks "had lost their existence as a nation."[79] Due to the rise of the Ottoman Empire after the fall of Constantinople, Goldsmith concluded, "The modern Greeks, without the least political importance, and sunk in slavery to a military government, retain but little of their original character. . . . Tyranny too effectually quieted this tumult of passion; the oppressed Greek, humbled to the dust, was forced to kiss the hand that was lifted up for his destruction."[80] Not only does this observation support existing expression of Ottoman degeneracy, but it also further confirms that early Americans viewed the modern Greeks as being in need of aid on the eve of their revolution.

For a broader American audience, readers obtained and read materials that did battle, literarily speaking, with the Barbary pirates. These pieces of literature emphasized that Muslims and their way of life were barbaric, ignorant, vicious, weak, and idle. Such attitudes were not new or necessarily unique to the period, but they climbed in popularity due to the contemporary conflict.[81]

Perhaps the most widely read genre of literature that reflected negative sentiments toward the Ottoman Empire in the late eighteenth and early nineteenth century was the captivity tale. The captivity narrative became especially popular during the Barbary Wars.[82] These tales portrayed the Turks as part of an ignorant and despotic civilization that Americans, now steeped in the rhetoric of the Revolution, must overcome in order to completely secure the liberty Americans had already achieved domestically.

Some of these tales were fictional, and others were written from firsthand experience. John Foss, one of the few surviving members of the brig *Polly*, which was captured by Algerian pirates in 1793, related his experiences as a slave in Algiers as well as his impressions of the different people he encountered. Published in 1798, his account described the different punishments that could potentially be inflicted on a Christian captive as well as an Algerian who broke local laws. Throughout the narrative, Foss juxtaposed his experience and observations with life in the United States.

Foss's narrative revealed his overall judgment of life in Algiers and intentionally contrasted this strange life, with its cruel and unusual punishment for white prisoners like himself, with life in the United States. Foss wrote that life in Algiers was directed by the Turks, who "have all the government and power in their own hands, and no man can hold any post of great distinction among them except he is a real Turk." Foss viewed the Turks as "savage barbarians" and wrote that they were a "well built robust people, their complexion not unlike Americans, tho' somewhat larger, but their dress, and long beards, make them appear more like monsters, than human beings." As to why Foss received such treatment, he explained that the Turks are "taught by their religion to treat the Christian Captives with unexampled cruelty."[83]

This distinction resurfaced once again in Foss's journal, where he related the initial efforts of the United States to free the American prisoners in Algiers. Once freedom was negotiated, Foss related how he came to hear that he was set free from his guards. Foss's guards were astounded at the dedication of the United States to freeing its citizens and wondered that "the American people must be the best in the world to be so humane and generous to their countrymen in slavery."[84] Foss saw the biggest difference between Americans and Turks in their different types of government. He even seemed to suggest that if liberty were instituted in Algiers, such cruel atrocities against the different people residing there would no longer exist. Foss's account ultimately confirmed what many Americans already believed to be true of life within a Muslim state.

The most well-known fictional captive story was first printed in 1797 by the American lawyer and playwright Royall Tyler. *The Algerine Captive* was a novel about a Doctor Updike Underhill, who was described as a well-educated man from New England. While sailing near the North African coast, Underhill was taken captive aboard an Algerian ship and held as a slave for six years. The book was dedicated to David Humphreys, an American minister to Portugal, who negotiated the release of American sailors from Tripoli. These negotiations eventually led to freedom for the American captives, including John Foss.[85]

Just as John Foss had concluded in his captivity narrative, Tyler's fictional character declared that no nation in the world was as free as the United States, while contrasting it with his experiences in Algiers. As a captive, Underhill worked under excruciating conditions and eventually had to be sent away for medical attention. While in the hospital, Underhill conversed with a Muslim man who tried to convert him to Islam. Instead, Underhill proudly proclaimed he had held on to "the religion of my country."[86] After his release, Underhill returned to "the freest county in the universe" eager to "contribute cheerfully to the support of our excellent government, which I have learnt to adore in schools of despotism."[87] Both Tyler and Foss's captivity narratives heavily influenced subsequent additions to the genre.[88]

Men wrote most of the captive tales published in the late eighteenth and early nineteenth centuries, but there were a few exceptions. A woman named Mrs. Maria Martin allegedly wrote one of the most popular captive tales published in the early years of the nineteenth century. The story's authorship and whether it is nonfiction remain dubious, but readers were intended to believe the story was true.[89] *The History of the Captivity and Sufferings of Mrs. Maria Martin*, first printed in 1807, was reprinted many times in the United States over the next ten years.

Although Maria Martin was English, the 1806 volume began with *A Short History of Algiers* by Mathew Carey, an Irish-American philanthropist who later supported the Greek cause. First printed in 1794, Carey's history introduced the Maria Martin volume with an American perspective on Algiers stating that it "retains the title of a kingdom; an epithet which might, without regret, be expunged from every human vocabulary." Though a "military republic," Carey continued, "it certainly can reflect no lustre on that species of government."[90] American readers would have approached the Martin narrative with this foundational information in mind.

The Maria Martin narrative conveyed the idea that the Turks were unfeeling and bloodthirsty toward women. Martin faced years of unspeakable torture.

As a captive, she attempted to escape after several years of servitude but was discovered and carried back into slavery for another two years. Martin viewed her captors as fierce, barbaric, and in many regards lacking any distinguishable human characteristics. Martin was chained in a small cell by the neck, waist, and ankles. The Turkish prison guards provided her with only moldy bread and slimy water.[91]

The Maria Martin narrative provides an important gendered distinction for captivity narratives and aids in defining the differences Americans perceived between life in the United States and in the Ottoman Empire. Martin was presented as the embodiment of feminine virtue, a quality that was desired in mothers of the new American republic. American revolutionary rhetoric provided a place for American women in society in which their role as nurturing wives and mothers was imperative to the sustainment of a healthy republic.[92] Early American readers in the late eighteenth and early nineteenth centuries would have viewed women in this light. The popularity of Martin's tale provides evidence of this sentiment. While an early American reader would have been horrified at such injustices inflicted on an American white male, a member of the supposedly weaker and more virtuous sex bearing such inhumane conditions was unthinkable. The tale also suggested to American readers that the Turks did not value women in the same way as Americans in postrevolutionary society did.

Yet another popular female captivity story was a play titled *The Sultan: A Peep into the Seraglio*. The play was performed in New York the first time in 1794 and was revived many times until 1840. *The Sultan* was originally published in Britain, with the central character being Sultan Solyman. The storyline in the play was likely based on the relationship between Sultan Suleyman I and his favorite concubine, Roxalana, who later was made his chief consort and legal wife. Roxalana was believed to have been of Slavic descent and captured by Turkish invaders. An American adaptation of the play changed the title to *The American Captive* and made Roxalana, recently captured and brought to the sultan's harem, the new central character. In this version of the play, Roxalana was elevated as the sultan's consort after convincing him that he would be happier if he accepted her as his equal.[93]

Because much of the play was set in a harem, early Americans might have viewed the tale of Roxalana as inappropriate or socially taboo to perform onstage. Written within the captive story genre, however, *The Sultan* served as a lesson on how the Muslim world's brand of tyranny oppressed women and employed despotism to effectively rule.

Roxalana was a Christian and therefore an outsider to the culture of the harem. She presented herself to the sultan as being worthy of respect and received it. In some ways these characters represent what early Americans would have seen as a confrontation of Eastern versus Western values. When Roxalana was first introduced to the sultan's court, she bluntly explained to the sultan and his adviser that in order to be a truly successful leader the sultan should free the women from the seraglio and "let inclination alone keep your women within it." She went on to state that women should be made his advisers instead of men because "we women have certainly ten thousand times more sense."[94] The sultan's adviser was shocked, while the sultan himself was at first amused. By the end of the play, Roxalana successfully appealed to the other women in the harem to a revolution of sorts by leading them in singing, "They're our masters but in name; Let them say whate'er they will, Woman, woman, rules them still." Roxalana won over the sultan, and she also requested that she be made not only his wife, but his equal. After voicing cultural and legal misgivings, the sultan agreed to elevate Roxalana's status after she pointed out that the emperor of the Turks "may do as he pleases, and should be despotic sometimes on the side of reason and virtue." Through the ideals of virtue and liberty, this young woman's revolution was complete when she "overturned the customs of a mighty empire."[95]

The assumed perils of the harem and the oppressive status of women under the Ottoman Empire played on the emotions of both male and female readers. For early Americans who saw the moral stability of a nation as originating in the home and with the wife and mother, the harem or seraglio was viewed as the ultimate manifestation of depravity and despotism.[96] Captivity narratives with female subjects were common and especially titillating reads for American audiences at the end of the eighteenth and early nineteenth centuries.[97] Early Americans viewed women within Ottoman society as being an exploited sex in the harems or seraglios of Western Asia. The harem, as it existed within the early American lexicon, was founded upon fantasy and imagination.[98] American men and women believed that women in these harems were literally locked up within the sultan's palace and kept for his every erotic whim. Americans perceived this cultural and social practice as the ultimate subjugation of the female sex. Advocates for women's rights, most notably Mary Wollstonecraft, referred to the status of women in Islamic culture as one of complete exploitation that "kills virtue and genius in the bud." According to Wollstonecraft, if women could not pursue reason and respect within society, then they would be condemned to the same kind of subjected status as Muslim women.[99]

Yet another source sometimes attributed to Thomas Paine held that the status of women in the Ottoman Empire was no different from slavery.[100] The author blamed the "seraglio" for "the domestic servitude of woman, authorized by the manners and established laws" of the region and argued that "the excess of oppression" was derived from "the excess of love."[101] Although Wollstonecraft, Paine, and others did not primarily intend to generate interest in Muslim society and culture, their works had that effect. By comparing the status of women in the West with their status in the despotic East, these writers implied that Western women should never be allowed to sink to such depths.

Americans in the Ottoman Empire

Early American interest in diplomatic and commercial ties in the Mediterranean were defined in part by existing Western prejudices and Americans' pride in their revolution. While the Jefferson administration was more concerned with commercial trade in the Mediterranean than with diplomacy, American sentiments soon changed on this subject by the end of the War of 1812.[102] Americans naturally saw their approach to both commercial trade and diplomacy through a republican lens rather than a traditional European one. Theodore Lyman for example, friend of Edward Everett, wrote a two-volume history on early American diplomacy in these terms. Lyman wrote that the early American approach to foreign diplomacy was different from other European powers, defining it as having a "commercial character," whereas "our treaties, for the most part, have consisted of arrangements for the regulation of trade and navigation." Viewing English navigation laws as "despotic," American diplomacy instead sought trade and commerce on "equal terms" with other nations.[103] Yet another early American historian observed that other nations who desired to emulate the United States should "look to *commerce and navigation*, and not to *empire*, as her means of communication with the rest of the human family. *These* are the *principles* upon which *our* confederated Republic is founded."[104] It was within this intellectual framework that protrade Americans desired to spread American ideals concerning democracy and free trade to other regions of the world where they desired to conduct business.[105] The Sublime Porte was one business ally these protrade supporters desired to possess.

Colonial merchants desired an established and independent commercial trade in the Mediterranean long before the Revolution. No longer restrained by regulations imposed upon them by Britain, American merchants began to pursue that objective not long after independence. Trade with Western Asia was especially desirable. Western Asia included the Middle East as well as the Levant. Raisins shipped from Smyrna (modern-day Izmir), for example, could be found in Boston by the 1780s.[106] American merchants were able to conduct trade at Smyrna, for example, under British protection by posing as British subjects and flying a British flag on their ships. When the relationship between the United States and Britain became strained, however, Barbary pirates attacked American ships, leading to several conflicts that would last three decades. Indeed, without the power of the British navy and its established connections with the Barbary States and the Sublime Porte, it was unlikely that American merchants could do business under their own flag. With merchants often leading the way, the full realization of the American Revolution's objectives concerning international commerce became the underlying driving force for the procommercial interest camp.

American merchants made some gains in the Levant on the eve of the War of 1812. In 1811, two Philadelphians, Edward Woodmas and David Offley, established the first American commercial house in the bustling Turkish trade city of Smyrna.[107] When Offley first arrived in Smyrna, conflict between the United States and Britain concerning trade had pressed them once again toward war. As a result, officials of the British-controlled Levant Company induced the Sublime Porte to issue an edict stating that American ships should pay double duties. Offley refused to pay, leading to the confiscation of one of his ships by Ottoman authorities.

Offley immediately traveled to Constantinople and displayed natural talents at negotiation, managing to secure a private treaty for American vessels in all Ottoman ports, thus placing American merchants at the status of the "Sultan's guests."[108] This would be the first of many instances where David Offley the merchant took on the role of unofficial diplomat in the Levant.[109] Despite this, American merchants were so accustomed to deferring to British protection that Offley "had the extreme mortification to find my countrymen . . . had been fully persuaded of the necessity of continuing under the English protection for the security of their property." This went on until 1815 when he was "able to prevail on my countrymen to abandon a protection unnecessary, expensive, and dishonorable to our national character."[110] Though he had negotiated this private treaty, American commerce in the Levant was not necessarily on secure footing, as there did not exist an official treaty between the United States and the Sublime Porte.

Aside from the interruption in trade due to the War of 1812, business for American merchants in Smyrna excelled. Offley himself handled two-thirds of all American goods arriving in Smyrna until 1820. Some of the largest ship-ments of goods from Smyrna included coffee, sugar, cassia lignia, figs, and opium. However, without a formal treaty with the Sublime Porte, American merchants continued to be dependent upon the negotiating prowess of men such as Offley. One American visitor to Smyrna, a Bostonian named George Barrell whose family fortune enabled him to travel extensively throughout Europe and Western Asia, observed this about his countrymen: "Not having an ambassador at the Porte and without which a consul would not be recognized in any other part of the Turkish empire, they remain at the mercy of the na-tives."[111] Though Offley had managed to secure a private trade agreement, it was by no means a formal understanding between the Sublime Porte and the United States, and it only permitted American merchants to conduct business at Smyrna.

Offley cultivated friendships with local merchants while living in Smyrna, writing home about his interest in Turkish customs and Islam. Offley also cul-tivated a friendship with Koca Husrev Mehmed Pasha, the *kapudan pasha* (sometimes referred to by contemporaries as the captain pasha), the head of the Ottoman navy and advocate for Westernization in Constantinople.[112] While in Smyrna, George Barrell noted the kapudan pasha's interest in American commerce, stating, "The Captain Pacha has taken the Americans under his protection; why, I cannot ascertain, but presume it arised from his observing the evident increase of our commerce in the Levant seas."[113] American politi-cians hoped that Offley's respected presence at Smyrna would help to benefit American commercial interests overall. With Offley's connections and knowl-edge of both Turkish and European commerce, a treaty between the United States and the Ottoman Empire, it seemed, was close at hand by 1820.

Newly elected president James Monroe desired to continue improving re-lations with the Ottoman Empire in the hope of signing a commercial treaty with the Sublime Porte. Under the authorization of his secretary of state, John Quincy Adams, an agent from New York by the name of Luther Bradish was dispatched to Constantinople with the explicit purpose of "collecting such in-formation in foreign countries, in relation to the commerce of the United States, as may prove useful and interesting to them."[114] Bradish's ultimate goal was to initiate negotiations and hopefully secure a formal treaty between the United States and the Sublime Porte through which, like their European counterparts, American merchants would have access to all ports within the Ottoman Empire.[115]

Another American was present in the Mediterranean at this time who would later play an important role in the initial negotiation for this commercial treaty.

George Bethune English, a native of Boston and a Harvard graduate, joined the Marine Corps in 1816. The Mediterranean Squadron was the American naval force dedicated to protecting commercial trade in Smyrna from pirate attacks. English was looking for a dramatic change of scenery after a controversial year in his hometown of Cambridge, Massachusetts. As a result of the publication of *The Grounds of Christianity Examined*, in which English expressed controversial views concerning Christianity, he was excommunicated from the First Church in Cambridge in 1814 on the grounds that he had proven "himself to be, not merely an apostate from the Christian Church, but an enemy to the Christian Religion."[116] English had pitted himself in this controversy against a classmate and intellectual adversary, Edward Everett, who wrote a lengthy response to *The Grounds of Christianity Examined* ultimately condemning English's argument. The public outcry against his views prompted English to join the Marines and travel to the Mediterranean.

Evidently life as a Marine did not prove to be what English was searching for. He subsequently resigned his post in 1820, leaving his crew in Alexandria, Egypt. English converted to Islam, adopted Turkish dress, and joined the Egyptian army under Mohammad Ali Pasha.[117] During his time in the Egyptian army, English went by the name Mohammad Effendi. Mohammad Ali Pasha was one of Sultan Mahmud II's troublesome pashas, reluctant to swear complete subservience to the sultan. English served as an artillery commander under Mohammad Ali as the pasha continued to expand his power into Sudan. English is believed to be one of the first Americans to travel to that part of the world.[118]

Although English's opinions and experiences were exceptional for the time, he was surprisingly not the only American in Egypt who had "taken the turban." While in the Egyptian army, English encountered at least two other Americans who had converted to Islam and endeavored to assume a new life in the region. English served with a New Yorker who took the name Khalil Aga and a Swiss-American named Achmed Aga.[119] Another American adventurer was Josiah Harlan, a Pennsylvania Quaker who left the United States in 1819 to travel throughout Egypt and the surrounding regions for two decades.[120] It was through English's experience in the Mediterranean and his familiarity with Ottoman politics that upon his return to the United States he was added to a short list of potential secret agents the U.S. government intended to send to the Sublime Porte in order to continue negotiations for a navigational and commercial treaty.

In addition to American merchants, American missionaries were also present in Western Asia.[121] Interest in American missionary work abroad first emerged in late eighteenth and early nineteenth-century New England. Religious revival during this time stressed the importance of conversion as something that could transcend social, geographical, and ethnic boundaries, resulting in the movement being national, and later, global.[122] The Reverend Samuel Hopkins was a member of the early stages of this movement. Hopkins and other critics of traditional Calvinism believed they had improved upon Calvinist teachings. The doctrine of predestination remained, but instead of emphasizing that Christ died for an elect few, Christians were obligated to secure the happiness of all mankind by bringing the gospel to all the world.[123] Hopkins was assigned to a congregation in the Massachusetts frontier in the 1740s, where he preached to and educated the native population. An early proponent of abolition, Hopkins also viewed slaves as prime candidates for conversion.[124] He is credited as being one of the first religious figures (perhaps even the first) to conceive of an American foreign mission.

Founded in Massachusetts in 1810, the American Board of Commissioners for Foreign Missions (ABCFM) was one of the first American missionary organizations and was in part inspired by Hopkins and his religious perspectives on Christianity. The organization of the ABCFM was modeled after similar ones in Britain because of their earlier successes in establishing a presence in India. With the intention of bringing the gospel to "heathen lands," American missionaries were inspired by this urge to convert all the world to their particular Protestant perspective.[125] This urge also inspired interest in the Greek Revolution. Missionaries would later play an important role in philhellenic efforts at providing aid and relief to Greek soldiers, civilians, and Greek refugees during the revolution.

Recent graduates of Andover Theological Seminary, Pliny Fisk and Levi Parsons were selected by the ABCFM to lead the first American mission to Jerusalem in 1819. Called "the Palestine Mission," its purpose was to spread a reformed Calvinist viewpoint that had begun to emerge in the United States in the early nineteenth century to the people of Western Asia, which included Jews, Muslims, and Catholics. There was particular excitement surrounding this mission, as it would mark the first time American missionaries formally began efforts to settle in and convert the "Holy Land." For months prior to their departure, Fisk and Parsons raised funds throughout the country, even traveling to Savannah, Georgia. Their travels were widely reported in American newspapers throughout the 1820s, reflecting the widespread interest the public had for their adventures in the East as well as the potential for spreading the gospel among a non-Christian population.[126]

The two men arrived in the Levant from Boston late in 1819. Fisk wrote home requesting that several friends keep up a regular correspondence with him while he was in Smyrna, as he felt divided from "Christian society and deprived of the ordinary means of grace; in danger from irreligious European society, and the influence of a moral atmosphere wholly corrupt."[127] Fisk observed that while this at times made him feel uneasy, he concluded that it was this fact that made Smyrna "a good missionary station."[128] The two young Americans traveled to the island of Chios a few months after arriving in the Mediterranean and began to learn modern Greek so that they could more easily converse with the local populations.

For the remaining months of 1820, the young men spent their time traveling to see the Seven Churches of Asia, teaching English, and meeting with locals as they handed out religious tracts and copies of the New Testament in a number of different languages. Upon arriving in Ephesus, Fisk recorded in his journal sentimental thoughts concerning ancient Greek history that would be common in American philhellenic literature in the months that followed: "While wandering among the ruins, it was impossible not to think, with deep interest, of the events which have transpired on this spot. Here has been displayed . . . all the skill of the architect, the musician, the tragedian, and the orator."[129] Fisk and Parsons, as well as many American and European philhellenes, saw the ancient history of these lands as pure, a purity that could once again be rediscovered by the modern Greeks if they were properly educated and evangelized. Their belief that they could help return glory to the eastern Mediterranean provided momentum behind their missionary spirit. Change appeared imminent, for not long after Parsons and Fisk returned to Smyrna they discovered the Greeks had begun an uprising against the Ottoman Turks.

★   ★   ★

Fisk, Parsons, English, and Offley were all in the Mediterranean as conflict between Greece and the Ottoman Empire began to unfold. Though none of these individuals could have anticipated the Greek Revolution, the events would affect their interests and goals in the years that followed. Early American interest in Greece was varied, inspiring merchants, Christian missionaries, politicians, intellectuals, and adventure seekers alike to take notice of the evolving situation within the Ottoman Empire. With Greece perceived as the intellectual and political ancestor of the American Republic, each of these groups at times disagreed but also worked together toward advancing an American presence in Greece and Western Asia.

American perceptions of Greece were at first molded by European and American prejudices against the Ottoman Turks. While early Americans saw themselves as having a unique and particular interest in Greece and the Ottoman Empire as a result of their own revolution, the origins of American philhellenism should be understood as being part of a global conversation concerning commerce, diplomacy, and humanitarianism. Existing conflict within the Ottoman Empire combined with European and American interest in the region played an important role in the outbreak of the Greek Revolution and influenced how an American audience came to perceive the war.

Chapter 2

European Philhellenism Crosses the Atlantic

"Lord Byron, the celebrated Poet, is about to enter the service of the Greeks," reported the *Essex Register* in June 1823. "If he can cause them to be sung into invincibility, he will confer a blessing on the world."[1] Though many Americans read about the Greek Revolution and expressed sentimental support in local newspapers, no major organized movement for aid emerged during the first two years of the war. That all changed in the summer of 1823. The popular romantic poet George Gordon Byron, commonly known as Lord Byron, had just publicly pledged to devote himself and his fortune to the service of the Greek army. Byron himself used the opportunity to call on Londoners to procure "means for aiding the cause of the Greeks."[2]

News of Byron's pledge and the mobilization of philhellenic efforts in England were widely reported in American newspapers. "The noble bard," reported a widely reprinted article, "is enthusiastic in the cause of [the Greeks'] emancipation from the shackles of Turkish despotism." Newspapers from Hartford, Connecticut, to Charleston, South Carolina, followed and reported on Byron's plans to devote his fortune toward chartering a vessel "with the avowed object of aiding the Greeks."[3] One newspaper editor opined that Byron was "personally brave; and his sword as well as his pen, would probably be employed in the cause of freedom and the emancipation of Greece." The editor further speculated that his presence in Greece would serve as an agent "of philanthropic individuals of other nations, in making a proper application of such supplies as may be forwarded, and in soliciting such aid as may be most needed."[4] The editor was more correct than he could have imagined.

The interest shared by early Americans in Lord Byron's activity in Greece was born out of a romantic sensibility about Greece's past rather than a mere connection with the classical tradition. The romanticization of ancient Greece was a European and American phenomenon that identified Greece as the original cradle of democracy and freedom. The nostalgic connection to Greece combined with the fact that the modern Greeks were living under Ottoman rule cultivated patriotic pride in both European and American understandings of their intellectual and cultural past. The Greek cause, as some philhellenes called it, also promoted early notions of humanitarianism.[5]

Still other factors that must be considered as a part of the American philhellenic experience are religion and race. For many Americans, especially those in New England with enthusiasm for foreign missions, the Greek Revolution was not only a war to revive the glories of ancient Greece but was also a religious war. American ministers combined efforts with philhellene organizers, infusing religious rhetoric with the patriotic. These joint efforts helped to expand the list of donors and effectively laid the groundwork for an evolving American philhellenic movement that became more clearly defined as the Greek war continued.

News reports and philhellenic speeches emphasized the differences between the Greeks and the Turks, noting not only that the Greeks were Christian but also that they constituted a superior race to that of the Turks. One news report stated that the "Hellenic race" was an "illustrious" one and worthy of support. Another asked its readers, "Would not every arm be uplifted to snatch so large a portion of our race from being consigned by their ruthless oppressors to slavery, dishonor, and death?" Regardless of whether or not they believed the Greeks were of a unique race or of a race that they shared, the consensus among early Americans was that the modern Greeks were a people worthy of support. Philhellenes contrasted their perspective on the Greeks by describing the Turks as "a race of merciless and incorrigible barbarians, whose ignorance, fanaticism, brutality and ferocity, render them enemies of mankind, and fit objects of execration to all civilized nations." These reports frequently referred to the Ottomans as being part of a race of "infidels" or "barbarians," suggesting that they were set apart from the civilized world and perhaps from the human race as a whole.[6]

Philhellenism in the United States has frequently been characterized as merely an extension of the European movement. However, it is clear that although the American philhellenic movement initially drew some momentum from its European counterpart, it quickly became a unique one in its own right. Many early Americans believed they better understood the hardships the Greeks faced because of their own recent experience with revolution. The Greek cause was also largely a bipartisan one that seemingly united early Americans both in the North and South. At the request of their constituents, state legislatures from New York to South Carolina put forward resolutions urging the U.S. Congress to openly support Greek independence. More than any other revolution of the nineteenth century, the Greek War of Independence saw Americans in both the North and South quickly connecting it with their own revolution, and they regarded it as their duty to raise public awareness and support for the cause.

A rapid transition in the philhellenic movement took place within the United States. Lord Byron represented the sentimentalism of the early Greek cause, but Americans quickly mobilized an active cause when it became obvious that the U.S. government would neither officially recognize Greek independence nor would provide the Greek army with military aid. The sentimentalism of the Greek cause was frequently expressed through news reports, public opinion pieces, and poetry. This sentimentalism gave way to the organization of Greek committees and calls for active monetary and military support for the Greeks. This mobilization of popular support for the Greek cause generated what many newspapers termed "the Greek Fire."

Philhellenism in Europe

The philhellenic movement as a whole does not have a clear origin but developed over several hundred years. It has traditionally been defined as a European movement that developed primarily in late eighteenth and early nineteenth-century England, with Lord Byron as its leader.[7] More recently the philhellenic movement has been described as being important in other European countries, such as France and Germany.[8] These European philhellenic movements linked their own national roots with ancient origins, claiming a direct cultural inheritance with Greece. More likely, the Greek cause was not something that emerged fully developed at one time but rather was a set of ideas that arose among the Greeks themselves as early as the late Byzantine period. Ideas concerning Greek independence were then spread as part of the Greek diaspora through Greek intellectuals living in Europe in the eighteenth and early nineteenth centuries. This at least played an important part in the emergence of the Greek intellectual circles throughout Europe and an important role in the founding of the Filiki Etaireia, a Greek revolutionary secret society. In all likelihood it was through a combination of factors that included

the evolution of nationalist ideas, seeing political and/or societal value in linking European culture to Greek intellectual origins, as well as the reinforcing
voices of intellectuals residing and writing within places such as Britain, Germany, and France. From this the concepts of philhellenism were transferred
onto a sympathetic audience in both Europe and the United States.[9]

Both American and European philhellenes held that the modern Greeks
had been living so long under Ottoman rule that they required assistance in
returning their society to what they imagined it was in Greece's Classical Age.[10]
If the modern Greeks could overthrow Ottoman tyranny and establish a free
society, then perhaps the once great Greek civilization would reemerge. The
philhellenic interest in "saving" the Greeks did not stem exclusively from the
fact that the Greeks were Christian; in fact, many Europeans and Americans
viewed the Orthodox Greeks as the wrong kind of Christians. Instead, they
held a romantic hope that ancient Greece could somehow be revived through
their intercession. This element of condescension was yet another common
aspect of the philhellenic movement. It was widely held that the Greeks could
not obtain freedom without assistance, a belief that fueled a sense of urgency
behind the movement.

Edward Everett was perhaps the most central philhellenic leader in early
America. Everett was just twenty-six years old at the outbreak of the Greek
Revolution, and his philhellenism was especially influenced by his German education. Before assuming his post as professor of Greek literature at Harvard
in 1820, Everett spent several years in Germany studying the classics at the University of Göttingen beginning in 1815. A close friend of Everett's named
George Ticknor accompanied him. Ticknor wrote home that the professors
at Göttingen had convinced him that in America "we do not yet know what
a Greek scholar is, nor even the process by which one is made." Ticknor also
observed that Everett was so determined to prove himself a scholarly equal
that he looked "as if he had fasted six months on Greek prosody and the Pin-
daric metres." Everett eventually resigned himself to the fact that he would
never be able to achieve the levels of knowledge the Germans had reached,
but he comforted himself that he had managed an "aesthetical view of the
subject, which is more adapted to the American market."[11] Everett's reference
to the aesthetic of the Greek language referred to the German school's emphasis on a comprehensive appreciation for Greek art and culture rather than
mere memorization of the ancient language, which had dominated classical
language curriculum in the United States for generations. Although Everett
felt he had fallen short of the German classical school's rigorous standards, his
time in Europe had introduced him not only to classical studies but to impor-

tant members of the European philhellenic movement in Britain and France as well as Germany.

In France, the popularity of the philhellenic movement largely stemmed from French nationalist sentiments linking French cultural origins with ancient Greece. Paris after all was the first European city where a philhellenic society was established, with some of the founding members later becoming active members in the Filiki Etaireia. With Enlightenment ideals and the memory of Napoleon fresh in many French minds, pro-Greek pamphlets printed in France played on these supposed cultural and intellectual links. In a pamphlet titled *Appeal to the French People*, one French philhellene wrote, "Can you be the only people who will not help the descendants of Themistocles, Alcibiades, and Demosthenes? Can you allow your brothers in religion to be massacred? Are you no longer the descendants of the Crusading St. Louis?"[12] Not to be outdone by British philhellenes, their French counterparts began to organize relief efforts and even traveled to Greece in the earliest months of the war to join the Greek army.

Greek expatriates were especially instrumental in cultivating a philhellenic following within France, which also helped inspire similar ideas in the United States. Thomas Jefferson's early writings on the subject of Greek independence long predate the founding of the Filiki Etaireia, and yet they simultaneously reveal the influence of the European philhellenic movement and the perceived bond Americans thought they should feel for the Greeks. While in Paris, Jefferson made acquaintances with several Greek Enlightenment thinkers. John Paradise, who was English but born in Greece while his father served as a diplomat, was an accomplished linguist, instructing Jefferson in modern Greek. Jefferson's relationship with Paradise was a close one, as Paradise had married into the Ludwell family, a wealthy and well-connected Virginia family. Jefferson also became acquainted with Adamantios Korais, or Coray as Jefferson called him, a Greek Enlightenment scholar and later a Greek revolutionary.[13] Korais and Paradise played important roles in the rise of philhellenism as a political endeavor, having melded their own love of Greece to Western Europe's classical tradition.[14] Through these relationships Jefferson's interest in Greece reflected many of the same sentimental and humanitarian attributes future American philhellenes would share.[15]

In a letter to his long-time mentor and friend George Wythe, Jefferson expressed some of these philhellenic attitudes: "I cannot help looking forward to the reestablishment of the Greeks as a people, and the language of Homer becoming a living language as among possible events. You have now with you Mr. Paradise, who can tell you how easily the modern may be improved into the antient Greek."[16] In Jefferson's mind, the modern Greek language needed to be purified and returned to its ancient Greek form. Jefferson conveyed the same sentiment to yet another friend, Charles Thomson. Jefferson observed that in the contemporary European conflict between Russia and the Ottoman Empire, Russia would likely prove victorious, paving the way for Greek independence. Should the Greeks gain their independence from the Ottomans, he told Thomson, the language of the ancient Greeks could be revived and could bring about a rebirth of classical Greek culture.[17] In a sense, independence was not enough. In order to be entirely free, philhellenes expected that the Greeks had to remake themselves into the image and likeness of Socrates and Pericles. Philhellenism routinely expressed the feeling that the Greek language and culture had been degraded as a result of the Greeks' subjugation to the Ottoman Empire. Only through independence and republican reform could the Greeks reclaim the purest form of themselves.

Jefferson was also cautious in his hope for Greek freedom. In a letter to Richard Henry Lee in 1785, he commented, "A lover of humanity would wish to see that charming country from which the Turks exclude science and freedom, in any hands rather than theirs, and in those of the native Greeks rather than any others. The recovery of their antient language would not be desperate, could they recover their antient liberty. But those who wish to remove the Turks, wish to put themselves in their places. This would be exchanging one set of Barbarians for another only."[18] Jefferson seems to indicate that while freedom for Greece was a possibility in the 1780s, the Greeks themselves were not capable of holding onto their freedom in the face of another neighboring power.

Thomas Jefferson did more than just express personal feelings concerning the possibility of Greek independence. Jefferson's friendship with Admontios Korais in Paris in the 1780s later helped introduce young American scholars traveling in Europe, such as Edward Everett, to French philhellenic circles. Everett's connection with Korais would later further link American philhellenes with the Greek cause, as some of the earliest pleas for American support were written from Paris by Korais.

A more general American audience became familiar with philhellenic sentiment through popular British literary figures and the movement they inspired. Works by Lord Byron, John Keats, and Percy Bysshe Shelley were particularly popular, with their romanticized depictions of the ancient world. Showcasing the ancient glories of Greece and Italy through an emotional and individual-driven style of poetry, Byron almost single-handedly propelled ancient Greece to the utmost importance in British and American cultural and literary identity.[19] Byron influenced a romantic movement that was further advanced by the widespread interest in his poetry as well as his involvement in the Greek army. Thought of as the ultimate philhellene, Byron inspired Europeans and Americans alike to support the Greek cause.[20]

George Gordon Byron was born in 1788 and is one of the most well-known poets of the nineteenth century's Romantic movement. He traveled throughout Europe extensively, which further cultivated his love for ancient history. Byron spent several years living in Italy and traveled to Greece for the first time when he was twenty-one. By 1816, Byron was an infamous character, estranged from his wife and accused of having an incestuous relationship with his half-sister. As a result of the scandal associated with him, Byron left England for the last time and spent the rest of his life living abroad. Despite his reputation, Byron's popularity as a foremost romantic poet and champion of the philhellenic cause helped to direct both European and American interest toward the Greek war effort.[21]

Byron visited Greece for the first time in 1809 and stayed for a couple of years, touring many ancient sites including the Acropolis in Athens, the field at Marathon, and the ruins at Delphi. During this time, Byron wrote one of his most popular epic poems, *Childe Harold's Pilgrimage*, which was first published in 1812. This poem, based on Byron's experiences in the Mediterranean, combined the travel narrative with philhellenic sentiment through observing the loss of ancient Greece to the sands of time and at the hands of the Ottoman Turks. Though Byron did not invent philhellenism, he certainly popularized it in his poetry and through his devotion to the Greek cause. Byron's poetry was defined by the period's anti-Turkish discourse and mythologization of the Orient and his belief that Greece could be redeemed from Turkish subjugation. *Childe Harold* articulated what many other philhellenes professed: 'Fair Greece! Sad relic of departed worth! . . . Greece! Change thy lords, thy state is still the same; Thy glorious day is o'er, but not thine years of shame.'[22] After the publication of *Childe Harold*, Byron became an almost overnight celebrity and was perhaps one of the most famous men in the world at the time of the Greek Revolution.[23]

The inspiration Byron gathered from his travels nurtured an already existing preference for the Greeks over the Turks. By the time his visit was complete Byron was prepared to advocate for the Greeks as a political cause at home.[24] It was largely because of Byron's empathy for the Greeks and his desire to make philhellenism an active political endeavor that showing support for the Greeks became a large-scale transatlantic movement.[25] Byron's poetry sparked a renewed interest in tourism to both Italy and Greece, which only further promoted the romantic sentiments toward the ancient world. In many cases, travelers left home with copies of *Childe Harold's Pilgrimage* in hand expecting to also experience the ruined former glory of Greece and Rome. Indeed, even Edward Everett traveled to Greece with a copy of Byron's poem. When travelers arrived in Greece, Greek nationalists played on these expectations and further promoted the claim that the suffering Greeks were the downtrodden inheritors of the ancients.[26]

Another way in which philhellenism and Lord Byron came to command attention in both Europe and the United States was through the acquisition of the Parthenon marbles, a group of large marble statues by the great ancient sculptor Phidias that once adorned the exterior of the Parthenon in Athens. Byron was ardently against the efforts of Thomas Bruce, Earl of Elgin, to remove the Parthenon marbles, now commonly known as the Elgin Marbles, from the Acropolis. Lord Elgin served as British ambassador to the Ottoman Empire from 1799 to 1803. During this time he took a special interest in collecting antiquities, including the Parthenon marbles. This debate engrossed many philhellenes at the time primarily because they believed that removing the marbles from Greece diminished their connection to the ancients.[27] While it is debated as to how Lord Elgin acquired the marbles, he claimed that he had appropriately done so from Turkish authorities in Athens. He sought the support of Parliament to purchase the marbles, which he eventually secured despite opposition.[28]

In 1816 a committee was appointed to consider the issue and assign a value to the marbles for purchase. "But if it be true, as we learn from history and experience," the committee observed in its decision, "that free governments afford a soil most suitable to the production of native talent, to the maturing the powers of the human mind, . . . no country can be better adapted than our own to afford an honourable asylum to these monuments of the school of PHIDIAS, and of the administration of PERICLES; where secure from further injury and degradation, they may receive that admiration and homage to which they are entitled."[29] The committee's decision was printed in London papers and subsequently reprinted in many American papers. Purchased for £35,000, the Elgin Marbles were placed in the British Museum, where they remain. This debate achieved much attention throughout Europe as well as the United States and contributed to the rising interest in philhellenism in general.[30]

Prior to the attention Byron gave to the Greek cause, British sympathy for the Greeks was widely held, but it was also abstract and lacked the urgency necessary to support a revolution. The poetry of Byron and his close friend Percy Bysshe Shelley generated a rising public interest in both Britain and the United States to support the Greeks militarily, financially, or both.[31] Despite popular support for the Greek cause in Britain, the members of Parliament were not as easily swayed. Robert Stewart, Viscount Castlereagh, was the prime minister at the time, and like his peers he was more concerned over the rising power of Russia than in supporting a Greek revolution. The first priority in Castlereagh's mind was to avoid the downfall of the Ottoman Empire given the rising threat Russia posed to Europe. The outbreak of the revolt in Greece brought Russia and the Ottoman Empire all the closer to war due to their common interest in the Balkans as well as the potential violation of the 1774 Treaty of Kutchuk-Kainardji, which allowed Russia the right to protect Orthodox Christians living under Ottoman rule.

Castlereagh quickly began diplomatic efforts to avoid an expansive war. This is not to say that Castlereagh had no sympathy for the Greeks. In fact, he wrote to Tsar Alexander I in 1821 in an effort to smooth over tensions between Russia and the Ottoman Empire. He stated that he did desire for the Greeks to overthrow the yoke of the Turks at some point in time but that European sympathy could not "be tempted, nor even called upon in moral duty under loose notions of humanity and amendment, to forget the obligations of existing Treaties, to endanger the frame of long established relations, and to aid the insurrectionary efforts now in progress in Greece."[32] Despite the unwillingness of Parliament to intercede on the Greeks' behalf, popular support for the war remained strong. The Greek Committee of London was the central organization in Britain that collected aid for the Greeks and at least initially was entrusted with the funds raised by American committees.

Some of the first American tourists in the Mediterranean demonstrate early American consciousness of a philhellenic movement inspired by Europeans. Four notable American philhellenes were some of the first Americans to journey to the Mediterranean: Joseph Allen Smith (first American tourist in Greece), Joel Roberts Poinsett (future politician and first American ambassador to Mexico), Nicholas Biddle (future president of the Second Bank of the United States), and Edward Everett. Each desired to travel to both Italy and Greece so that he might visit the ruins of the civilizations to which he believed Americans owed the greatest debt.[33] Through their travels these men heightened an already existing romantic and intellectual interest in ancient Greece among Americans. While Smith and Biddle did make their way to Greece, the closest Poinsett came was his visit to the Greek ruins in Sicily in 1802. Ironically enough, despite his enthusiasm for ancient Greece, Poinsett would be one of the many congressmen in the 1820s to stand in the way of congressionally recognizing the Greek Revolution with financial aid.

Joseph Allen Smith of Charleston was one of the first American tourists (perhaps even the first) to make his way to Greece. Smith traveled extensively throughout Europe and Asia in the 1790s, returning to the United States sometime around 1806. A philhellene, Smith traveled to Greece for reasons not dissimilar from those of the typical Grand Tourist of Europe: to learn about ancient history through personal experience and to collect classical art, whether original or copies. Smith also carried ambitions of receiving an appointment as minister to Russia in the hopes of improving American trade agreements with the Ottoman Empire. Contemporary newspapers and magazines reported on Smith's return and observed that they anticipated printing an account of his adventures.[34] There was overwhelming interest in his travels not only from those hoping to travel to Greece but also from those who wanted to know more about the ancient ruins that remained. Despite the public encouragement to write an account of his travels, Smith never obliged. What is known about his visit to Greece can be gleaned from the writings of others who knew him and through the objects he brought home. Smith donated a portion of his collection to the Pennsylvania Academy of the Fine Arts for the purpose of making the objects open to the public.[35]

Traveling a short time after Smith, Nicholas Biddle became the second American tourist in Greece, making his journey in 1806. Biddle's architecture played a part in the popularity of the Greek revival in the early nineteenth century, but it directly influenced the use of Greek architectural elements in the construction of the Second Bank of the United States.[36] Like so many other European and American tourists, Biddle kept a travel journal and wrote home about his adventures. He wrote about his love for Greece as well as his impressions of the land and the people he encountered. With American independence still fresh, Biddle's thoughts on his travels in Greece reflect his perspective on independence, his devotion to the classics, and early philhellenic notions. "The men of Greece are the descendants of the people who enlightened their country by their virtues," Biddle began, "& who gave by the reflection of their science & their arts the empire of the world to Rome. Shall I be insensible to the pleasure of treading on the ground which had felt the footsteps of Epaminandas of Plato of Demosthenes?"[37]

After traveling in the Mediterranean for several months, young Biddle at last arrived in Athens and was immediately thunderstruck by the ruins and by thoughts of how they must have looked in their heyday. His first letter from Athens to his brother encapsulates the enthusiasm as well as despair for looking upon the ancient city with his own eyes:

My heart beats as I date my letter from the venerable presence of the mistress of the world. . . . Having now seen many of the objects which distance & fiction have exaggerated into greatness, I am able to appreciate the value of Athens. . . . Rome gives but half the ideas of destruction, but Athens reflects the perfect picture of desolation & despair. The recollection of her greatness becomes doubly distressing amidst the traces of her misfortunes, & the mind sickens over the melancholy contrast between the glory of ancient Athens & the misery of her present condition.[38]

Biddle's reflections closely resemble prevalent philhellenic sentiments concerning the current state of Greece. Like so many philhellenes, Biddle seems to argue that the modern Greeks had somehow failed Western civilization because ancient structures nearly two thousand years old were not in the same condition as when they were first completed.

Biddle also lamented that the Greeks had not yet overthrown the Turks. "But it is on the holy spot where this great people assembled to hear their orators," Biddle related to his brother, "to frame laws for themselves to indulge in all the license of freedom, it is here that the fall of Athens is most acutely felt. . . . Where are her people? Are these few wretches, scarcely superior to the beasts whom they drive heedlessly over the ruins, are these men Athenians? Where is her freedom? Alas! this is the keenest stab of all. Bowed down by a foul oppression, the spirit of Athens has bent under its slavery." In another letter also dated June 1806, Biddle observed that the "time does not seem very distant when this country will be relieved from its oppressors," but he first wrote and then struck out "rise against its [oppressors]."[39] This suggests that while Biddle sensed an interest at least among intellectual circles to achieve Greek independence, he was not so sure the Greeks themselves would be able to accomplish it on their own. Indeed, Biddle later personally donated three hundred dollars to the Philadelphia Greek Fund in December 1823.[40] For many philhellenes, this romantic sense of loss, contrasted with the ancient achievements of the Greeks and combined with the notion that only Americans understood how to successfully achieve independence, later provided fuel for the American philhellenic movement.

The influence of philhellenism on Edward Everett, however, proved to be the most pivotal in terms of growing philhellenic sentiment in the United States. Everett was first inspired to become a philhellene while a student at Harvard. In 1814 he gave an oration at Cambridge titled "The Restoration of Greece," reflecting his budding enthusiasm for the Greek cause and his increasing desire to tour that region. Byron's *Childe Harold's Pilgrimage* was a favorite of Everett's and undoubtedly influenced his early perspective on Greece. In fact, the young Everett had his copy of *Childe Harold* signed by the author when on a visit to London. Everett admired Byron's adventures in Athens, supported his opposing opinion on the subject of Lord Elgin's effort to remove the Parthenon marbles from Athens, and was even given letters of introduction to go on his own trip to Greece by Byron himself.[41] In more than a month in Greece, with nearly two weeks in Athens alone, the young American scholar marveled at the ancient Greek ruins. Everett took the enthusiasm instilled in him from his studies, his encounters with European philhellenes, and his scholarly pilgrimage to Greece back home with him, where he found a receptive audience for his lectures on all things Greek.

Upon his return to Boston, Everett helped organize a public exhibition of a well-known painting called *The Panorama of Athens*. Everett had managed to persuade Theodore Lyman, author and personal colleague, to purchase the painting while traveling in Europe. Lauded as the "best executed of the famous Panoramas," the painting was large and impressive to its Boston audience: "The Parthenon, the entrance of the Acropolis, the Temple of Jupiter Olympius, the ruins of the Stadium, the Islands of Aegina and Salamis, the Academy, and the Temple of Theseus, the most perfect ancient ruin in Athens, all unite their attractions in the picture to gratify the classical." *The Panorama of Athens* conveyed the picturesque views of the modern city along with the decaying ruins of the classical age.[42] The arrival of the painting was advertised in the local Boston papers and stimulated public enthusiasm and discussion of Greek history and art. The public praised Lyman's purchase, as this painting was considered a highly desirable work of art at the time. Bostonians were all the more proud of the painting when it was reported that the English universities of Cambridge and Oxford had made efforts to acquire the painting and had failed.[43] Americans also enthusiastically followed the popular classical trends in Europe that dictated popular fashion, interior design, art, and museums, so the acquisition of this painting was a boon for the residents of Boston.[44]

The display of the *Panorama* heightened the importance of Everett's new position at Harvard. The arrival of the *Panorama* and the initial interest in Everett's lectures took place in 1820, two years before Americans would dedicate themselves to supporting the Greek War of Independence. Everett's use of art as a method for inspiring enthusiasm for ancient Greece was an active employment of the philological pedagogy Everett learned in Germany, which clearly resonated with the students of Harvard and the people of Boston in general. The romantic connection between early Americans and Greece had clearly manifested itself, at least within educated circles, before the Greek Revolution began and could be mobilized to attract a broader audience among the general public.

Everett also published numerous pamphlets and articles in newspapers and magazines, especially through his involvement with the *North American Review and Miscellaneous Journal*.[45] Everett's vocal support for the Greek cause helped him win national notoriety as the voice of the American philhellenic movement. In fact, as Everett began to call for support for the Greeks, he discouraged interest in supporting revolutions in South America, stating that early Americans had more in common with Europeans than "our sister states in South America." "We are sprung from different stocks, we speak different languages, we have been brought up in different social and moral schools," explained Everett to his *North American Review* readers. Seeing no reason why Americans should support South American revolutions with aid, Everett observed, "They would not act in our spirit, they would not follow our advice, they could not imitate our example."[46] Greece, however, was the ancestor of their own cultural tradition and therefore deserving of American support.

American taste for things Greek in many ways followed the same patterns as those in Europe. The common principle that bound these different philhellenic movements together was the hope of returning modern Greece to its former glory. While the United States in many ways lagged behind its European counterparts in terms of sponsoring archaeological expeditions and sending visitors to Greece, Americans nonetheless were just as devoted to the philhellenic cause due to their own experience in overthrowing tyranny.[47] On the eve of the Greek Revolution, much had already been written by American intellectuals and politicians on the subject of Greek nationhood, but the idea that Americans would provide aid to the Greeks to bring about this result was not necessarily what they had in mind. This rapidly changed as interest in the Greeks grew. The belief that the United States desired to be competitive on the global stage of politics and commerce combined with an overwhelming sentiment that Americans understood the task that lay before the Greeks better than Europeans would transform the American philhellenic movement into a unique and independent one.

The Greek Revolution Begins

The combination of increasing international philhellenic support for Greece with internal conflict within the Ottoman Empire precipitated the outbreak of the Greek Revolution. Sultan Mahmud II ascended to power in 1808 and was determined to reverse the decline of his empire. One issue that had plagued the empire was the conflict between the sultan and his pashas, whose roles were to govern various provinces within the empire while still also remaining ultimately under the direction and rule of the sultan. Many of these pashas were independent and were reluctant at best to pay tribute and allegiance to the sultan. One independent pasha that Sultan Mahmud wished to assert authority over was Ali Pasha of Ioannina, the ruler of Albania and northwestern Greece.[48] In 1820 the sultan ordered Ali Pasha to come to Constantinople in person in order to address certain crimes for which he had been accused. Ali Pasha refused and was therefore declared a rebel.[49]

Many philhellenes and Greek intellectuals worried that if the sultan proved successful in suppressing Ali Pasha, then Ottoman power in Greece would be strengthened, making a revolution in the future more difficult to achieve. If a rebellion began before a conflict between Ali Pasha and the sultan were settled, then the Ottoman forces would be divided and weak. Plans for a revolution within the Filiki Etaireia, therefore, began to take a more solid shape in 1820.[50]

Ottoman officials may have been aware of rumors concerning a potential revolution in the weeks that led up to the outbreak of war, but there is little evidence to suggest that the Ottomans possessed knowledge of a planned insurrection made by an organized secret society consisting primarily of Phanariot members. Ottoman documents reveal a general sense of surprise at Alexandros Ypsilantis's plans for inciting insurrection and assumed at first that the conflict was orchestrated by Russia. Phanariotes later were targeted for blame, with the sultan issuing orders to punish important members of the Greek community linked with the uprising. The Ottoman perception of the impending conflict suggested disbelief that the Greek *reaya* would carry out an unprovoked rebellion. The Greeks knew that the Ottoman army lacked the resources needed to suppress a widespread rebellion. They increasingly realized that if they desired to strike out against the Turks, time was of the essence. In October 1820, Ypsilantis and members of the Society of Friends met in Izmail, Moldavia, to make solid plans, including for the dispatching of Society "apostles" to Greek regions and the Greek diaspora.[51]

Alexandros Ypsilantis and members of the Filiki Etaireia seized the moment. Ypsilantis expected support from the Russian court, as he planned to incite rebellion among Christian subjects of the Danubian principalities Wallachia and Moldavia, then within Ottoman suzerainty. His plan churned up already existing tensions between the Ottoman Empire and Russia when the sultan received word that Ypsilantis, who had connections with Russian elites, was planning a rebellion against him. Sultan Mahmud II began to weigh his options in engaging Russia or mobilizing subjects in Rumelia, a region north of Greece in the Balkan Peninsula. The sultan was faced with a difficult situation—a rebellion on the one hand and a possible war with Russia on the other. If the sultan were to call for general mobilization against Ypsilantis, it would be to "ostensibly punish the rebellious subjects in Moldavia and Wallachia without disclosing any news of a campaign against Russia."[52] The sultan waited to see what kind of support Ypsilantis would receive, either from locals or from Russia.

When the expected support from Christian subjects within Wallachia and Moldavia did not come, Ypsilantis issued a proclamation in October 1820 that alluded to supposed support from Russia for a rebellion against the Ottomans. This proclamation, which was reprinted throughout Europe and the United States, drew on Greek nationalist and religious rhetoric to generate enthusiasm among the Greeks: "Turn your eyes, fellow citizens, and observe our deplorable situation; see our temples defiled, our children torn from our arms by our barbarous tyrants, for their shameful pleasures; our houses despoiled, our fields devastated, and ourselves vile slaves."[53] Ypsilantis never did incite general support among Romanians and Slavs for a Greek uprising, despite the assumption the Filiki Etaireia made that such an effort would benefit not only the Greeks but other Balkan peoples.[54] The Russian tsar also publicly denounced Ypsilantis, despite his previous support of Greek intellectuals. With slow progress and lack of military planning, the Ottomans defeated Ypsilantis and his band of Greek expatriates. The Filiki Etaireia, however, had managed to organize support for Greek independence within the Morea, where Ypsilantis and his army had been expected to arrive.[55] Though Ypsilantis's efforts to lead the rebellion had been quashed by the Ottomans, the revolutionary efforts of the Filiki Etaireia remained within Greece and began to resonate with Europeans and Americans on a sentimental and political level.[56]

In order to diffuse a potential conflict, Turkish officials ordered the Greeks to turn in their weapons to local authorities and for local Greek leaders to come in person to Tripolitsa, the largest town in the Peloponnese at the time. Ottoman efforts to avoid conflict had the precise opposite effect on the Greek populace. In February 1821 the Greeks, led by bishops and priests, unleashed a spree of ruthless bloodshed, slaughtering thousands, including women and children. With pockets of rebellion emerging in Greece and elsewhere within the empire, Mahmud II responded with force. The status of many Greeks was reduced within the Ottoman government, most notably the patriarch of Constantinople, though he had not played a role in the organization of the rebellion.

He was publicly hanged on Easter Sunday, fanning the flames for an extended conflict.[57]

After the immediate outset of the conflict, newspapers in the United States enthusiastically reported that the Greeks had engaged in an insurrection "of a most formidable kind."[58] Still other reports detailed that bloodshed had taken place in Tripolitsa, where "all the Turks . . . who could not save themselves by flight were massacred, and the city itself almost wholly laid in ashes." In one example alone, the Greeks were said to have massacred 26,000 Turks.[59] The Greek cause had attracted many European volunteers in the early months of the war, many of whom were present at the time of the massacre at Tripolitsa. For these European volunteers, Tripolitsa proved to be so horrifying and disgusting that many abandoned their philhellenic ideals and quickly returned home. Philhellenes in Europe and the United States, however, either dismissed reports that portrayed the Greeks committing gross atrocities against civilians or excused their behavior as a result of so many years living under tyranny.[60]

Numerous Americans were especially taken with Alexandros Ypsilantis's call to arms for Greek subjects within the Ottoman Empire. Ypsilantis used philhellenic language to appeal to Europeans to assist the Greeks: "The civilized people of Europe are busy in laying the foundations of their happiness, and, full of gratitude for the benefits they received from our forefathers, desire liberty of Greece. Showing ourselves worthy of our virtuous ancestors, and of the age, we hope to deserve their support and their aid, and many of them, partisans of our liberty, will come to fight by our sides."[61] At first printed in Europe and then reprinted in the United States beginning in May 1821, Ypsilantis's appeal generated widespread interest and enthusiasm for the possibility of Greek freedom. Indeed, some Americans were so inspired by Ypsilantis's leadership in the Greek Revolution that one community in the Michigan Territory named its town after him. Whether one lived in the north, south, east, or west, Ypsilantis's call to arms to spread independence to Greece resonated with early Americans.

Public interest only increased as news arrived from abroad about the Greeks' progress. Hundreds of news reports were printed via intelligence from European sources as well as from American merchants in the Mediterranean.[62] Addresses from European philhellenes such as Admontios Korais were printed as well, which solicited aid for the Greek cause. One such address, titled "Proclamation of the Messenian Senate," was sent by the provisional Greek government to Greek expatriates living in Europe in order to rouse support for the Greek cause. Korais translated the proclamation and sent it to his American philhellene contact in Boston, Edward Everett. The article was printed and reprinted throughout the country, notably linking the Greek cause with the American Revolution: "It is now for you to perfect your glory, in aiding us to purge Greece from the barbarians, who for four centuries have polluted it. . . . No, the country of Penn, of Franklin, and of Washington, cannot refuse her and to the descendants of Phocion, Thrasybulus, Aratus, and Philopoemen."[63]

By December 1821 foreign intelligence revealed that "many foreigners had arrived in the Morea and joined the Greeks."[64] In the months that followed, newspaper editors continued to print news of the enlistment of European philhellenes. Recruits from across Europe, including England, France, Russia, and Germany, formed whole battalions of volunteers assembled for the purpose of serving in the Greek army. Though few American volunteers joined the Greek army at this time, they began to do so in greater numbers a few years later. In the first two years of the war, the American public followed the events in Greece with interest and supported the Greek cause, but primarily on a sentimental and romantic level.

American philhellenes frequently expressed this romanticism through popular literature such as poetry. American poets captured similar themes found in the poetry of Lord Byron, making reference to Greece's ancient achievements. They referred to Greek nationalism and the obligation to be in democratic solidarity with the Greeks. While the poetry does not always directly call for political or charitable activism, it is implied. This rhetoric provided some of the earliest momentum for a more active Greek relief effort in the United States. One noteworthy American poet named James Gates Percival reflected some of these early themes. Percival's published volumes of poetry were widely advertised in newspapers, which suggest his popularity as well as widespread access to his works. Percival wrote several poems on the Greek Revolution over the course of the 1820s with the first being printed in 1821. His poems drew heavily upon philhellenic rhetoric, referenced the classical world as a major reason for why the Greeks should ultimately triumph, and inspired American readers to support the Greek cause. By aiding the Greek War and "her ancient liberty," Americans would be fulfilling a philanthropic obligation to their intellectual forebears and thus might "live immortal." Percival's language, like other philhellenic rhetoric of the time, would eventually motivate a widespread effort to support the war.[65]

One of Percival's first poems on the subject of the Greek Revolution was "Ode on the Emancipation of Greece: Greek War Song." The poem combined ancient and modern history and urged modern Greeks to take courage from their ancient past. Percival wrote that Greece was undergoing a new beginning at that time in which "the demigods of old arose, / And, mantled in the patriot's might, / Drove back in shame their myriad foes, / And crown'd their brows with civic wreaths of light."[66] Percival's use of "civic wreaths of light" contrasts with the supposed darkness that had blanketed the Greeks under Ottoman control. Now through an awareness of their ancient past, the Greeks could once again be guided by civic duty in order to achieve freedom. Only through the guiding light of civic duty could the Greeks succeed "where tyrants shall make their last stand for their thrones." At last the Greeks had awakened from their "long, long, dream of prostrate thralldom" and had chosen their moment to rise up against the Turks.[67]

What made supporting the Greeks exciting and attractive to the American public was that by doing so they were, in a romantic sense, becoming part of an ancient struggle against tyranny. They connected themselves with a story containing, in their minds, some of the greatest heroes of all time. This is the sort of abstract, romantic enthusiasm that permeated American society at the beginning of the war. The unity that the Greek cause inspired among the general American population in many ways was also linked with the nationalist sentiment that emerged after the War of 1812. This period is characterized by an awakening of American nationalism and a move toward national unity. The display of nationalist sentiment and public celebration of American achievements was intentionally linked to the American Revolution, and through the print culture of the time, it must have made it seem that Americans from both the North and South shared in the same traditions and celebrations. President James Monroe in particular cultivated this new mode of politics that, at least for white Americans, endeavored to create unity—an era of good feelings.[68] The Greek cause was adopted as part of this common celebration and unity in the early 1820s. Even though division on the issue of slavery had begun to emerge with the Missouri Crisis, that the Greeks were viewed as white and Christian made the cause palatable for both North and South.

American Philhellenism in Motion

A shift in interest from mere romanticism to activism emerged in response to James Monroe's December 1822 State of the Union address. For many American philhellenes, public interest and support for the Greeks led them to expect that the president would perhaps announce some kind of formal recognition of Greek independence or at least provide aid, as had France. But Monroe showed no signs of providing official acknowledgement or aid. He observed, rather, "The mention of Greece fills the mind with the most exalted sentiments, and arouses in our bosoms the best feelings of which our nature is susceptible. . . . It was natural, therefore, that the re-appearance of those people in their original character, contending in favour of their liberties, should produce that great excitement and sympathy in their favor, which have been so signally displayed throughout the United States."[69] Monroe therefore only recognized the validity of the general public's interest and support for the Greeks. The public understood his not pledging official support to mean that his administration planned to stay out of the conflict. Monroe's address signaled that the United States, which for many early Americans should have been at the forefront of philhellenic support, would be outdone by its European counterparts. This was not a revelation American philhellenes were willing to accept.

In response, 138 notable citizens of Washington and Georgetown submitted one of the first memorials to Congress calling for financial support for the Greeks. Pointing to Greece's classical past and its influence on the American Revolution as the foundational reason for supporting the Greeks, the signers of the memorial called for a hefty sum of money to be appropriated by Congress that totaled two or three million dollars in "provisions, and whatever may be necessary" to the Greeks. Henry Dwight of Massachusetts introduced the memorial to the House of Representatives. Dwight stated that he was certain it was not an exaggeration to assert that there was a deep sympathy throughout the country in support of the Greeks. Although his remarks were not intended "to commit himself to any ulterior measures upon the subject," Dwight argued that given the vocal national interest in the Greek Revolution, he supported at least debating the topic on the House floor.[70]

Debate over the memorial commenced, with Robert Wright of Maryland arguing in opposition. Wright said that he "trusted this House was not prepared to commit the peace of this nation, by interfering, in any manner, in the contests of Europe." He acknowledged it was natural for Americans to sympathize with any people struggling for liberty, "but this petition is from a number of philanthropists petitioning for others, not with the purview of the Constitution." Wright went on to say that once Greece became independent, the United States would acknowledge the fact, just as it had "in the case of the Governments of South America, in our own hemisphere."[71] Wright made reference to the public support for revolutions within Spanish colonies of Latin America.[72] There was therefore already a precedent in place for neutrality, not military activism. John Rhea of Tennessee concurred, stating that neutrality was the best path and pointing out that to support the memorial would place the Congress in opposition to the Executive, referring to Monroe's recent address. Though members of the public had expressed enthusiasm for the spread of independence within the Western hemisphere, officially supporting the Greeks was deemed ill-advised by members of Congress. It was then decided, with bipartisan support, that the memorial be tabled, to the disappointment of the memorial's signers.

American philhellenism as a popular, national movement surged again late in the summer of 1823. This time it was in response to the poet Lord Byron. The Greek Committee of London had long been trying to persuade Byron to lead its efforts in Greece by commanding a brigade of light artillery. Edward Blaquiere, a leading member of the Greek Committee of London, wrote to Byron, who was living in Genoa at the time, promising that should he join the Greeks his "presence will operate as a talisman." He continued: "The field is too glorious, too closely associated with all that you hold dear to be any longer abandoned. . . . The effect produced by my mentioning the fact of your intention to join it, has been quite electric."[73] After months of flattery, Byron finally agreed to join the Greek army and departed Genoa for Greece on July 13, 1823, on a chartered vessel that included several other volunteers, horses, cannon, medicine, and 10,000 Spanish dollars in cash. To philhellenes throughout Europe and the United States, the Greek Committee of London had just proven that its dedication to the Greek cause was sincere.

Though Byron had initially agreed to set sail for Greece as the Greek Committee of London's champion in April, news of his departure did not arrive in the United States until June. One enthusiastic report observed, "The lovers of freedom and of genius . . . will rejoice to hear that Lord Byron is going to quit the shores of Italy, and take his departure for Greece, there to join the standard of the oppressed."[74] For the next several months, reports on Byron, the officers that traveled with him, and the fortune he spent on supplies for the Greeks were discussed throughout the United States in both newspapers and magazines. One article printed and reprinted several times in October noted in awe that Byron "intends to buckle on the armour, to breast the storm of war, by aiding these persecuted people in their struggle for liberty. If so, probably the star of his glory will shine in the eastern hemisphere, and his literary talents be lost to the world, as the chances are against his life's being preserved."[75] Newspapers noted any updates from the war front, especially if they concerned Lord Byron. There were reports concerning the philhellenic efforts of other European nations besides Britain, France in particular. In the months that followed, many American philhellenes assumed that the United States would no longer ignore Greece's war for independence and at last would provide assistance. This assumption was proven wrong in December 1823.

Monroe's seventh address to Congress is primarily remembered for outlining a foreign policy that came to be known as the "Monroe Doctrine," in which the president warned European powers against new colonization in the Americas. However, Monroe also addressed the conflict in Greece: "A strong hope has been long entertained, founded on the heroic struggle of the Greeks, that they would succeed in their contest, and resume their equal station among the nations of the earth."[76] Monroe's comments acknowledged public interest in Greek affairs but did not extend any kind of monetary or military commitment to the cause. Neutrality would continue to be Monroe's course on the subject of the Greek question. Although he did not outline the details for this decision in the address, it became clear in the years that followed that it was part of a complicated matter concerning the United States' long-standing efforts to secure a commercial treaty with the Sublime Porte.

Days later, on December 8, Daniel Webster, member of Congress from Massachusetts and ardent supporter of Greek independence, responded to Monroe's statements by proposing that an agent be sent by the U.S. government to Greece. Webster's proposal offered up the possibility of the United States recognizing Greece as a free nation and raised the question of direct assistance to its war for independence.[77] Congress addressed the proposal in a series of debates beginning on January 19, 1824, with Webster leading the way in a now famous speech.

Webster directly addressed the president's statements from the previous month in his speech: "If the sentiments of the message in respect to Greece be proper, it is equally proper that this House should reciprocate those sentiments." He emphasized that unless the United States sent an agent to Greece the country would be supporting "principles not only utterly hostile to our own free institutions, but hostile also to the independence of all nations, and altogether opposed to the improvement of the condition of human nature."[78] Webster tied the Greek cause to the freedom of all Americans, essentially arguing that independence throughout the world was an American interest. Webster claimed that Greek independence, especially because of the influence ancient Greece had imparted to "the admiration and the benefit of mankind," was worthy of recognition and action on the part of the federal government.

Webster's speech stirred up much discussion and debate but resulted in political gridlock in Washington. Representative Samuel Breck of Pennsylvania wrote to a friend in January 1824 complaining that public and private business in Congress "is postponed to make room for idle debates in relation to the Greeks, who are no more entitled to our money or sympathy than the hindoos."[79] Even Joel Poinsett, who as a young man dreamed of traveling to Greece, similarly complained about those who supported the Greek cause: "Nothing in my opinion can be more absurd than a romantic statesman, and I am opposed to chivalry in politics."[80] Support or opposition to the Greek cause does not appear to have been a specifically partisan issue. Men from both sides of the aisle supported and opposed the cause. Those who did not support Webster's resolution generally supported independence for Greece but either favored neutrality in European affairs or desired to cultivate a trade relationship with the Ottoman Empire and therefore saw supporting Greece as counterproductive.

Although President Monroe himself was pro-Greece, his sympathy was met with a negative reception from his secretary of state, John Quincy Adams. Adams thought philhellenism was purely sentimental and not in the best interests of the United States in the long run. Adams was in the midst of yet another attempt to negotiate a commercial treaty with the Sublime Porte and was not about to allow a sentimental cause to jeopardize it. There were historical reasons for not wanting to actively support revolutions abroad for fear of those ideas making their way back to the United States. There were also immediate reasons for not viewing support for Greece as diplomatically wise.[81]

In fact, the extent to which Adams had discouraged support for Greece came to light in late December 1823. With heightened interest in the Greek cause combined with Webster's call for a commissioner to be sent to Greece, the House requested that the president provide a report and accompanying documents relating the present conditions and future prospects of the Greeks. The report and documents were presented to the House on December 31.[82] The accompanying documents included letters written between Adams, Richard Rush, American minister to Britain, and Andreas Luriottis, agent for the provisional Greek government. These documents were printed in newspapers and magazines nationwide in January 1824. In these letters it was revealed that the Greek government had been directly appealing for American support for over a year and that the Monroe administration had denied the requests.[83] This revelation, in addition to Webster's words on the House floor, made waves in public circles across the country and initiated a proactive philhellenic movement in the United States.

As Congress began its debates concerning whether or not to support the Greeks, communities throughout the United States answered Webster's call for organized support in their own way. Local organizations consciously linked ancient Greece and the Greek Revolution to the American Revolution, using this connection to appeal to others to become involved in the cause. Calls for support once again cast the Ottoman Turks as members of a "race of merci-less and incorrigible barbarians" and linked early Americans culturally, reli-giously, and racially with the Greeks. "Can the heart of sensibility endure for a moment the thought," wondered members of a Greek relief committee in Hartford, Connecticut, at the reports of the suffering Greeks, "would not every arm be uplifted to snatch so large a portion of our race from being consigned by their ruthless oppressors to slavery, dishonor, and death?"[84] These organ-izations included literary, political, community, and religious groups. Com-mittee members frequently organized fund-raising efforts around patriotic holidays, especially Washington's Birthday and the Fourth of July, in order to gather support from the American public.

The Greek Committee of Boston was one of the leading philhellenic organ-izations in the United States with Edward Everett, the noted philhellene and classical scholar, a founding member. This group became the central organ-ization not just for the Boston area but also for the region, with smaller New England philhellenic organizations sending donations to it on a regular basis. Created on December 19, 1823, Boston's Greek Relief Committee immedi-ately began to mobilize fund-raising efforts.[85] Due to Everett's connections, the committee later published correspondence from American philhellenes fighting in Greece, including George Jarvis, Jonathan Peckham Miller, and Samuel Gridley Howe. Everett's reputation as a philhellene, as well as his con-nections both domestic and abroad, led to him being added to a short list of potential delegates that President Monroe considered sending as an agent to Greece.[86] As the preeminent American philhellene, Everett also corresponded with other American philhellenes and philanthropists on the subject of the Greeks. Mathew Carey, noted Philadelphia printer, also became an important organizer for the American philhellenic movement, frequently combining his efforts with those of the Boston committee.

Carey was born in Dublin, Ireland, in 1760 and at a young age entered the publishing industry. A Catholic, Carey criticized the treatment of Irish Cath-olics under British rule by printing and distributing pamphlets. Threatened with prosecution, Carey left Ireland for Paris in 1781. In Paris Carey met Ben-jamin Franklin and became his apprentice. Carey accompanied Franklin to Philadelphia in 1784 and quickly became a noted and well-connected printer, bookseller, philanthropist, and political economist. Carey fully embraced his American citizenship and lauded the achievements of the American Revolu-tion. His American nationalist sentiments had developed in the popular spirit that followed the War of 1812 and influenced his printing, which publicly sup-ported philanthropic causes devoted to uplifting and educating a number of groups of people at home and abroad. With regard to his undying support for the relief of his countrymen in Ireland, Carey's rhetoric on this subject eventually was defined in terms of his own experience of living in the United States, where he thought Irish Catholics stood the best chance for freedom and prosperity.[87] It is perhaps due to his background as a persecuted Irishman and his devotion to the ideals of liberty that he came to support the Greek cause. Though not specifically a philhellene, but a well-known philanthropist in his time, Carey was an important element to the success of the Greek Committee of Philadelphia. He was able to attract notable figures to serve with him on the committee as well as obtaining monetary aid and supplies for the cause.

Initially formed by Dickinson College's Union Philosophical Society, Mathew Carey became a leading member of the Greek Committee of Philadelphia.[88] Other notable members of the committee included Joseph Hemphill (congressman from Pennsylvania), Joseph Watson (mayor of Philadelphia), Roberts Vaux (jurist and philanthropist), William Meredith (president of Schuylkill Bank), James Ronaldson (philanthropist), James N. Barker (playwright), and James C. Biddle (of the prominent Philadelphia Biddle family). The Greek Committee of Philadelphia was formed at approximately the same time as many other American philhellenic organizations and regularly corresponded with other philhellenic relief groups, often coordinating efforts.

Greece became part of a national conversation by January 1824, by which time the Philadelphia-based organization was fund-raising actively. Mathew Carey was then the committee's secretary, with George M. Dallas the chairman. Dallas was a noted public figure. Then the deputy attorney general of Philadelphia, he was later elected mayor of Philadelphia, U.S. senator, and vice president of the United States under James K. Polk.

In a printed letter dated January 5, 1824, Dallas requested that recipients and their friends attend a theatrical production to be performed for charity the following week. He expressed dismay that such entertainments for charity had not yet proven successful in gathering a substantial amount of funding for the Greek cause in Philadelphia "notwithstanding the acknowledged liberality of its citizens."[89] It is not possible to know for certain how many of these letters were sent out, but it was enough so that a form letter was printed. Given the quick reaction to the president's address from just a few weeks prior, it seems likely that Dallas was attempting to play on the sympathies of the reader and was exaggerating the Greek Committee's failure at raising relief in order to guarantee support. The printed letter was additionally noteworthy because it was intended for women. Philhellenic leaders began to mobilize community-based ladies' societies in the service of the cause. In the coming years of the American philhellenic movement, women would play one of the most important organizational roles in gathering aid and contributions.

Dallas's letter was obviously worded in order to convey a sense of urgency. His efforts were not in vain. The Greek Committee account books for the last week of December 1823 indicate that more than four hundred dollars in donations had been deposited into the Schuylkill Bank; by the end of the following month that amount had grown to almost $2,600. If the Greek Committee got off to a slow start, subsequent donations made up for it. The committee maintained an active membership and a constant level of donations for the duration of the war. By 1826 the committee's treasury books reveal that it had deposited thousands of dollars into the Schuylkill Bank.[90]

In addition to the fund-raising of the Greek relief societies in Boston and Philadelphia, the Greek Committee of New York also became important, serving as a national collection point for all donations made to the Greek cause. The Committee of the Greek Fund of the City of New York was formed officially on December 3, 1823. At its inception, the Greek Committee of New York resolved that it would appoint a seventy-person committee to "solicit subscriptions from this and neighboring States" as well as to "prepare a Memorial to Congress praying that the Independence of the Greek nation be recognized by the American government."[91]

On December 12, the Greek Committee of New York printed a pamphlet stating that the group intended to correspond "with the Friends of the Greek Cause, in the other Cities and Towns of the Union, and to request them to call Public Meetings, and to take such other measures as may be adapted to promote the success of that Cause." The pamphlet went on to articulate the shift from philhellenic sentimentalism to activism that would take place in the coming months:

> The Citizens of New-York have desired to manifest their sentiments on this subject, by something more substantial than the mere expression of their good wishes and fervent aspirations for the triumph of regenerated Greece; and they now seek the cooperation of their fellow-citizens in every part of the Union, whose hearts are engaged in this noble work. . . . We also request that . . . the amount of any pecuniary contributions which may be raised in your City, may be remitted to Charles Wilkes, Esquire, the Treasurer of the Greek Fund.[92]

A few weeks later the New York committee submitted a memorial to Congress. Read on December 29, 1823, the committee requested that the federal government acknowledge the Greek nation and asserted that the Greeks "have proved themselves competent to maintain their independence."[93] The memorial dismissed previous notions that questioned the modern Greeks' ability to rise up against the Turks and defend themselves against tyranny. The document pointed out to Congress that the Greeks had clearly proven themselves worthy of liberty and, ergo, deserved American support. The Greek Fund's acknowledgment of the modern Greeks' worthiness, and the unworthiness of the Turks, was something the organization repeatedly emphasized as a reason to become engaged in the cause.

Even though the Greek Committee of New York enjoyed the longest lasting success of the many Greek committees in the United States, it was not the first to be created. A Greek aid society in Brooklyn predated the New York committee and had much success in the early years of the war in generating enthusiasm for the Greek cause. Women played a leading role in the society's success. The women of Brooklyn organized their own subcommittee in 1822 and endeavored to raise funds for a memorial cross to be erected to the Greek cause on the Brooklyn Heights. They published a pamphlet comprised of a collection of newspaper articles that had been published over the course of a year concerning the acquisition of funds for a "Grecian Cross" to be placed to honor the Greeks. Calling themselves the "Grecian Ladies," the women described their efforts in a New York newspaper:

> Some ladies of this city . . . have caused a Grecian Cross to be prepared, 40 feet high, which was yesterday conveyed to General Swift at Brooklyn. . . . It is, we understand, to be planted on the Brooklyn Heights, facing the city. Its elevation, however, is delayed until the committee who have it in charge can ascertain of what material the Grecian wreath of victory was composed, as they desire to surmount the Cross with such an one. We are authorized to state that a "Golden Token" will be presented to any "Grecian" who will furnish the requisite information on this subject.[94]

The Grecian wreath of victory that is mentioned refers to the material used in ancient Greek victory garlands. The entire pamphlet is focused on this debate, as the Grecian Ladies desired to accurately recreate a similar garland for the cross, thus combining symbols of Christian charity and ancient Greece. There was also discussion as to whether to include an inscription. One suggestion was to use a line from Byron's famous pro-Greek poem *Childe Harold's Pilgrimage*, "Sons of the Greeks arise."[95]

This debate went on for months. In fact, the cross itself was erected on the Brooklyn Heights in 1823 but awaited decorative embellishments from its creators. The pamphlet, published in December 1824, was over one hundred pages long. The essence of the argument boiled down to a desire to commemorate Greece's revolution while also connecting the conflict to an American audience. One contributor responded to some who did not think the cross should be adorned with any ancient garlands or classical references. The contributor's reply was to suggest that the cross itself was an "ensign or banner, and by it we are to recognize modern Greece in the same manner as our own land is to be recognized by an Eagle and star-spangled banner. . . . Their Cross, to them, is the banner of freedom. . . . Let the daughters of Columbia decorate it with the wreaths of Victorious Greece."[96] The author thus suggested that even if modern Greeks might associate their identity more with the cross, American philhellenes saw the Greek Revolution as a potential rebirth of democracy in Greece and therefore viewed the use of classical motifs in the monument as essential. The monument then would be a fusion of Christian charity and classical devotion that American philhellenes felt and assumed they shared with the modern Greeks fighting for their independence.

Though the united effort at erecting a monument to the Greeks was sentimental, the conversation about the memorial by the end of 1824 reflects the changing interest in providing aid to the Greeks. The pamphlet itself was a publication intended to be sold so that the Grecian Ladies might "present to the Grecian Senate some memorial of their country's sympathy, which, whenever it meets their eyes, may remind them of those, who, though parted from them by a wide expanse of waters, are yet with them in their every effort for national deliverance."[97] The Grecian Ladies were confident their call for aid would not go unnoticed, as they were certain their countrymen understood the importance of Greece's success to the "friends of humanity and liberty."[98]

Grecian societies also existed outside the urban cities of the North. One of the first groups was the Periclean Society, a debate and literary society in Alexandria, in the then–District of Columbia. Founded in September 1821, this organization was comprised of prominent men from the surrounding area. The Periclean Society's meeting minutes reflect a keen interest in exchanging original, classically inspired poetry and engaging in debate on classical history and politics. By the fall of 1823, however, the society was struggling with a declining attendance record.[99] The philhellenic cause proved to have, at least for a brief period of time, a rejuvenating effect on the society's membership. The

Periclean Society also reflects the shift that took place in the United States from sentimentalism to activism toward Greece.

The Periclean Society met the week Daniel Webster first proposed supporting the Greeks on the House floor. On December 13, 1823, the members of the society convened their weekly Saturday meeting. This was not an ordinary meeting, however. Meetings typically consisted of leisurely debate on topics ranging from ancient history to politics, but business as usual was postponed to discuss what could be done for the Greek cause. Meeting at the Alexandria Town Hall, members spent the evening drawing up the society's official stance on the revolution and how they might respond. More than just holding a debate on the merits of Greece's war for independence, the members of the committee feverishly planned a public declaration of support for the war by incorporating their devotion to the Greek cause into the upcoming celebration of "the birth of the illustrious Washington." With plans to advertise their fund-raising efforts in all the newspapers of the District of Columbia, the society drew up a resolution to join their celebration of Washington's birthday with fund-raising for the Greek cause::

> Whereas the Greeks are the descendants of those illustrious statesmen, philosophers, orators, poets, historians, artists and commanders, who, by their writing, works and actions have conferred immortal honor on themselves. . . . Understanding the severe oppression under which they [the Greeks] have labored for ages that they are destitute of those means of defence . . . and this society having agreed to celebrate the 22d of February next by the delivery of an oration to be pronounced by one of its members, a day consecrated in the sympathy of mankind by the birth of the illustrious Washington, and considering it a suitable period for the collection of funds to aid the cause of the Greeks, Therefore it is Resolved that an appeal be made by the orator to the citizens in favor of the suffering Greeks and that a collection be taken up, the proceeds of which are to be applied to the assistance of that virtuous and heroic people.[100]

In fact, society members scrutinized the word choice and phrasing of this declaration, going through several drafts before they settled on a final resolution two weeks later. To the members of the Periclean Society, Greek independence from the Ottoman Empire, it seemed, was perhaps the most important issue they could help advance as a Greek-inspired literary society.

As they considered this proposal, members also suggested creating a separate society to be known as the "Grecian Society" that would serve as a philhellenic organization devoted to supporting the Greeks "by contribution of money." Every member would thus "obtain an increase in friends to the Holy cause in which we are engaged."[101] The proposal was adopted. By creating the Grecian Society, this literary organization could solve two problems with one step: the philhellenic appeal to the community would boost its membership numbers, and the organization would be devoted to something more exciting than listening to each other's poetry.

The first effort the Grecian Society made in gathering money was its organizing a public debate for January 17 where admission would be charged. The editor of the *Alexandria Gazette* endorsed the event with a separate memorandum in the January 13 issue and assured his readers that the admission fee would be well spent. In addition to his endorsement, the editor stated that however little one could spare for the cause, "it will prove that the young men of our town, sympathise with the Greeks, in their effort to shake off a yoke, more galling than that under which any people ever labored."[102] For the residents of Alexandria, the Greeks had long been enslaved by the Turks and had suffered a gross indignity as a people for centuries. The editor did not hint at any sense of irony in that Alexandria had a thriving slave market where humans of a different race were bought and sold as property without a second thought.

Interest in supporting the Greeks was more widespread and enthusiastic than the Grecian Society initially expected. The society immediately perceived an opportunity to expand its numbers and influence within the community. Society members quickly organized a public debate on "Which of the two should be more admired, Pericles or Epaminondas?" Admission to the event was twenty-five cents, a moderate amount for the time, given that on the same day the event was advertised in the *Alexandria Gazette*, residents could expect to pay three cents per pound for spare ribs, six and three-quarter cents per pound for sausage, and eight to ten cents for salted pork. It is unlikely that those in attendance would have been of a low socioeconomic circumstance. Due to increasing enthusiasm for the Greek cause, however, and because this debate was open to members of the public, attendance was three times greater than a typical meeting of Periclean Society members. The event was so successful that the society put on two other debates that month.[103]

The society also organized a larger fund-raiser for the Greeks, combining it with the local celebration of Washington's Birthday. In the weeks leading up to February 22nd, the Grecian Society received letters of support from several organizations, including a group of officers in the 1st Artillerists. This group was selected to escort the members of the Grecian Society to the community festivities on Washington's Birthday. In thanks for the society's efforts, the officers wrote that they claimed "the Greeks as brother patriots in distress, persevering in a cause peculiarly dear to Americans, as it brings to their recollection their own contest for liberty though opposed to a more honorable enemy."[104]

The Grecian Society also received a supportive letter from a local youth debate club called the Ciceronian Society. The Ciceronian Society expressed its enthusiasm for the Greek cause in the pursuit of liberty from the "cruelties excised by the barbarous Turks over the illustrious Greeks." The youth group also observed that enthusiasm for the Greek cause had excited the sympathies of "the whole American family." The letter continued: "Every bosom beats high at the name of Greece and every hand is ready to give her that relief which she so much needs." The youths of their community "felt how much they owed to Ancient Greece for their present felicity and they thought it their duty to aid the descendants of such men as Leonidas, Pericles, Miltiades, and Epaminondas." This group of fourteen youths had gathered $7.75 and requested that their club president send the money to the Grecian Society to aid the Greek cause.[105] These young boys had managed to do this two months after the Grecian Society held its first fund-raising debate and less than one month after the Grecian Society connected its fund-raising with Washington's Birthday.

The Grecian Society would not have been successful unless its message had resonated within the community. While the society's organized efforts ignited an activist approach to philhellenism, it is safe to say that the society could not have made such an immediate impression in the community if receptivity to philhellenism had not already existed within popular culture. The society's connecting of the Greek Revolution to Washington's Birthday also suggests that Greece's war for independence was linked to the tradition of liberty secured by the American Revolution.

The first few months of 1824 were fruitful for philhellenic groups. In a similar fashion as the Periclean Society in Alexandria, committees in many other cities paired their Washington's Birthday celebrations with the Greek cause. In Providence, Rhode Island, for example, community festivities were advertised in the local paper, which reminded prospective attendees that after the entertainment, "a collection will be taken up, for the benefit of the enslaved and suffering nations whose cause has been a warmly espoused in this land of freedom."[106] The people of Petersburg, Virginia, held a ball on Washington's Birthday with "the nett proceeds to go to the benefit of the Greeks."[107] Greek supporters in Cheraw, South Carolina, raised $225 in just one evening, while another group in Savannah, Georgia, raised $350.[108] Enthusiasm for the Greek cause was so high in South Carolina that the state legislature submitted a resolution to the U.S. House of Representatives on January 2, 1824, asking the government to formally recognize Greek independence.[109]

Hundreds of news reports, advertisements for Greek committee fundraisers, and meeting minutes were printed in newspapers across the country, with the most numerous being in Massachusetts and Rhode Island. However, newspapers in Virginia, South Carolina, and even the territory of Arkansas engaged in the national discussion on the Greek cause. In a sample of forty-six newspapers printed throughout both the North and the South from December 1823 to April 1824 on the subject of the Greek cause, there was an increase in organizational efforts that peaked in January. In December there were 133 articles printed on the Greek cause, and in January 1824 there were 180—a 35 percent increase in a one-month period.[110] That so many articles were printed in January coincides with the increased interest in the Greek cause generated by Monroe's annual address and Daniel Webster's response. Most of these articles advertised efforts to raise funds for the Greeks. Many of the newspapers in the sample included reprinted articles from other newspapers, suggesting that the editors were aware of the demand for current information on the Greek Revolution.

Frequently, newspapers not only reported on individual Greek aid society efforts at fund-raising, but also on coordinated efforts between societies in different cities. Organizing a ball in the community was one common way of raising interest and funds for the Greek cause. Greek enthusiasts organized these balls at the local level by soliciting funds and advertising in the local newspaper. Frequently, advertisements were also printed in newspapers farther afield, sometimes even in different states. For example, an article printed in the *Salem Gazette* reported on cooperative fundraising efforts in Philadelphia and New York. The Salem, Massachusetts, paper reported that a "Fancy Dress Ball" was to take place in Philadelphia with "about one hundred ladies and gentlemen" expected to travel from New York to attend. The idea that a hundred New Yorkers planned to make the journey to Philadelphia to attend a benefit for the Greeks is interesting. Even more interesting is that the report stated these ladies and gentlemen would be attending dressed in "garments of their great grand-fathers and grand-mothers."[111] One must assume that none of these attendees were of Greek descent and were also not likely planning to attend in ancient Grecian garb or togas. So what connection could the organizers of this ball be making to the Greek Revolution? One must conclude that these attendees intended to dress as their own great-grandfathers and great-grandmothers from fifty years before—the theme of this ball was the American Revolution.

In Baltimore a ball was also held on Washington's Birthday, "to give some public expression of the feelings of Baltimore towards the cause of the Greeks, and at the same time to raise a contribution for their aid."[112] The Baltimore advertisement succinctly described the shift to an activist interest in philhellenism that took place at this time throughout the country during the early months of 1824. The organizers identified sympathy for the Greeks and activism for their independence as two separate endeavors, as they had been in the first year of the war. As this notice indicates, however, the organizers hoped to combine the two in order to generate wider support for Greek independence.

Community Activism and Support

In addition to reports on fancy dress balls organized to raise funds, newspapers reported instances of non-elite individuals outside of the philhellenic organizations donating funds. These individuals came from all walks of life. For example, a barber in Troy, New York, pledged that "he would give the avails of his labor, on Thursday and Friday last, to the committee appointed to receive donations for the benefit of the Greeks."[113] The barber's donation was reported in newspapers from as far away as Baltimore. The same newspaper reported that the local Washington Hose Company had collected fifty dollars to aid "the suffering and persecuted Greeks." The report was accompanied by a call for other members of the community to follow suit, noting, "The Greeks are our brothers, both in a political and in a Christian point of view. . . . There is in this, a uniform, pervading American feeling, and we are confident that our fellow citizens of Baltimore will testify their participation by their benevolence."[114] Still another example of individuals raising money for the Greeks on their own accord includes the General Society of Mechanics in New Haven, Connecticut, which raised fifty dollars and presented it to the local Greek committee. Members of a number of different churches devoted to the Greek cause also emerged during this period, with their efforts widely reported. One particularly successful Methodist Church in New York collected $120 in one January evening alone.[115]

American philhellenic activism touched many other religious groups in the United States as well, inspiring additional membership in Greek relief societies. Philhellenic organizations often worked with local church groups, hoping to mobilize already existing community organizations for the cause of the Greeks. Committees asked local pastors to remember the plight of the Greeks in their Sunday sermons. These committees also printed and distributed pamphlets appealing to philhellenic sentiments as well as to Christian charity within the community.[116] In many cases, sermons given on the subject of aiding the Greek cause were printed and distributed by the Greek committees. For example, on December 12, 1823, the Greek Committee of New York stated that the people of "an enlightened, free, and Christian Nation" like the United States would naturally take a deep interest in the "struggle of that race of men who have been the Parents of Civilization, and the Instructors of the rest of mankind in Letters and Art—in the principles of Civil Liberty, and the precepts of our Holy Religion—and who are now endeavouring to shake off the yoke of their barbarian task-masters."[117] In this case, both religion and race were used to set the Greeks apart as deserving of support.

In a similar way, the Greek Committee of Boston wrote to the "Ministers of the Gospel" within the community asking them to call their congregations' attention to "the cause of *civil liberty*, of *human happiness*, and of *Christianity*" and to help support the Greek cause.[118] Likewise, the Greek Committee of Philadelphia asked Gregory T. Bedell, rector of St. Andrew's Church, to speak about the Greeks in a sermon. Bedell compared the plight of the Greeks to that of the Israelites, stating that even a casual observer must note that "when we view the subject, as the struggle of a people professing christianity [*sic*], against the followers of the imposter; and when we see the danger they are in, and think what would be the consequence to them and to christianity, should the Turks regain their former ascendency, every individual, whose bosom is not lost to the impulse of sympathy, and genuine christian sensibility, will feel that his heart trembles for the ark of God."[119]

Sereno Edwards Dwight, pastor of the Park Street Church in Boston, also devoted an entire sermon to the subject. He asked his congregation, "Were the case of the Greeks our own; were our country thus oppressed, invaded and desolated by a cruel and blood-thirsty enemy; would it not be demanded of every minister of Christ, that he should raise his voice in behalf of his suffering countrymen? And is the great rule of christian benevolence—'Though shalt love thy neighbour as thyself'—to have no influence here?"[120] Dwight continued his appeal, pointing out "how delightful" it will be, once independence is achieved, "to overspread Greece with bibles, and to furnish her the chosen heralds of salvation. . . . Missionaries loaded with bibles will feel their way into the farthest retreats of Mohammedan darkness." In doing this "the recovery of Jerusalem, the liberation of the eastern churches, and the admission of the Gospel to Western Asia" will be achieved.[121]

The sentiments American ministers shared with the Greek cause were not separate from the larger philhellenic movement. Ministers combined patriotic holiday celebration, philhellenism, and religion in a number of these sermons, most of which were printed by Greek committees. One sermon given on Washington's Birthday in 1824 was delivered at a Presbyterian church in Lebanon, Ohio. The minister acknowledged that most of the congregation had probably already heard about the Greek cause from the local newspaper, but he did not intend to merely ask for charity for the Greeks. "We come to solicit in favour of one of the most ancient nations of the earth," minister John P. Durbin explained, "a nation that once rose to the highest prosperity, to a degree in learning, in science, in civilization, perhaps never since equaled; a nation that conferred the benefits of her improvements on all succeeding generations . . . and at this very time suffers an accumulation of the most sickening and unheard miseries."[122] Durbin argued at length, citing history and current events, that the Greeks could in part reclaim their liberty from the Ottomans not just from inspiration from the ancients but also specifically from American charity.

Yet another example of philhellenism joining with patriotism and religion was an oration given at the First Baptist Church in Providence, Rhode Island, by Solomon Drowne, professor of botany at Brown University and an army surgeon during the American Revolution. "Novel and important is the occasion of our assembling," Drowne began, "and great the sympathy, so generally and generously expressed for the much injured people, whose cause we now espouse." He continued: "This, too, is an anniversary of the birth of the illustrious Father of American Liberty: and may we not presume, that his benignant spirit will regard, with approbation, the doings of this day." Invoking the spirit of Washington himself, Drowne apologized to the crowd that while they had most likely heard about the case for the Greeks repeatedly, and acknowledged how "almost impossible it is to offer anything new," he hoped his speech would in some small degree help to promote "so glorious a cause" that "would afford a solace to the evening of my days."[123] Once again this oration was printed by a Greek committee, the Greek Committee of Providence in this case, and was distributed in order to generate support for the Greek cause.

Not only was this appeal to ministers and their congregations effective, but it later proved to play an important role in the transformation of the American philhellenic movement. In this early stage of the war, American ministers, especially in the more urban areas of the North where Greek relief societies enjoyed the highest levels of membership, helped mobilize interest in sending aid for the Greeks. The funds collected by various philhellenic organizations were at first directed toward supporting the Greek army. The only major group that opposed supporting the Greek army was the Quakers, whose pacifism prevented them from supporting a cause devoted toward making war. Quakers, at least in London, however, were reported to have raised funds to relieve civilians and wounded soldiers.[124]

As was reflected in these early sermons, American Christians believed not only that independence in Greece would provide an opportunity to extend their influence into the East, but also that they as Americans had a special duty to pledge their support for the Greek war effort. Charitable aid for Greek citizens would come later, with church organizations, especially led by women, spearheading a different kind of philhellenism. This initial mobilization of American Christians, however, laid the groundwork for subsequent activism.

★ ★ ★

"The Greek Fire seems spreading through the U. States," wrote a Virginia author for the *Richmond Enquirer* in January 1824, "Meetings have been held in a variety of places, resolutions adopted, and contributions made for the Holiest of all causes." Hundreds of dollars had been raised in the last few months from Connecticut to Georgia to aid the Greeks in their revolution against the Ottoman Turks. Church groups, students, literary societies, comprised of men, women, and children all had come together for this common purpose. Urgently calling on equal Virginian support for the Greek cause, the anonymous author opined, "The money which we may contribute to the Greeks will be repaid to us with interest—it will be repaid in that pride and holiness of conscious virtue which ennobles a nation as well as individuals." The author then appealed to his readers to "unite our feelings in the cause of the Greeks—the cause of the whole human race."[125]

In the first years of the Greek Revolution, interest in supporting the Greek cause stemmed from a number of different facets of early American popular culture. The romanticism and sentimentalism of the philhellenic movement provided a basis of knowledge of Greek history and informed early Americans that their own identity was linked to Athenian democracy and culture. In addition, the knowledge most early Americans had of the Ottoman Empire was steeped in an exoticized understanding of the Orient in which the Turks allegedly engaged in the enslavement of the Greeks and had degraded the modern Greek culture from its pure ancient form. That the Greeks were Christian and the Turks were Muslim also contributed to rising enthusiasm for the Greek cause among religious circles in the United States, especially in the Northern states. Race also appears as an underlying reason for supporting the Greeks, though there is not always a consensus concerning whether the Greeks were of the same race as early Americans or if they were a separate race though superior to the Turks due to their ancient contributions to Western society. As was believed by the Virginian who pleaded with fellow readers to support the Greeks, by uniting with the Greek cause they would also unite with "the cause of the whole human race," suggesting that the Turks were outside of the human race and were different creatures all together.

The Greek Fire spread throughout the United States and enjoyed national support for the next several years. Philhellenism in the United States transitioned into a movement that seemed for many of its supporters especially suited for their attention, with links to their own revolution as well as to ancient Greece. In fact, one individual who had previously supported the South American revolutions looked on in disbelief at the response Greek aid societies received, noting, "Our diary of news details repeated resolutions by our Southern brethren to support the cause of religious and civil liberty among the Greeks . . . and the same popular sentiment has excited our own citizens to make a common cause." Convinced that citizens should be more concerned with successful revolutions in their own hemisphere, the author conceded, "The favorite theme is Greece, and her suffering people."[126] Greek committees collected funds not only from philhellenic elites within their communities, but also from church groups, benevolent groups, and tradesmen. Some of the charitable efforts of these groups were ambitious, indicating just how widespread and enthusiastic the cause was early on in the war. Soon the scope of the philhellenic movement would expand farther afield, taking on a reformist roll in both foreign and domestic affairs.

Chapter 3

Philhellenism Joins with American Benevolence

Frustrated with the government's unwillingness to aid or recognize Greek independence, constituents began to write letters to their congressmen. Support for the Greeks was so intense that members of Congress began to reply in earnest; in so doing, however, they held firm to neutrality. Lewis Williams of North Carolina wrote his constituents in April 1822 that although the Greeks, "the most renowned people of antiquity 'both in arts and in arms,' have risen against the Turks who have held them for centuries past in degraded and slavish subjection," the United States would not be the country to provide aid. In 1825, Congressman Williams continued to defend the government's decision not to officially support Greek independence by observing, "It must be satisfactory to behold Russia taking an interest in their defense." Joseph Gist, a congressman from South Carolina, did not even offer his constituents hope for other sources of aid to Greece, but simply apologized: "I pray to God [Greece] may be restored to her ancient liberties in a tenfold degree, and become one of the republics of the world." A congressman from Tennessee, Robert Allen, wrote to his constituents explaining that the House of Representatives supported "the heroic struggle of the Greeks" but that "prudence pointed out many objections to a legislative act, that could be construed into any thing like an interference in the internal concerns of other nations."[1] Rather than defusing popular support for the Greeks, congressional inaction helped spread American philhellenism at the local level and inspired new groups of people, both men and women, to join.

The Greek Fire continued to spread in the United States, kindling a sense of historical and moral obligation among both men and women to support the cause. The American philhellenic movement emerged as a fully defined entity separate from its European counterpart by 1824 and enjoyed popular support on a national scale. Though as with any movement interest in the Greek Revolution ebbed and flowed, there is evidence of consistent support for the Greek cause especially in the more urban areas of the United States throughout the 1820s. Greek relief society leaders, especially Mathew Carey and Edward Everett, continued to encourage and organize support from the public by connecting the Greek Revolution to the American Revolution. In order to continue expanding national support, however, philhellenic leaders began to alter the focus of the Greek cause to encompass a benevolence element, where aid would be raised for civilians instead of the Greek army. This expanded appeal made participation in the movement an especially appropriate outlet for women.

There are a number of reasons why this transition of sending aid to civilians took place. On the one hand, philhellenic leaders perceived that they would more likely be able to engage a broader base of interest, especially from women, if they directed their efforts toward the Greek populace rather than the military.[2] There is also evidence, on the other hand, that American agents in the Mediterranean directed members of the Monroe and Adams administrations to discourage public support for the Greek army if they desired to successfully negotiate a trade agreement with the Ottoman Empire. With this in mind, Presidents James Monroe and John Quincy Adams advocated for neutrality in the Greek Revolution in favor of advancing a strategic foreign policy. Adams, while secretary of state, certainly made it known to pro-Greece members of Congress that the executive branch would not support their foreign policy plans. With Everett's close connections to government officials, it is possible that the government's wish that philhellenic societies redirect their efforts toward civilian relief helped shape the American philhellenic movement in the final years of the war. The core beliefs and goals of a fully mature American philhellenic movement would inspire similar movements in the decades that followed.

Whether a more humanitarian-focused Greek cause was directed by philhellenic leaders or by members of the government, a transition toward exclusive humanitarianism began to take shape by the end of 1824. Instead of merely relying upon philhellenic rhetoric to inspire citizens to donate funds and supplies to the Greek troops, societies turned their attention to Greek citizens, especially Greek women and children displaced by the war. Greek committees spearheaded this effort as they collected supplies, sponsored American volunteers in the Greek army, and even later sent and financially supported agents to Greece.

Still inspired by the philhellenism of Lord Byron, speeches, poems, and other literary pieces that were printed at the time reflect the shift from passive sentimentalism to a more active focus. One poem entitled "The Song of the Greek Amazon" was first printed in 1824 and was so popular that not only was it reprinted in poetry collections throughout the nineteenth century, but it was also set to music. William Cullen Bryant, proclaimed to be the "author of America" by his friend James Fenimore Cooper, was an aspiring young poet when war broke out in Greece. Bryant became a supporter of the Greek cause in December 1823, when so many other Americans were drawn to the Greek question, and he wrote several poems on the subject. "The Song of the Greek Amazon" tells the story of a young Greek maiden whose betrothed had been killed in battle by the Turks. Rather than merely grieve her loss, the maiden took matters into her own hands by shedding her femininity and becoming a Greek klepht.[3] The violence the young woman intended to embrace as she declared, "I buckle to my slender side the pistol and the scimitar and in my maiden flower and pride am come to share the tasks of war," was justified because of the injustice she had suffered at the hands of the Turks. Dressed in a Turkish costume and wearing pantaloons beneath shortened skirts, the Greek Amazon was depicted making this vow on the cover of the musical setting of the poem.[4]

The subject matter of "The Song of the Greek Amazon" would have especially appealed to female readers by pulling on their heartstrings to support the Greek cause. Bryant's contrast of femininity with masculine violence must have been a shocking as well as a provocative storyline for early American readers. At the conclusion of battle, the young Greek maiden tends to the arrangement of her hair—"My mirror is the mountain spring, at which I dress my ruffled hair"—but this Greek maiden's feminine self-care continues to the unexpected: "My dimmed and dusty arms I bring, and wash away the bloodstain there." She explains that because the Turks had slain her beloved "and my virgin years," she had "vowed to Greece and vengeance now; and many an Othman [sic] dame, in tears, shall rue the Grecian maiden's vow."

Though women who supported the Greek cause did so within their own socially constructed gender roles of the time, that this Greek maiden had experienced such grief and anguish at the hands of a non-Christian adversary called American women to action. Further contrasting the violence of war, Bryant's Greek Amazon recalls her life prior to the war, in which she was

Bufford's Lithog 114 Nassau St. N.Y.

SONG
of the
GREEK AMAZON
„I buckle to my slender Side

the Poetry by

WM. CULLEN BRIANT ESQR.

To whom the Music is
Respectfully Inscribed

by

Principal of the Philadelphia Musical Seminary

PHILADELPHIA
Published by John F. Nunns 70 South 3ª St.

Figure 3.1. Elam Ives Jr. set Bryant's 1824 poem to music sometime between 1830 and 1836, when he taught and wrote music at the Philadelphia Musical Seminary. That Ives composed the music at least six years after it was first published suggests the ongoing popularity of the Greek cause in the United States. The illustration on the cover sheet is illustrative of the philhellenic sentiments surrounding the Greek cause, in this case justifying the romantic as well as violent actions of the poem's heroine. William Cullen Bryant and Elam Ives Jr., *Song of the Greek Amazon*, The Library Company of Philadelphia.

accustomed to playing music and dancing with friends, a setting that would have been recognizable to many young women and their families living in the United States. Now, however, the maiden was all too happy to pursue victory on the field of battle in the name of her lost love and for Greek independence.[5] For the women who became involved in the more humanitarian-focused philhellenic movement, by sewing clothes or gathering food for Greek civilians perhaps other Greek maidens could maintain their femininity while remaining within the domestic sphere.

Benevolent societies and community charity groups frequently centered around local churches were popular especially among elite and middle-class Protestant women in both the Northern and Southern states by the early nineteenth century. Dedication to Christianity and family justified participation in the civic and political affairs of local communities.[6] With philhellenes actively requesting the participation of church societies, along with local ministers blessing the Greek cause as an appropriate Christian charity, women quickly became involved. Enthusiasm for ancient Greece entwined with dedication to the Greek cause led to global outreach for social and religious reform. Perceiving the Muslim Ottoman Turks as the ultimate tyrants, female benevolent societies increasingly organized their efforts toward the aid of Greece. Ultimately, while early Americans donated time, money, and supplies to aid the Greek cause, the goal was to provide relief to a Christian population and effect an independent Greek republic.

The Death of the Famous Philhellene

If not for a series of setbacks sustained by the Greek army, American philhellenic interest may have fizzled in 1824. The first of these setbacks was the death of Lord Byron in April. From the earliest stages of the war, popular interest in Lord Byron had sustained interest in the Greek cause. The American public learned about Byron's life and experiences in the Greek army on a regular basis by reading any newspaper. Lord Byron was portrayed as a patriot and hero for the Greek cause not only because of his membership in the army but also because of his monetary support. Lord Byron's willingness to seemingly sacrifice everything for the cause had inspired American interest just as the national government declared its neutrality.

Lord Byron was already ill in March 1824, just one month after the widespread joint celebrations of Washington's Birthday and the Greek Revolution. He made a partial recovery, which was happily reported in both European and

American newspapers. However, he relapsed, developing a serious fever most likely brought on by a combination of the unhealthy climate and diet. After several doctors attempted to save him through a regime of bloodletting, Lord Byron died on April 19, 1824, at Missolonghi, a city that was at the time under Greek control and had been the focal point of two sieges. The city would later fall in 1826 to Ottoman forces. As a result of the siege and Byron's death, Missolonghi became the center of interest in the Greek Revolution.[7]

News from Greece took about six weeks to arrive in the United States. By mid-June, newspapers began to report that Lord Byron was ill; at the end of the month the news of his death arrived. American newspapers printed the official proclamation of his death reported by the provisional Greek government:, "His munificent donations to this community are before the eyes of every one, and no one amongst us ever ceased, or ever will cease, to consider him with the purest and most grateful sentiments, our benefactor."[8]

American men and women eulogized Byron at Fourth of July celebrations in 1824. In Saratoga, New York, toasts were given in honor of the Greeks and Byron, who was described as a Hercules who had "expired in his cradle."[9] In Washington, D.C., Greece was toasted as "the land of ancient renown, and modern glory," and Byron was eulogized as "the Poet who has immortalized modern Greece by his pen, and defended her liberties by his sword."[10] In Salem, Massachusetts, Fourth of July celebrants toasted Greece with these sentiments: "Her ancient greatness has been immortalized by the genius of her Homer; her modern glory will be coeval with the fame of her Byron."[11] And in Boston, Byron was toasted as a "martyr to liberty." While mourned by Bostonians, they rejoiced "that his *heart* is left with Greece."[12] The people of Boston intended this as both a sentimental and a literal observation: it was reported in American newspapers that the Greeks requested that Byron's heart be removed from his body and placed in a mausoleum in Missolonghi.[13] The body was then sent back to England for burial.

Byron's death increased public interest in providing support for the Greek cause. Many Greek committees published and distributed pamphlets that promoted the campaign. Newspapers reported that the Greek Committee of New York alone had sent its first contribution in the amount of $6,000 in the early summer, with $5,000 more by August.[14] Though Lord Byron was not an American, he was a symbol of the transatlantic philhellenic movement. In addition to his poetry, Byron's sacrifice represented a noble and virtuous gesture. While most Americans did not wish to emulate him literally, they felt inspired to at least support the Greek cause through donations.

Americans by this time were not, however, content with their efforts being jointly associated with the larger European philhellenic movement. Though donations were at this point collected by the Greek Committee of New York and forwarded to its London counterpart, American philhellenes wanted their donations to be recognized as separate from those of European aid societies. Upon request by the Greek Committee of New York, Andreas Luriottis, agent of the Greek government in London, assured Americans later that summer in a letter to Richard Rush, American ambassador to London, that the American contributions were duly noted and that the Greeks were aware of the sacrifices made by their benefactors in the United States. The correspondence between the Greek Committee of New York, Luriottis, and Rush was printed in late August 1824 in both Northern and Southern newspapers, including the *City Gazette and Commercial Daily Advertiser* (Charleston, SC), the *Rochester (NY) Telegraph*, and the *Rhode-Island American*.[15]

In addition to this, philhellenes had concerns that the Greeks would not in fact establish a republic once independence was secured. Luriottis tried to reassure Americans on this subject by stating that it was the desire of the Greek government to "establish the system of politics which [Americans] possess in our own country; when we consider this, we feel a secret and gratifying assurance that our efforts will not be baffled, and that Greece will issue, like the United States, from the honorable struggle which in so many respects resembles their own." Apologizing for the delayed public statement of gratitude, Luriottis continued that at last the provisional Greek government wished to publicly express to "the people of the universe of the benevolence of the freemen of the United States, who so kindly co-operated to open the path of Independence to those that seek that flowery way."[16]

Lord Byron's philhellenism and his service in the Greek army inspired a number of Americans to contribute more than money and supplies.[17] George Jarvis was the first American volunteer in the Greek army. Jarvis was the son of a New York merchant who had established himself in Denmark. After receiving his father's permission, Jarvis appeared with his father before the American consul in Hamburg in order for the young Jarvis to acquire the appropriate papers. In April 1822, George Jarvis arrived in Greece and officially entered into the service of the Greeks.[18] Named a general in the Greek army, he served for the duration of the war only to die of an illness in 1828. While alive, he kept the Boston Greek Committee informed of the Greeks' successes and setbacks.

The Boston Greek Committee sponsored other Americans in Greece, including Jonathan Peckham Miller of Vermont and Samuel Gridley Howe of

Massachusetts. Miller was a veteran of the War of 1812 and had attended the University of Vermont prior to his service in Greece. It was Byron's death that inspired young Miller to present himself as a volunteer to the Boston committee in November 1824.[19] Samuel Gridley Howe, a member of a well-established Boston family, was a recent graduate of Harvard in medicine. Also influenced by Byron's philhellenism, Howe desired to follow in the heroic poet's footsteps. Assuring his father that he desired medical and surgical experience on the battlefield, Howe arrived in Greece in early 1825.[20] These three Americans reported regularly to the Boston committee. Their letters were printed and reprinted in newspapers, providing invaluable information on the status of the Greek cause to the American public. The correspondence received from these three men, which provided updates on civilian and military needs, kept the Greek Revolution in the public eye.[21]

Philhellenes at Home and Abroad

In March 1825 the first news from Jonathan Peckham Miller arrived and was quickly printed in the Boston newspapers. A note of explanation from the Greek Committee of Boston was printed alongside Miller's letter stating that he had left for the Mediterranean as a sort of agent from the committee itself. The committee had appropriated a portion of its funds to help Miller with his passage to the Mediterranean and to assist him with the costs he would incur upon arrival. The newspaper stated, "These letters are now published, in the belief that they may prove interesting to the friends of Greece and the community at large."[22]

American volunteers also played an important part in mobilizing the American philhellenic movement into humanitarian relief for Greek civilians. Upon arriving in Greece, Miller observed that the Greek soldiers had been fighting all summer and were "now coming to their commander to beg bread to keep them alive. But such is the sight to which my eyes are every hour witness." Miller stated that European philhellenes were not as devoted to the Greeks as he and George Jarvis, with whom he met immediately upon his arrival. Instead the Europeans came "with abounding titles." He continued: "Most of them I am informed instead of assisting the Greeks, have only lived upon them, until reduced by poverty, sickness and death; and there now remain but few of them in Greece." Miller concluded his letter with "May you gentlemen, and my beloved country, continue to receive the smiles of heaven . . . and exhort the friends of liberty in America to remember Greece."[23]

Miller's description of the starving Greeks conveyed two points to his fellow Americans: that an American presence was needed in Greece and that the need for American assistance remained. Reporting that European philhellenes were less devoted than their American counterparts to the Greek cause would have played on American pride, encouraging continued support. Stories about the pitiable circumstances the Greeks found themselves in compelled American audiences to adjust their thinking toward the Greek cause. Rather than focusing solely on military assistance, humanitarian aid might go further in helping secure Greek independence.

It is at the least coincidental that Miller suggested philhellenic efforts should be redirected toward humanitarian instead of military aid. Just one year before, George Bethune English, by appointment of Secretary of State John Quincy Adams, had written that his prospects at negotiating a trade agreement with the Sublime Porte would be improved if philhellenic efforts would remain focused within local communities rather than be a movement endorsed by the national government.[24] With Edward Everett's close association with the leadership of the Greek Committee of Boston as well as with members of Congress such as Daniel Webster, it is possible that Everett encouraged this new direction in fund-raising at the request of the government. In response to Miller's call, the Greek Committee of Boston proposed "to make him immediately a remittance of two hundred dollars. Any contribution toward this object will be gladly received by Nathaniel P. Russell Esq. Treasurer of the Greek Committee."[25]

In fact, for the next several years, Jarvis, Miller, and Howe continued to provide the Greek Committee of Boston with letters relating the state of affairs in Greece, requesting support from their fellow Americans. In a letter dated January 21, 1825, Miller wrote, "The misery of the people is so great, that I have often wept to see their extreme distress."[26] In September 1825, the *Essex Register* of Salem, Massachusetts, printed a letter written by Miller relating the dire situation of the Greek army. Miller described how he and General Jarvis were with the Greeks attacking the Castle at Lepanto for "nearly three weeks; but the delay of the payment of the troops has detained us, till I have the satisfaction to see an American ship anchor in the harbor."[27] Miller then summarized his life in Greece. While difficult, he said, "my life is devoted to the overturning of the Turkish empire." In another letter, Miller wrote the committee, "I wish to be understood, that I have no claim upon the committee whatever, and wish them to act in this case for the good of Greece and not for me."[28]

More than just American volunteers, Miller, Jarvis, and Howe also served as agents for these Greek aid societies and to some extent played nonstate diplomatic roles in the war. Sanctioned with such leadership roles, these volunteers saw themselves as American Lafayettes, hoping to not only help the Greek cause but to inspire a future independent Greece.[29] For example, both Jarvis and Miller met with Alexandros Mavrokordatos, secretary of state for foreign affairs of the provisional Greek government. In a letter Miller wrote to the Greek Committee of Boston in December 1824, he described the meeting and stated that Mavrokordatos expressed interest in the American support of the Greek cause, asking many questions "in reference to the views which were entertained by the Americans of the character of the Greeks." Miller replied that the exertions made by members of the different committees were for the liberty of Greece, and it was his opinion "that nothing further would be done by the Americans, if the Greeks should consent to accept of a foreign king." Mavrokordatos quickly replied that only by foreign force would the Greeks place themselves under a king.[30] Pleased with this reply, Miller pledged that he would remain in Greece, fighting for its independence for as long as the prospect of freedom remained.

American philhellenes worried whether European expansionist interests would curtail Greek independence. Some Americans even wondered if the Greek Revolution was nothing more than a Russian instrument to extract power from the Ottoman Empire.[31] Britain also had long been concerned over Russian ambitions and sought to gain the confidence of the Ottomans in order to prevent Russia, and other European powers for that matter, from having a greater say in some future negotiation over Greece or lands in the Balkans. Each British ambassador who served during the Greek Revolution wrote his foreign office constantly on matters pertaining to the health of British trade and the diplomatic and commercial interests of Austria, France, Russia, and the Sublime Porte.

Due to the complicated as well as delicate political situation in the region, Mavrokordatos was perhaps holding back that the Greek government would be willing to place itself into the hands of European powers if it meant securing independence. This is precisely what took place beginning a little more than a year later. In a coded message written in May 1826, British ambassador to the Ottoman Empire Stratford Canning wrote to Prime Minister George Canning, his cousin, that he had received word from the Greek insurgents of "a formal application for the mediation of Great Britain to effect a peace between that country and the Ottoman Porte."[32] In any case, the possibility that Greece might not achieve independence free and clear of the intervention of

another European power was of the utmost concern for many American philhellenes and added momentum behind not only providing aid to the Greeks
but also gaining the confidence of provisional government officials such as
Mavrokordatos.

Reading between the lines in the exchange between Miller and Mavrokordatos in December 1824, it seems that Miller was all too aware that a larger
political game was taking place between Greece, the Ottoman Empire, and
the rest of Europe. Interestingly, Miller, as an agent for an American Greek
relief society, had taken on a role as a nonstate actor and clearly hoped to influence the political future of Greece, despite the wishes of the more conservative powers of Europe as well as the U.S. government. Greek aid society
agents were not acting with any official sanction on the part of the U.S. government; in fact, their actions were in opposition to the decisions that had
been made by both the executive and legislative branches. Without official
trade relations in the region and given the U.S. government's official stance of
neutrality, there was no force that could stop nonstate actors like Miller from
serving in this unofficial capacity.

While Jarvis, Miller, and Howe were perhaps the most well-known Americans serving in the Greek army, there were others. For example, Miller mentioned a Kentuckian named John M. Allen in the army as well as a distant
relation of George Washington by the name of William Townsend Washington.[33] Jarvis himself even proposed to the Greek Committee of Boston an
effort to recruit Americans willing to travel to Greece to serve in the army. By
the close of the war, at least fourteen Americans had served in the Greek army
during the revolution.[34]

Miller, however, made it clear that serving in the Greek army would not
be an easy venture. The letters repeatedly testified that service in the Greek
army was not as glamorous as Byron-inspired poetry made it seem. In fact,
Miller forthrightly stated in one letter, "I hope, gentlemen, to hear from you
soon; and in the meantime I beg leave to caution all persons, who have not
resources of their own, from coming to Greece. My health is good. I believe
that Greece will yet be free, and with this hope I take cheerful part in the war."
Immediately after this warning, Miller continued that the most recent American arrival at that point, Samuel Gridley Howe, "was prompted last summer,
not less by a generous zeal for the cause of oppressed and suffering humanity,
than by a desire to accomplish himself in his profession, to repair to Greece,
and enter her service as an army surgeon."[35] Miller informed the American
public that while a philhellenic sensibility was certainly important in devoting oneself to the cause, anyone considering the journey to Greece should

understand that life was hard and that the Greeks were struggling though hopeful for independence. If a potential candidate understood these facts, he was welcome to join.

Realizing that this would not sound attractive to most able-bodied young men, Miller instead concentrated on humanitarian relief by appealing for donations of money and supplies: "We would exhort the friends of Greece in America, to exert themselves for this suffering people, remembering that the struggle is not yet over." Miller's letters continued to carry this same message for the next several years, relaying the situation in Greece while also reminding supporters that their exertions had "no relation either to war or pirates, but are made to clothe the naked and feed the hungry, to snatch from famine its victim, to administer to the necessities of decrepit old age, and to save youth and beauty from a premature grave."[36] This pleading reminder became increasingly crucial by 1826 when enthusiasm in America for the Greek cause began to plateau.

An important setback the Greeks sustained was inflicted upon them by an American shipbuilding company with connections to the Greek Committee of New York. This proved to be a national embarrassment that incited public outrage and rejuvenated any momentum that had been lost from the initial emergence of popular philhellenism in the United States. In the spring of 1825, Johannis Orlandos and Andreas Luriottis, both deputies of the Greek government, contacted the shipbuilding house Le Roy, Bayard & Co. in New York and were provided an estimate for the cost of two new frigates for the use of the Greek navy. The two Greek officials contacted this company over any other because the head of the house was also the current chairman of the Greek Committee of New York.[37] These two ships were named *Liberator* and *Hope* (later renamed *Hellas* by the Greeks). By the fall there were rumors of mismanagement on the part of the shipbuilders. The shipbuilders continued to bill the Greek deputies for the building of the two frigates, but completion was nowhere in sight. In the spring of 1826, an agent from London arrived to go over the accounts only to discover that the frigates were not only not finished, but required additional expenditures to make them seaworthy. By the height of the controversy, the shipbuilders billed the Greeks for several hundred thousand dollars more than the Greek deputies were initially quoted. For the Greek agents, this revelation was a disaster.

At the request of the builders, the naval committee in the House of Representatives contacted the secretary of the navy and inquired whether the U.S. government could purchase one of the vessels so that the account could be settled. The *Liberator* was purchased in August 1826 in the amount of

$230,570.97 for the U.S. Navy and later joined the Brazil squadron. This decision enabled the Greek deputies to settle payment for the *Hope*.[38] This is the closest the U.S. government came to directly aiding the Greeks. It was not until October 1826 that the *Hope* set sail for Greece. The Greek frigate controversy, as it came to be called, combined with news of a military setback at Missolonghi to revitalize the philhellenic movement in the United States.

American philhellenes thought the whole Greek frigate controversy was a disgrace, and Greek aid societies redoubled their efforts to gather donations. They specifically mentioned the controversy as the basis for their efforts. One newspaper article declared that the United States had narrowly "avoided the indelible disgrace which would otherwise have attached to this country." "Such a blow," it was said, "would probably have annihilated the last hopes and hastened the concluding agony of a country more interesting than any other to the scholar, the philanthropist, and the Christian."[39] News of the controversy spread from New York to as far south as South Carolina, where similar reactions of dismay and embarrassment were shared with readers. One Charleston paper reported, "If there be fraud, robbery, disgrace, to any of our own citizens or to strangers, let it be exposed—but let not the Greeks suffer from this abuse of confidence; their cause demands all our sympathy."[40]

Newspapers also played a part in generating discussion regarding what could be done about the frigate controversy. The *New-York Post* openly supported the Greek cause by calling on the U.S. government to "make a present" of the *Liberator* to the Greeks. This opinion was reprinted not just in New York, but in newspapers as far south as Charleston, South Carolina, suggesting that this opinion was widely shared.[41] Yet another New York newspaper, the *New York Spectator*, reported on a Greek Committee meeting intended to raise interest in procuring a "vessel of war" for the Greek cause. The *Spectator* observed that, "Unless we mistake the feeling and the spirit of this community, the Greeks will not be disappointed in receiving the naval aid from America for which they have paid so dearly."[42]

In the midst of the Greek frigate controversy, news arrived that the Greek army had lost control of Missolonghi, a center for the Greek army as well as the seat of the provisional Greek government at the time. The Ottomans had redoubled their efforts early in 1826 to take the city, with the siege culminating in April when Ibrahim Pasha, son of Mohammad Ali of Egypt and a commander of the Egyptian–Ottoman forces, arrived with reinforcements. When supplies began to run perilously low, the Greeks, including not only soldiers, but women and children as well, attempted a *sortie en masse* in order to escape the city. The Greeks failed, however, and the Ottomans ultimately destroyed the city. The American public associated Missolonghi with Lord Byron's death and had followed the military action there for more than two years. By the spring of 1826 when Missolonghi fell, the city had become a symbol of the Greek War of Independence and was a focal point of philhellenic sentiment in both Europe and the United States.[43]

Rumors first arrived in the United States that Missolonghi had fallen beginning in June 1826. On June 8, a Boston paper reported information sent home by William Townsend Washington that the city had indeed fallen to the Ottomans.[44] A Baltimore paper reported on the same day that Greece was fighting its last battle and that the fall of Missolonghi was imminent. The article further reported that Sultan Mahmud II had ordered Ibrahim Pasha to "give no quarters to the inhabitants of Missolonghi, no matter what their age, sex, or condition may be."[45] Another newspaper played down the battle, however, stating that "Missolonghi had not fallen, but was in jeopardy; our gallant countrymen, Jarvis and Washington were on their way to throw themselves into the besieged city."[46] By early July the worst fears were confirmed: the Greeks had been defeated at Missolonghi, and their hopes of independence were in all likelihood lost.

The American public was shocked at the news of the fall of Missolonghi. Philhellenic interest groups gathered or even reformed defunct committees and once again began to appeal to the public for support. One newspaper noted, "On an occasion so peculiarly appropriate as the fiftieth anniversary of the day of our Independence, something should be done, however slight it may be, to awaken the remembrance of a heroic people, at this moment engaged in the most devoted manner for their liberty and national existence. . . . We are confident that many would require nothing further than the sight of a subscription and the name of Greece to contribute for their assistance."[47] Though joining national celebration with raising funds for the Greeks had been fruitful in previous years, excitement over the fiftieth anniversary of the ratification of the Declaration of Independence especially aided in stirring support for the Greeks.

Beginning in the summer of 1826, a revitalized philhellenic frenzy spread throughout the country. Poems written in the style of Lord Byron appeared in newspapers mourning the loss of Missolonghi and romantically urged readers to offset the loss through active support. One poem printed originally in the *New-York Evening Post* and then distributed and reprinted in other newspapers recaptured the philhellenic sentiments that had initially charged the movement just three years earlier: "Sons of Greece awake: they come!—/ The Turk! The foe is near, / They come—in thunders loud and far, / Rolled on the echoing tide of war." The author referred to the Greeks residing in

Missolonghi as the Turks arrived at the city. The author blamed the loss of Missolonghi in part on European philhellenes. Suggesting that European devotion was not resolute enough, the author continued: "They struck in vain—O Europe! shame / Upon thy sons,—the cold and tame, / Where were your sabers then?"[48] The belief that American assistance was an imperative element to eventual Greek victory formed the crux of the American philhellenic argument. Given the widespread distribution of information provided by Americans Jarvis, Howe, and Miller, it was a common belief that Americans were more devoted to the cause than were European philhellenes, who had reportedly abandoned the cause and returned home. In resting blame on the European philhellenes, the author intended to appeal to American philhellenes that they should continue their support for the Greek cause.

The loss at Missolonghi aided in renewing interest in the Greek cause on a national scale, with enthusiasm reaching outside of the more urban cities of the North. For example, one young Ohio woman named Eliza Snow specifically used the image of a young Greek maiden to persuade readers to support the cause. In a poem printed in a local newspaper, she connected American liberty with that of ancient Greece and suggested to her readers that Americans owed a debt to the suffering modern Greeks. Expressed through the eyes of a "Grecian daughter," the poem portrayed an embattled war zone where the Greeks had fallen to the Turks with the powerless young woman looking on: "See with what anxious tenderness she plies, / Unmindful of the grief that swells her heart, / Some healing balm—some kind of restorative / To save a husband, brother, or a sire, / On whose joint efforts hang the fate of Greece."[49]

Snow's poem appealed to the sympathies of her readers, calling for "healing balm," which presumably would have taken the form of monetary assistance, food, and clothing for Greek civilians. Though Snow's Greek maiden did not personally seek vengeance as had William Cullen Bryant's Greek Amazon, the message behind the poem was the same: a call to action. The poem not only signaled the changing interest the philhellenic movement had toward humanitarian relief instead of military aid, but it also showed that even on the Ohio frontier there was a keen interest in the Greek Revolution.

Similarities between Snow's poem and others such as Bryant's "Song of the Greek Amazon" reveal that philhellenes hoped they would influence the American public to take an active part in the Greek cause by suggesting they had a moral obligation to do so. Many American philhellenes expressed the opinion that if not for the delayed completion of the frigates, "Missolonghi would not have fallen!"[50] The urgency expressed in popular literature concerning the Greek cause was made real through an appeal for donations.

Many American philhellenes tried to compensate for the shipbuilding fiasco.[51] Mathew Carey of Philadelphia presided over a meeting early in November calling for a national effort to raise subscriptions in order to purchase a frigate for the Greeks "as an indemnity for their loss by the extravagance and inattention of the agents at N. York."[52] News of the meeting was reprinted in several states, including Massachusetts, Connecticut, New Hampshire, and New York. A few weeks later, relief societies began to organize their efforts at gathering food and supplies rather than supplies for warfare. A warehouse was secured for the specific purpose of receiving such contributions.[53]

As philhellenes began to collect contributions to compensate for the frigate debacle, another scandal erupted. Despite the reassurances made by Greek agents such as Luriottis, some philhellenes had long expressed concerns over sending all American donations to the London Committee. Fear of mismanagement or simply that American philhellenes would not be recognized as having donated at all was of paramount concern for many potential donors. It was confirmed by the fall of 1826 that the Greek Committee of London had indeed wasted or mismanaged the funds sent by American philhellenes.[54] If any kind of relief continued, concluded many American philhellene organizers, it would be focused on civilian relief exclusively and would come directly from American donors, not through European intermediaries.

The shift toward organizing and collecting donations on behalf of the Greek cause was complete by December 1826. Edward Everett received letters from George Jarvis and Jonathan P. Miller describing the "amount of suffering for want of food" by the Greeks. It was noted that "the Committees for the relief of the Greeks in France, Holland and Geneva have sent twelve cargoes of provisions and an agent to superintend their distribution." Not to be outdone, Everett made a public appeal: "Let not the United States among so many states and nations be indifferent to the sufferings of this dreadful, but not desperate conflict."[55] Everett's sentiments were not in vain. Now engaged in a humanitarian effort, American philhellenic leaders appealed for food and supplies for suffering civilians. American philhellenic organizations were determined to let the world know that the Greek cause was of the utmost concern to the American public.

The Greek Fire Resurges

With the Greek cause now refocused as a humanitarian effort, Mathew Carey published several addresses to the citizens of Philadelphia on the subject in the early months of 1827. Referring to the scandals that had recently plagued the philhellenic movement, Carey's appeals expressed the hope that "the good work is only postponed for a while, and that it will now be promptly and zealously undertaken, so as to make amends for lost time."[56] Greek aid societies employed a range of methods for exerting interest in the cause. Carey printed his correspondence with Everett as well as updates from the American volunteers in the Greek army in March.

In his correspondence, Everett discussed the humanitarian efforts that were so important to the Greek cause. Everett stated to Carey that "a Great amount of suffering might be relieved, by the dispatch of a vessel loaded with provisions."[57] Carey ultimately challenged his readers that if European nations could furnish twelve cargoes of provisions to Greece, then surely the United States could furnish twelve more. At the least, Carey said, Pennsylvania itself could supply two. Unlike in the early years of the American philhellenic movement, the object of these donations would not be for military purposes but rather to assist the Greek civilian population. In adjusting the focus of their charity, philhellenes managed to gather a broader base of support that included women and church groups, people who were more inclined to raise funds for relief than for war.

Carey hoped that he could generate interest in a humanitarian effort by once again using philhellenic rhetoric to describe the shared experiences between war-torn Greece and the United States during the American Revolution. This comparison was not a difficult sell given that the United States had just commemorated fifty years of independence. Instead of appealing to "passions or feelings—which frequently lead us astray, and whose effects are generally evanescent," Carey made his argument from the belief that the Greeks deserved aid because of their extended period of subjugation under the Turks. "The more severe and grinding the tyranny under which it has groaned, the more imperative the claim for sympathy," he argued in a printed address. Carey's readers were then reminded about why the American colonies had departed from Great Britain: "Taxation without representation is slavery." Carey contrasted this publicly accepted truism with the Greek Revolution: "The whole of the grievances of the British colonies, from their first settlement to the declaration of independence, were not equal to those suffered by Greece in a single month." Carey intended to give his readers pause by stating that the civilized nations of the new and old world "look with heartless indifference . . . on one of the most heroic nations of ancient or modern times—for no nation ever maintained a more glorious struggle with barbarous oppressors, under such immense disadvantages."[58] As hard-won as American independence had been, the Greeks deserved more sympathy and support, philhellenes believed, as they were subject to a Muslim power.

Even the smallest communities throughout the country contributed supplies to the cause. In the first few months of 1827, tens of thousands of dollars were collected by aid societies. While the romanticized philhellenic rhetoric that had dominated the discussion during the early years of the Greek war persisted, the activist urge to assist the Greeks took on a more pronounced humanitarian intent with the raising of funds as well as clothing and food for Greek civilians.[59] Taking the lead in these efforts was the Greek Committee of New York.

On January 8, 1827, a large meeting of New York citizens convened by public notice at the City Hotel with the specific purpose of deciding how best to harness local and national forces to collect supplies for the Greeks. These supplies were to aid the citizens of Greece, not provide arms or munitions to assist in the war itself. The public nominated new officers for the committee, including Stephen Allen, former New York mayor and New York State assemblyman, who became chairman. The meeting was reportedly "filled with sentiments of compassion and sympathy towards the Greek nation, in their present extreme suffering of all the complicated evils of war and famine." These sentiments had "a peculiar claim upon the sympathies and charities of every citizen of this free country."[60]

Ultimately, it was agreed at the meeting that the main goal should be to provide food for the Greeks. The group also supported a resolution written by native New Yorker and Louisiana congressman Edward Livingston requesting $50,000 from the national treasury to purchase food and clothing. Reports of this meeting were reprinted in multiple states, thus generating interest in rekindling efforts to support the Greeks. That relief for Greek citizens did not necessarily convey the same diplomatic, political, and moral complications as had calls for military aid, and a revitalized philhellenic movement enjoyed even more interest than it had in the previous years, joining new participants with the Greek cause. The New York committee hoped that this new approach to providing aid to Greece would allow Congress to openly support Greek civilians if not the Greek army. Their motion, however, was defeated in the House of Representatives 109 to 54.[61] Though efforts to lobby Congress for aid were again foiled, the Greek Committee of New York came to be viewed as the central collection point for Greek aid throughout the country. With New York in control of American donations, the fear some philhellenes had expressed previously over the mismanagement of these funds by European philhellenic groups receded.

The Greek Committee of New York's goals were exceeded in just a few months of local community fund-raising. A Richmond, Virginia, paper reported in mid-March that the committee had raised $20,972.40 from citizens throughout the state of New York and neighboring states. While the committee had proven phenomenally successful in its efforts, the donations would "go a very little way in feeding and clothing the many thousands of destitute women and children who compose the unhappy population of Greece."[62] One philhellene speculated, after the initial receipt of donations from across the country had arrived in New York, that the total amount of donations gathered from American citizens in 1827 would reach over $70,000.[63]

The first shipment of supplies in 1827, with over 2,300 barrels of provisions, clothing, and medicine, was sent off on the *Chancellor* along with Greek Committee of New York agent Jonathan P. Miller.[64] Miller and his fellow Americans in the Greek army had dealt primarily with the Greek Committee of Boston, especially Edward Everett. Miller returned to the United States in November 1826 in order to receive supplies from various aid societies. He did this not only to expedite the acquisition of the supplies but also to relieve the uneasiness over the previous mismanagement of funds. Miller issued a statement that circulated widely in newspapers concerning the necessity of acquiring supplies and connecting the Greek cause with the American Revolution: "The Greeks are struggling, as our fathers did, for freedom and independence."[65] Miller's statement received much attention and contributed at least in part to the success of the fund-raising efforts.[66]

The Greek Committee of New York was more than successful in gathering supplies for the Greeks. Even after the massive collection of supplies was dispatched to Greece in March 1827, fund-raising continued. The following year, the committee sent more money and supplies. George Newbold, the committee's treasurer, deposited cash received by the committee into the Bank of America, where he was director and later president. Greater New York and Connecticut communities forwarded their donations to the committee in New York City. For example, Catskill, New York, forwarded $183.27 in May 1828, and Greenville, New York, sent $66.38. Newbold was determined to keep the committee donation books and receipts in order, not surprising given the outrage over the London Committee's mismanagement of funds from previous years.

Since Newbold kept detailed records on all donations, receipts name those who provided donations and the amounts they gave. Deposit slips indicate that while much of the money came from various New York and Connecticut Greek aid societies, private citizens donated funds as well. One resident of the small town of Bloomingdale, New York, donated five dollars. Citizens from various wards of New York donated one or two dollars to the cause. Philhellenic sentiments were so prevalent that one donation of thirty-one dollars was given by a group of men "belonging onboard the Jersey City Steam Ferry Boats."[67] Especially worth noting is that these men were apparently not solicited for a donation but rather took up a collection themselves and forwarded the money to the bank on their own accord.

Committee members often solicited donations by actually going out into the community to collect from the different wards of the city. In the case of the Greek Committee of Philadelphia, subscription collectors were hired and paid a wage to go out into the community.[68] For example, one committee collector from New York wrote in his receipt of deposit to the bank, "The inclosed amount is all I could collect in the 9th district of the first ward, for the benefit of the Greeks, from the following persons . . ."[69] Small donations from three persons were listed. A receipt written for the first ward, however, lists fifteen individuals who donated cash as well as clothing totaling $76.25.

Despite the fact that there were few organized philhellenic groups in the Southern United States, George Newbold received donations made by individual citizens from the South. Several residents of Virginia in 1828, for example, sent their personal donations to New York. A struggling businessman and resident of Richmond named Hezekiah Belden, a native of Connecticut whose business brought him to the South, wrote to Edward Everett requesting that his donation of ten dollars be forwarded to the Greek committee in Philadelphia, New York, or Boston "as you shall think most advisable."[70] Belden explained to Everett that in Richmond "something is said, but nothing is done for the cause, here—Would to God that less was said, & more done, & that benevolence did not dwell upon the tongue alone."[71] That Everett forwarded the donations to Newbold suggests that even the great American philhellene saw New York as the central collection point for the Greek cause.

Newbold received one donation from a resident of Staunton, Virginia, who requested that his five dollars be handed to the proper person for the use of the Greeks. He wished to remain anonymous. Another Virginian named H. M. Thompson gave $66.38, a sizable individual donation. Although many Southerners supported the Greeks, they did not form as many groups or organizations to aid the cause as Northerners did. This does not appear to be a point of difference based on sectionalism; rather, it stemmed from the fact that the North offered more organizational opportunities in its urban centers than did the more rural South.

While there were certainly exceptions, these receipts indicate that Greek aid societies were active primarily in urban areas in Northern states. The receipts also repeatedly indicate that the New York committee was viewed as an established and legitimate group that could be trusted with individual donations. Although the Boston committee was one of the larger Greek committees in the union, the New York committee compiled donations on a national level. That Everett forwarded the donation from Virginia to the New York committee supports this organizational cooperation and understanding. The Virginia letters also indicate that even though there was no organized Greek society in Virginia, there was nonetheless the same kind of philhellenic-driven humanitarian sentiment in these communities.

Although the Missouri Crisis of 1819–1821 had solidified sectional tensions over slavery immediately before the Greek Revolution began, Southern newspapers and personal letters do not indicate that the less organized effort at supporting the Greeks in the South was a direct result of this tension. The Greek cause and the philhellenic rhetoric used to promote it appealed at both the local and national levels, where sources from the period reflect a common intellectual and romantic bond with the Greeks. In addition to the Greek Revolution, congressional debates during the Missouri Crisis concerning foreign slavery in places such as Spanish America similarly avoided reference to the domestic slavery issue while promoting the idea of emancipation abroad. The connection between Ottoman subjugation of the Greeks and American enslavement of African Americans did not emerge as a point of domestic contention until the late 1820s with the second wave of the abolitionist movement and the emergence of immediatism.[72]

The Greek cause continued to elicit charitable donations for the Greeks across the country even after the Battle of Navarino was won in October 1827. Britain, in part because of philhellenic organizations within its own borders as well as concern over Russian ambition in the Balkans, consented to serve as mediator between the Greeks and the Turks. Despite the fact that the British had been reluctant to show official support for the Greek cause, their role became more active as a result of the Treaty of London, signed in July 1827. Fearing that Russia might act alone in hopes of territorial gains in the Balkans, Britain and France insisted on the inclusion of a secret article in the treaty, which compelled all three powers, Britain, France, and Russia, to cooperatively use force if the Ottomans and the Greeks refused mediation. When the Ottomans refused to back down, the three European powers entered the conflict on the side of the Greeks in a campaign that culminated at the Battle of Navarino.[73] American newspapers reported at length on any details that arrived from the battlefield.[74] News began to arrive at the end of December that Ottoman and Egyptian forces had been defeated at Navarino. This was quickly followed by news from American philhellenes in Greece that American aid was still needed for suffering Greek civilians.

Through the efforts of Mathew Carey and Edward Everett, the Greek Committees of Philadelphia and Boston enjoyed a successful partnership in the final years of the war while also nurturing philhellenic enthusiasm within their own respective communities. One letter printed en masse for subscribers of the Greek Committee of Philadelphia asked that the letter be distributed among "active citizens of your neighbourhood."[75] The letter concluded with a list of figures quoting the amount of money raised from various communities within Pennsylvania and sent to New York—a grand total of $17,168 as of April 2, 1827. Mathew Carey assumed leadership of the Greek Committee of Philadelphia in January 1827 and reinvigorated the committee through public appeals made through newspapers and pamphlets. Edward Everett continued to correspond with George Jarvis, Samuel Gridley Howe, and Jonathan P. Miller and made public news provided to him from Greece.

Howe and Miller returned to the United States on separate occasions in 1828 specifically to raise funds for Greek civilians through speaking engagements in New York and Boston. Howe explained that he had witnessed the suffering of Greek civilians firsthand and relayed these experiences to a meeting of the Greek Committee of New York early in 1828. Howe wrote: "Should I detail to you what I know of Turkish cruelty, you might deem it fable; you might think it impossible that in the nineteenth century such depravity exists." He continued with a brutal description of the atrocities committed by Egyptian-Ottoman forces under Ibrahim Pasha in the Peloponnese. "The men have the best fate," explained Howe; "they are generally massacred on the spot, though often with torments." Although men were slaughtered by Ottoman forces, it was Greek women and children, according to Howe, who suffered most: "The women are put to death—or if beautiful, are sold to some rich Turks." And what of the Greek civilians who had managed to survive? "Why one half of the inhabitants of the Peloponesus and Romelia have taken refuge in the mountains," Howe explained. The situation of many of these refugees, continued Howe, "principally women and children, is indeed deplorable, and not to be conceived of by comparison with any misery as seen in this country. . . . I could tell you of families with no other shelter than the shade of an olive tree; of emaciated, half-famished orphans, who go round to pick up the most offensive substances for food."[76] A portion of Howe's address to the Greek Committee of New York was printed and circulated among subscribers. It asked clergy especially to include Howe's remarks in their Sunday sermons in order to generate donations for the cause.

Newspapers and pamphlets, primarily in New York and New England, reported on Howe's efforts, calling on readers to assist in putting together food and clothing for thousands of Greek refugees. Howe's efforts were also supported by Jonathan P. Miller, who continued to send reports to the larger Greek committees in New York, Boston, and Philadelphia concerning the ongoing need for civilian relief. In one of these reports, Miller emphasized the important contribution American philhellenes had made, noting that Greek bishops had ordered prayers to be said publicly "for the blessing of Almighty God to rest upon those Americans who at the distance of five thousand miles have not forgotten their fellow beings in the hour of greatest need."[77] Howe wrote to the Greek Committee of New York that he, Miller, and George Jarvis had traveled around Greece and its islands dispersing aid provided by American philhellenes. In one case, said Howe, the three American philhellenes were greeted by "about 5,000 who received us with shouts of joy." "How often did I wish," Howe continued, "the charitable donors could have witnessed the gratitude of these poor wretches? It would be impossible to hear the story, and see the general distress of each individual without shedding tears."[78] Both Miller and Howe were so devoted to aiding Greek refugees that they adopted Greek boys and brought them to the United States to be raised and educated.[79] Miller's adopted son, Loukas Miltiades Miller, later became a congressman from Wisconsin. Howe's adopted son was John Zachos, who became an author, educator, and abolitionist.

While the organizational efforts of men such as Carey, Everett, Miller, and Howe quickly transformed the philhellenic movement into a nationally engaged, humanitarian endeavor, the role women played in responding to their calls for donations must also be examined. Female church groups and community relief societies especially answered the call for charitable assistance for the Greeks, becoming part of the driving force behind the philhellenic movement in the late stage of the war. Benevolence joined with the philhellenic cause, providing women an avenue for extending their influence from local communities to the international stage.

Philhellenism and Benevolence

Perhaps the most important way in which Carey, Everett, and many other male philhellenes successfully promoted the Greek cause in the final years of the war was through involving women in their organizations. As philhellenic efforts had shifted toward a more humanitarian emphasis, Greek committees recruited female supporters on the basis of their supposed natural inclination toward faith, community, and family. The Philadelphia committee, for example, wrote to the wife of one of the committee members requesting that she use her influence with her friends to rebuild support among the women of Philadelphia. Mathew Carey penned the letter and expressed the committee's "great surprize [*sic*] and regret" that the event that had been planned "was a total failure [because] not a single lady appeared."[80] The committee members wondered if no ladies attended the event because the Greek cause was viewed as a novelty rather than one deserving of the active involvement of local ladies' benevolent groups. Carey continued that "the happiness of probably 200,000 adult females" depended upon the action of the ladies of the city. He said that the committee "cannot allow ourselves to believe that the ladies of our city will be indifferent" to these Greek women. He concluded that without the assistance of women, the committee's success would be greatly reduced.

Why would it be appropriate to ask respectable women to become involved in a political cause? And why would Everett and Carey expect that women would consider such an appeal? With the Greek cause transformed into more than a call for military aid and political support, benevolent groups took a particularly active interest in the relief of Greek civilians. Beginning in the 1790s, elite and middle-class women began to form and participate in a variety of organizations, typically associated with church or community groups. These organizations engaged in a range of charitable efforts and social reform movements that included temperance, antiprostitution, relief for the sick, help for the orphaned and destitute, and education reform. Participating in these organizations allowed women to extend their domestic role outside the home, fulfilling local obligations to the religious community while also increasing their social status.[81] Instead of being viewed as improper or radical, women who participated in these charitable organizations were admired for their "true womanhood" in aiding the community and society in general.[82] Both Everett and Carey would have understood that the entwined roles of volunteer work and domestic duties had increasingly allowed women to pursue activities outside of the home. Female participation in the Greek cause grew into an international movement. Organized benevolence abroad allowed American women to expand their influence within "civil society" well beyond their individual towns and communities.[83]

In addition, middle class and elite women would already have been familiar with the stereotypes associated with the treatment of women in the Ottoman Empire. Captivity tales with female subjects as well as tales of Turkish harems were prevalent in early American society. Reports provided by Howe and Miller describing the fate of young women at the hands of the Ottomans almost certainly played on the sympathies of female benevolent groups. By joining forces and aiding Greek civilians, American women could rescue their Greek counterparts from a fate worse than death and also place Greece on a pathway to freedom.

Carey brought together "true womanhood" rhetoric with elements of American patriotism and philhellenism in pamphlets prepared for women. While relying on the usual philhellenic rhetoric, Carey also emphasized the parallels between the Greek Revolution and the American Revolution in making a particular appeal to female organizations to join the cause. Carey asked his female readers,

> Shall we appeal in vain for what is good, to that sanctuary, where all that is good has its proper home, the female bosom? The darkest day of our revolutionary struggle, was cheered by the beams of woman's benevolence. In this city, the ladies were distinguished for their active beneficence; and it is a part of our annals, of which we are most proud. . . . Come forth, then, ye who can mould the feelings, and direct the will of the ruggedest nature. Ye chaste and tender wives and mothers, ye affectionate daughters and sisters—come forth and exercise your well-deserved influence over those whom you can so easily move.[84]

The rhetoric of this letter draws on the vocabulary of benevolent societies of the time, suggesting that it would be unwomanly not to respond. Carey also argued that Greek independence was just as worthy as American independence; consequently, the ladies of the community should show their patriotism by openly supporting Greece.

From 1827 to the early 1830s, women served a central role in the American movement for Greek relief. In many localities where a Greek committee existed, there is convincing evidence to suggest that women were a driving force behind collecting subscriptions and coordinating events for the Greek cause. Many Greek committees had ladies' subcommittees, making women a recognized asset to each organization. In communities where there was no ladies subcommittee, women gathered on their own accord and collected funds.[85] At least in one instance, students of the Female Academy in Lexington, Kentucky, joined the efforts of the local male college to raise funds and even issued a pamphlet titled "Address to the Young Ladies of the West," which encouraged women throughout the United States to join their efforts at raising donations.[86]

Even though there were female aid societies prior to 1827, a brief glance at period newspapers reveals that women largely moved from being peripheral members of philhellenic societies to serving in leadership roles around this time, or at least coordinating with male leaders to provide clothing and other supplies. Women's involvement in providing relief for the Greeks continued longer than the relief work of most other philhellenic organizations in the United States. Many women remained active in the effort after 1827, when Britain, France, and Russia aided the Greeks in securing a victory at Navarino. American women understood that while the war might be coming to an end, Greek civilians would continue to require assistance.

Ladies' groups primarily directed their efforts at gathering food and clothing for Greek civilians. The ladies of Providence, Rhode Island, and surrounding communities alone produced over 3,000 items of clothing, which were sent to the Greek Committee of New York.[87] In Hartford, Connecticut, women advertised they were collecting subscriptions in order to purchase materials for clothing and provisions.[88] In Boston, a meeting of ladies designated "four places of deposit . . . where articles of money contributed for the relief of the Greeks" would be received.[89] Even in smaller communities such as Canandaigua, New York, local ladies made clothing for Greek women and children.[90]

African American women were at least minimally involved in the Greek cause. One paper reported that free "ladies and gentlemen of colour" in New York had given a benefit for the Greek cause in March 1827. Though it is not clear if philhellenism was an influential movement within the African American community, African Americans certainly understood the desire a group of people could have for freedom. According to the report, these ladies and gentlemen were enthusiastic enough over the benefit that "the company did not disperse until six in the morning."[91]

Newspapers and pamphlets publicized female efforts at raising funds and supplies, simultaneously providing local news of charity efforts as well as advertising for Greek aid. These reports also show that female organizations from different localities made active attempts to coordinate efforts. A newspaper in Hartford, Connecticut, described how women were "actively engaging their sympathies in behalf of the suffering Greeks." Addressing ladies of neighboring towns, the piece asserted, "We shall be pardoned for intimating the practicability of a co-operating exertion, as their intercourse with Hartford, or with New York would open to them, and to us, a common channel of communication with Greece."[92] In Boston, a meeting of ladies was so large that its members had to relocate to a larger meeting hall. With the meeting now in a nearby church, the building was quickly filled with ladies who "appeared to be strongly interested in the object of the meeting."[93] Surveying the women's efforts, one newspaper announced in 1827, "In other states, individuals, religious and Masonic societies, corporations, &c., have all contributed their aid in various forms; and the ladies have enthusiastically exerted themselves in the same noble cause."[94]

The language used to report female efforts at fund-raising or recruitment linked charitable outreach in Greece with benevolence. In one of the Philadelphia committee's printed addresses to the public, two examples of organized female support provided evidence of successful donation collections in other parts of the country. The examples provided were from committees in Buffalo, New York, and in Baltimore. In Buffalo, the ladies were "respectfully invited to solicit donations" in order that the "suffering mothers and daughters of Greece will find zealous friends and able advocates among the sex, who proverbially lend a grace to deeds of charity, while they borrow a charm from the exercise of its duties." In Baltimore, ladies did not wait to be invited to assist with the cause, but rather formed their own organization for the purpose of "devising measures, to assist as far as may be in their power."[95]

A resolution from Baltimore stated that it was the duty of the ladies of the United States to "depart from that retired circle, in which a judicious state of society requires the ladies of this country usually move, and use the influence which is allotted them, in relieving from starvation the suffering females of a foreign land, whose sons and husbands are fighting the battles of the cross against the crescent."[96] The Greek cause gave American women permission to become more active publicly. Among the successes of this Baltimore-based relief society was a Ladies Fair, which raised $1,700 for the cause.[97] In fact, one article written on the success of the Ladies Fair pointed out that the women of Baltimore had far outdone their male counterparts and that the men should be ashamed of their lethargy.

The New York committee collected donations of both money and provisions from female groups in New York, Connecticut, and Massachusetts. Most of these donations came from ladies' Greek committees in various localities. Some funds also arrived from ladies' church groups. With a few exceptions, donations made by women came from organized groups and not from individuals.[98] That charitable outreach was largely conducted by local benevolent groups rather than individuals again suggests that communities saw the Greek cause as a logical extension of women's charitable activism. It also indicates that this kind of public outreach was perhaps considered more socially acceptable if done in a group environment.

Female participation in benevolent societies was more common in the Northern states, but their Southern counterparts expressed similar interest in aiding the Greeks. An article originally printed in a Richmond, Virginia, paper that was subsequently reprinted in Macon, Georgia, reported, "The Ladies of the North have again roused themselves in behalf of the suffering Greeks. . . . This is generous design, which we must greatly admire, however little we may imitate it."[99] The article was printed alongside a letter written by a Mrs. Lydia Sigourney of Connecticut, a member of a ladies' aid society in Hartford and a nationally known poet.

Sigourney's poetry endorsed women's participation in political reform as an extension of the domestic sphere. In not requiring women to depart from the separate sphere of domesticity, Sigourney's call for support of the Greeks would have resonated with the more politically conservative women of the South.[100] The Richmond article provided a Southern female reaction to Sigourney's call for Greek aid and indicated frustration that there was no organized effort similar to those in the North: "Who can read the following effusion . . . without being penetrated with esteem for the fair authoress?" The letter written by Sigourney was addressed to the "Ladies of Greece" and described women's heartfelt sadness and joy for the women and children of Greece. The letter explained that the contributions accompanying the letter were limited in comparison to the donations given by the ladies of larger cities but that

> the poor among us, have given according to their ability—and our little children have cheerfully aided, that some of you, and your children might have bread to eat and raiment to put on. Could you but behold the faces of our little ones brighten . . . while they give up their holidays that they might work with their needles for Greece; could you see those females who earn a subsistence by labour, gladly casting their might into our treasury, and taking hours from their repose, that an additional garment might be furnished for you.[101]

Sigourney's letter was printed in its entirety, indicating at least some Southern interest in the Greek cause. Widespread organized efforts in the South, however, did not take place. Individuals living in the South who desired to send aid to Greece sent their donations to Northern aid societies.[102] For women involved in benevolence, the idea of aiding other Christian women and children was immediately appealing and, not surprisingly, interested women from both the North and the South. What made Greece all the more worthy of aid was that it was fighting against a Muslim power and if successful would require assistance with establishing new social infrastructure, especially schools for Greek children. Aiding the Greeks, therefore, provided a long-term outlet for social reform where American ideas of republicanism, female virtue, and Protestantism could be effectively advanced. As with many female reform movements of the antebellum era, women were more likely to mobilize in groups in the North and in urban areas.

The widespread efforts of American women were distinguishable enough from those of their male counterparts that the Greeks openly acknowledged their time and support. For example, in January 1829 a letter of thanks was printed in a New England newspaper written by a group of widows from Ipsara, a Greek island that was at the center of brutal fighting in 1824. The widows identified the "ladies of America" as their "dear sisters the friend of liberty." Their efforts, they said, had greatly lifted the Greek women's spirits.[103] Another letter was printed in a Baltimore paper penned by the "Directress of the American Hospital at Poros thanking the Ladies of America" for their assistance. A "Grecian mother" also offered her thanks "to the most lively acknowledgements of the whole nation, she dares hope and promise you, ladies, that the sensibility and consolations which you have bestowed upon the unfortunate, will be forever indelibly engraven [sic] upon their hearts, and that the example of a nation so glorious will incite them to imitate your virtues."[104]

Benevolence and philhellenic organizations built collaborative efforts through which agents were sent to Greece to act in the interests of both groups. The Reverend Jonas King, who was sent as a missionary to Greece by the American Board of Commissioners for Foreign Missions, was also provided money to assist the Greeks by the Ladies' Greek Committee of New York. King saw firsthand the impact American women had in providing aid to the Greeks.[105] Some of King's journal entries were printed in American newspapers, providing perspective on the conflict as well as the character of the Greek people. In one of these letters, King described an experience of attending a party in a small village. The locals, who were especially interested in him as an American, provided expressions of "gratitude for what the Americans had done, and for the sympathy expressed by the American ladies to the females of Greece." Later in the evening as toasts were offered, one was proposed to "the health of the American Ladies, which was instantly received with three or four loud cheers and clapping hands." This toast was carried out at length as "for 8 or 10 minutes, nothing was to be heard but long and reiterated cries of 'Long live the American Ladies!'—'Long live the American Ladies!' I must confess, that the hearing of this . . . excited in my bosom peculiar emotions of pleasure, and showed me, that the kind and benevolent exertions of my country-women had produced a powerful effect, even among those who had never received a single article of their charities."[106]

A few Greeks who came to the United States as refugees also lauded support provided by American women. For example, Samuel Gridley Howe brought a young boy named Christophoros Plato Castanis home with him to the United States. A Boston ladies association at Amherst provided Castanis with an education. He became a well-respected orator, primarily speaking on the subject of Greece.[107] In a memoir he wrote as an adult, Castanis detailed his life in Greece and his experiences in the Greek war. He especially acknowledged American women as being particular patrons of Greece. Dedicating the memoir to the "Ladies of America," Castanis expressed his gratitude for female philhellenic efforts, requesting that they "accept this work, as a token of the love and gratitude of the Matrons and Maidens who, through yourselves, have taught the heart of Greece to beat in response to the heart of Columbia."[108]

Another Greek refugee by the name of Joseph Stephanini, who wrote a history of the Greek Revolution, came to the United States after escaping from Turkish servitude. Stephanini's purpose of writing and publishing a history of the war was to "enable him to return to his own country, and to release from slavery a large and suffering family."[109] Published in 1829, Stephanini's history concluded with thanks to the people who had assisted him in his life in America. He singled out for special thanks "the ladies who have so kindly interested themselves to obtain subscriptions for my work."[110]

Female aid societies provided support for Castanis and Stephanini, each of whom acknowledged the singular efforts of women on behalf of the Greeks. With this in mind, both men spoke about the need for American education efforts in Greece, calling on American women to support the cause. Castanis captured the desire to educate the Greeks in his memoir: "Just as primeval Cretans nourished and educated infant Jove [i.e., Jupiter], about Mt. Ida, so the strong and refined arm of American philanthropy fed, clothed and educated many an infant descendant of those god-like fathers of the Grecian race."[111] Such observations encouraged Stephanini and Castanis to regard American women as the special patrons of Greece's women and children. Indeed, education in Greece would prove to be one important way in which women continued to exert influence in Greece even after the revolution was at an end.

Women's organizations raised an impressive amount of money for the period. It would not be an overstatement to suggest that the women of New York and New England alone assisted in raising thousands of dollars' worth of supplies for the Greeks during the final years of the war. Their contributions reflected the degree to which the American people engaged with the Greek cause, but they also demonstrate that benevolence in early America provided women with a means for expanding their presence abroad. Female support defined the revival of interest in the Greeks not in terms of the war itself but in the effects of war especially on Greek women and children. Though the war drew to a close, women continued their support for Greek civilians in the years that followed, especially through the establishment of schools in post-revolutionary Greece.

★   ★   ★

In its final years of fighting for independence, Greece received a tremendous amount of supplies and philanthropic interest from both male and female philhellenes. Fund-raising efforts resonated with Philadelphia residents as donations deposited into the bank and storehouses established by the Greek Committee increased significantly by April 1827. With Mathew Carey at the helm, the committee had criticized the dwindled enthusiasm for the cause. They pointed out that although Pittsburgh and Brooklyn contained a fraction of Philadelphia's population, they had outraised the citizens of Philadelphia, a city of 140,000 inhabitants.[112] The public appeal evidently succeeded in persuading Philadelphians to renew their dedication to the cause. At the end of January only $3,700 had been collected by Philadelphia's Greek Committee, but by the end of March the committee had collected $16,675.[113] Carey's work as a writer and publisher played no small role in keeping the Greek cause in the public eye, and he printed his addresses not only in English but in other languages as well, such as German.[114] The Greek Committee of Philadelphia continued to deposit funds into the local bank at least through the end of 1828.

Philhellenism as a romantic and sentimental phenomenon existed in the United States prior to the Greek War of Independence but evolved over the course of several decades. American identity as being bound to ancient concepts of freedom and liberty also had developed over time and became fused with the popular philhellenic movement. These sentiments provided the initial thrust behind American support for the war. As an outgrowth of these ideological connections to ancient Greece, American philhellenes identified their own country as possessing an inherent duty to support Greece; as such, they could not be outdone by other European nations. This competition with Europe, the seemingly selfless sacrifice of Lord Byron, and the Americans and Greeks serving in the army continued to engage public interest and support for the cause.

Edward Everett spent much of his time as a nationally recognized philhellene writing to other philhellenes, organizing relief efforts, and appealing to the president to send him as a special agent to Greece.[115] Everett was never successful in obtaining this appointment to Greece. He did, however, assist in keeping the Greek Revolution an ever-present issue in Washington through proposals printed in his own publication, the *North American Review*. Everett was also instrumental in highlighting the adventures of George Jarvis, Jonathan P. Miller, and Samuel Gridley Howe as a means of favorably discussing American support for the war and the Greek civilian population.[116] In an 1829 issue of the *North American Review*, for example, Everett reviewed Howe's *Historical Sketch of the Greek Revolution*, which was an account of his recollections in the Greek army's service. Everett explicitly stated that his object in writing the review was to "convince our readers, if they needed to be so convinced, that the subject of the work before us is of great importance and interest."[117]

Everett's activism in the movement strengthened his connections with other like-minded and politically connected men of his time. His interest also perhaps contributed to the ongoing tension that existed between those congressmen who desired to provide aid to Greece and those who did not.[118] Everett's enthusiasm as a philhellene and his success in making his opinion on the Greek Revolution known and widely circulated forced politicians as well as private citizens to consider with whom and to what extent the United States should be involved in foreign affairs.

Due to the shift from a romantic and sentimental support to an activist support of the Greek Revolution, Americans began to transfer their attention to assistance for the Greek civilian population. Confronted with reports of the realities of the conflict, especially from Americans serving in the Greek army, American philhellenes not only used traditional philhellenic rhetoric, but also increasingly employed benevolence rhetoric in their public appeals in order to expand their base of support. Charitable activism in support of the Greeks later inspired and became a part of future conversations on reform. These movements included abolitionism and women's rights with David Walker, William Lloyd Garrison, and Emma Willard using the Greek cause to advance their arguments.

The success of the American philhellenic movement was due in no small part to ladies' organizations throughout the country. American women insisted that independence was not won with military victories, but through benevolence-based support. American women could justify their involvement in a very public forum as well as support a political cause while simultaneously expanding their place outside of the home. Female support for the Greek cause

signified a growing scope within benevolent organizations that included domestic as well as global goals of social reform. With the help of American
women, Greek women could leave the battlefield behind and focus their efforts at growing and nurturing strong, healthy, and educated families.

Although the hope that Greece would gain independence and declare itself
a republic was dashed as a result of European intervention, American relief
efforts in Greece played an important role in the survival of the Greeks in the
last years of the war. Food, clothing, and other supplies provided by American philhellenic organizations in part helped stave off starvation for many Greek
civilians.[119] This aid allowed the Greeks to continue their war long enough
until the tide turned in the fighting beginning in the summer of 1827 when
Britain, Russia, and France entered into the conflict. After the Battle of Navarino in October 1827, independence for Greece became more of a reality.
Though the Greeks had formed a government, Britain, Russia, and France
continued to squabble over the details of Greek independence, which were
finally agreed to in February 1830. In the midst of this, Greek civilians continued to suffer from starvation, lack of clothing, and medicine. Americans
were not at this point concerned with influencing the political outcome in
Greece. American philhellenes, with the particular efforts made by female organizers, continued to send civilian aid and cultivated interest in establishing a
newly independent Greece.

Chapter 4

Philhellenes Clash with American Commerce

Early in September 1823, Percy Smythe, Sixth Viscount Strangford and the British ambassador to the Sublime Porte, wrote to Prime Minister George Canning concerning a confidential conversation his interpreter had had with Mehmed Sadik Efendi, the *reis efendi*, or foreign minister of the Ottoman Empire. It was Strangford's responsibility to promote British commercial interests, and he was attentive to news about foreign powers that wished to gain access to trade in the region.[1] Strangford was deeply concerned that the Sublime Porte intended to open trade to all flags in the Black Sea, and he worried what this could mean for British interests if the United States gained full commercial access there. The reis efendi confided that the Sublime Porte was "apprehensive of finding itself placed in a situation of great difficulty upon that point," especially given that Russia had made several demands that the "Americans should be allowed to navigate there."[2]

By this time, the Ottoman Empire had found itself increasingly caught in the midst of a larger European political intrigue. Russia, its oldest foe, was allied with other major European powers, though Britain, to some extent, viewed Russia with suspicion. Where did Britain stand on the subject of Russia and the Americans, wondered the reis efendi? As for the sultan, he and his government "had an exceeding antipathy to Republicans in general, and to the Americans in particular," Strangford wrote. "His Highness was firmly resolved never to enter into any relations of Amity or Commerce with a set of people, who ought to remain quietly in their own quarter of the Globe, without intruding themselves into this." Strangford openly revealed his relief to the reis efendi, confiding that he was "gratified to learn that my own notions on the subject of Republics and Republicans, were sanctioned by the enlightened judgment of the Sultan and His Ministers." This conversation revealed the complicated political landscape American merchants and reformers faced as they considered an expanded presence in diplomacy, commerce, and reform.

After the close of the War of 1812 and the Barbary Wars in 1815, many American men and women hoped that the United States had secured its place in the world of nations. The enthusiastic endorsement of philhellenism in America, however, brought to the fore issues concerning foreign policy and American identity that had long been brewing beneath the surface of American politics and public life. On the one hand, the lack of a treaty between the United States and the Ottoman Empire plagued American merchants and politicians conducting business in the Mediterranean and Western Asia. American merchants also wanted to negotiate a commercial treaty in which they would not have to suffer the insult of paying tribute. On the other hand, philhellenes and reformers openly supported the Greek Revolution against the Ottomans, which jeopardized treaty negotiations. American interest in the Greek Revolution became the impetus for the emergence of a conflict between American philhellenes and those who wished to foster better trading relationships with the Muslims of the Ottoman Empire. Though at odds, both groups had ambitions for expanding an empire of America ideals into the Mediterranean and Western Asia.

Americans committed to the Greek cause envisioned a presence in the Mediterranean with the hope of uplifting the Greek culture to its supposed former ancient glory through charity, the promotion of education, and evangelism. The redemption of the Greeks by various pro-Greek organizations assumed a "secularized missionary spirit," which endeavored to spread an American understanding of freedom and liberty to all parts of the world.[3] At first, Greek relief efforts by philhellenes such as Edward Everett, Mathew Carey, and countless community social groups made up of both men and women were largely responsible for the initial surge of interest and the continuing growth of the movement.

The New England–based American Board of Commissioners for Foreign Missions (ABCFM) posed similar issues for protrade Americans. First organized contemporaneously with other philhellenic groups, the ABCFM sent some of its first missionaries to Greece, where their efforts were focused upon aid, education, and conversion.[4] These American missionaries of the 1820s were an interesting combination of philhellenes and evangelists, who ultimately desired to redeem the Greeks from their present status as subjects under Ottoman rule.

While pro-Greek organizations in the United States had different goals, they all ultimately acted from a common nationalist mindset that had developed from the philhellenic ideology professed in the late eighteenth and early nineteenth centuries. Americans who glorified ancient Greece's significance in the founding of the United States also drew on the emerging nationalist rhetoric of the late eighteenth century, which emphasized American independence as a shining example of freedom to the rest of the world.[5] American philhellenes of the 1820s endeavored to preserve an abstract understanding of national identity by spreading their ideals abroad. These ideals included representative government, liberal education, ancient roots, charity, and Christianity.[6] Animated by growing nationalist fervor and the understanding that modern Greeks were the most deserving of any other foreign group of people because of their connection to ancient Greece, pro-Greek Americans set their sights on that part of the world.

Those on the other side of the debate built their case in similar terms. Revolutionaries had argued that an important reason to declare independence was the potential of the United States to enter into the transatlantic trade as an independent and free nation.[7] Americans applied the enlightenment ideal of self-determination to their emerging nationalist view of expanding free trade.[8] As one American statesman observed in 1819 on the subject of trade with the Ottoman Empire, the financial resources of the United States were exclusively dependent on commerce, and it was therefore "of primary importance that every facility should be afforded for its extension and security."[9] With the loss of British commercial protection, the first several decades of American existence were mired by conflict in this part of the world. This struggle strengthened a growing desire among American merchants and their supporters to conduct business on the basis of diplomacy, not through the paying of tributes.

The Greek War of Independence changed the foreign political landscape, making a more difficult situation not only for the Americans to negotiate but also for other European powers with interests in the Black Sea. Many Americans with different interests in Greece came together to help place Greek civilians on a path toward reinventing themselves as free citizens. Commercially minded Americans desired to put their free-trade principles to the test, turning their gaze toward the Mediterranean and the Black Sea, a trade network they had long been denied from entering.[10] Both groups hoped to embrace what they believed was the legacy of the American Revolution, but the Greek Revolution put these interests at odds with one another. Navigating a neutral course was difficult enough, but protrade Americans found themselves all the more embroiled in conflict when forced to explain to the Turks why many Americans so desired to officially support Greek independence. Particularly troublesome for American diplomats and merchants would be negotiating a commercial treaty with the Sublime Porte when the sultan knew all too well that American citizens were effectively aiding a group of his subjects to rebel against him. The Greek Revolution was a moment that both catapulted early Americans into international affairs and threatened to keep them isolated in their corner of the world.

The Complications of Greek Independence

American tourists and diplomats beginning in the early nineteenth century were among the first Americans to help secure American trade interests with the Sublime Porte. One of the earliest was Joseph Allen Smith, who toured Greece around 1804, five years before Lord Byron's first visit. While abroad, Smith had secretly hoped to accomplish something more than to take a philhellenic-inspired vacation. Smith was convinced that the key to the United States gaining navigational access to the eastern Mediterranean was with the Sublime Porte and not with the Barbary States themselves as President Jefferson believed. Smith's brother, William Loughton Smith, had been appointed minister to the Sublime Porte in 1799 under the Adams administration, but with Jefferson's election Smith never assumed the post, and the idea of establishing an embassy in Constantinople was dropped.

Ambitious for a diplomatic post himself, Joseph Allen Smith, an ardent Federalist, hoped that if Jefferson were defeated in 1804 then perhaps he would be chosen as minister to Russia. While on his travels abroad, Smith made his way to Russia, where he managed to gain audience to the court of Tsar Alexander I. Smith believed that through Russian cooperation, the United States could negotiate trade access with the Ottoman Empire.[11] At a time when Russia was attempting to expand its empire as the Ottoman Empire weakened, Smith believed that the situation in the East was a precarious one but that some European powers would benefit, commercially or otherwise. Unfortunately for Smith, Jefferson won reelection in 1804 and thus did not invest Smith with any authority to negotiate alliances on behalf of the United States.

Despite the fact that he lacked any official status as a diplomat, Smith managed to complete his journey to Greece through passage on a Russian warship. Joseph Allen Smith's philhellenic sympathies and American commercial interests were not yet in conflict with one another in 1804. Greek independence was nothing more than a wish at that point, with the potential for political and commercial gain of immediate concern. A special relationship with Russia did not fully materialize, though American merchants frequently entered the Black Sea under Russian flags.[12] American merchants understood that the best approach to gaining trade access in the Levant and the Black Sea could only come through a treaty with the Sublime Porte. Gaining favor with the Ottoman court would not come easily. American merchants such as David Offley would have to navigate not only the tense European political situation but also the mixed feelings Ottoman officials felt toward the United States. Twenty years after Smith's visit to Greece, the Greek Revolution only further complicated American interests in the Levant.

Nearly ten years after Smith's visit to Greece, David Offley proved to be adept at securing a place for American merchants at Smyrna, despite the efforts of the British. Without an official treaty, however, American commerce in the region was not on firm ground. By the end of the Barbary Wars, Americans realized that the best way to secure commercial interests in the Levant and expand into the Black Sea would be to negotiate a treaty with the Sublime Porte. No one understood this better than Secretary of State John Quincy Adams. He had accompanied his father to France and the Netherlands and later served as secretary to the American minister to Russia, providing Adams with extensive information on the larger world of European politics.

In April 1820, Adams selected New York lawyer Luther Bradish to travel under the guise of an American tourist but with the intent to gain an audience with the Sublime Porte on the subject of a commercial treaty. Bradish traveled with two sets of papers issued to him by Adams; one set identified him as a tourist, and the other introduced him as an appointed government agent tasked with collecting information for the purpose of securing a commercial treaty on behalf of the U.S. government.[13] Bradish tried to keep the contents of the second set of papers concealed from other European merchants and diplomats as much as possible so that the purpose of his voyage might not be compromised.

Bradish arrived at Constantinople in October 1820. Almost immediately, rumors circulated that he was not merely a tourist but an agent for the U.S. government. Desire for agreeable trade relations in the Mediterranean was so great among European powers that competition for the Sublime Porte's trust and admiration was intense. In addition, concern over Russian ambition in the Balkans was also very high, and there was particular opposition to Bradish's objective on the part of the British ambassador Lord Strangford. In his first letter to Adams, Bradish stated that within a few days of his arrival, European nations hostile to commercial relations between the United States and the Sub-lime Porte had presented a "formal and solemn protest against such negotia-tion, in which she [European nations] has even threatened, in case the Porte should conclude a treaty with the United States, to break off her present rela-tions, and declare war against the Porte."[14] Clearly, successful negotiation be-tween Constantinople and Washington would be a delicate matter.

Bradish realized that in order to conclude a trade agreement he needed the support of the reis efendi, the Ottoman foreign minister, who in 1820 was Halet Efendi. Halet had a long career in public service to the sultan, serving as ambassador to the court of Napoleon among other notable positions. Brad-ish described Halet as being a man of "extraordinary talents and considerable acquirements" who had managed to diminish the powers of the various other government offices in favor of his own. Halet therefore "notoriously possesses the will of the Sultan," and if Bradish could convince him to enter into a trade agreement with the United States, then surely the sultan would agree as well.[15] Writing in December 1820, Bradish reported that Halet was receptive to a treaty with the United States, but pressure from other European powers could potentially prevent the treaty from being secured on negotiation alone.

In addition, Bradish discovered that to secure such a commercial treaty with the Porte would require costly tributes. Tribute was a reality of foreign commerce at the time and one the United States wished to avoid.[16] Bradish estimated that the cost "to preserve Halet Efendi's opinion the same as at present" and negotiate a treaty would come to 350,000 Turkish piasters.[17] Despite this, Bradish advised Adams that a treaty with the Porte would be commercially useful to the United States provided that the country could afford the cost of tributes as well as the likelihood of hostilities from European ships in the Mediterranean. Bradish ex-citedly observed to Adams, "Turkey would afford an advantageous market for many articles . . . the produce of our own country; many, the returns of our Chinese, East and West India trade; . . . and many of increasing importance in the growing manufactures of our country."[18]

Any hopes of a speedy treaty were dashed when war in Greece broke out in 1821. Sultan Mahmud II became convinced that Halet Efendi's mismanage-ment was at least in part to blame for the outbreak of the war and growing discontentment among Ottoman elites. As a result, Halet was dismissed from his position and later assassinated.[19] With Halet's favored position within the Ottoman government at an end, so too were the negotiations between Bradish and the Sublime Porte. Bradish returned to the United States empty-handed.

At the same time, popular sentiment toward Greece in the United States quickly energized a public dedicated to supporting Greek independence from the Ottoman Empire. In 1822 when American philhellenes began to advocate for federal involvement in the Greek Revolution, American merchants joined the debate. With all of this interest and attention directed toward Greece, Americans desiring to quickly secure an improved relationship with the Ottoman Empire feared that Greek sympathizers would pose a serious threat to their interests abroad.

President Monroe found himself caught between overwhelming popular support for the Greeks on one side of the debate, and the pleas from American merchants to deny support on the other. As a result, he did not strongly pursue a treaty. In addition, public support for the Greeks only undermined hopes of a commercial alliance with the Ottoman Empire. Ottoman officials at the Sublime Porte perceived popular support in the United States for the Greeks as evidence of the United States' disrespect of their authority. David Offley reported to John Quincy Adams that the safety of American goods in Smyrna was at great risk due to the pro-Greek financial and military support from the United States.[20] Even though Monroe was indecisive, Adams continued to try to persuade him. Early in 1823, information from Bradish's former translator arrived indicating that negotiations might be renewed if an agent from the United States were once again sent to Constantinople.[21] This time, Adams sent a graduate of Harvard who had previously traveled the Mediterranean and converted to Islam to represent American commercial interests. The secret agent was George Bethune English, or as he called himself while serving as an officer in the Egyptian army, Mohammad Effendi.[22]

Adams did not anticipate the extent to which pro-Greek sentiment would spread. He sent English as a secret agent to the Sublime Porte just as popular support for the Greeks began to surge in response to Lord Byron's joining the Greek army.[23] English would represent those Americans who did not want to support the Greek Revolution, believing that in order to promote free trade and increase commerce in the Mediterranean and Western Asia, sentimentalism for Greece had to be set aside.

Edward Everett versus George Bethune English

No two individuals better exemplify the diverging mindset over the future of the United States in Western Asia than the philhellene Edward Everett and the philo-Turk George Bethune English. Their paths had crossed since their youth; both were Bostonians and classmates at Harvard, and at one time both were devoutly Christian. English's subsequent religious doubt and adventures in the Mediterranean and Egypt, however, proved to be the defining experiences of his life. They pitted him against his former schoolmate and helped him receive a position as American agent to the Mediterranean in the 1820s, a job Everett desperately wanted for himself. The contrasting opinions espoused by these men illustrate the convoluted and complex foreign policy debate that began to unfold in the first decades of the nineteenth century.

At Harvard, George Bethune English received his A.B. in 1807 and A.M. in divinity in 1811. When English graduated in 1807 he was at the top of his class and was selected to provide the salutary oration in Latin at commencement. A respected scholar, he received the Bowdoin Prize, which was awarded annually to students who advanced "useful and polite literature among the Residents as well graduates as undergraduates of the University" with the intention of inspiring emulation among such residents.[24] A few years younger than English, Everett graduated with his A.B. in 1811. He was also awarded the Bowdoin Prize the same year English received that honor. The two young men knew of one another as fellow students.

Their paths began to diverge shortly after English's graduation. In 1813 English published a work titled *The Grounds of Christianity Examined* in which he challenged the legitimacy of Christ's divinity. Through this work, English seemed to beg for a debate from his peers. Even the dedication sought to inflame argument: "To the Intelligent and the Candid who are willing to listen to every opinion that is supported by reason, and not averse to bringing their own opinions to the test of examination." In his concluding remarks, English challenged anyone to refute his argument: "Let him do it like a man" and "not avoid the principal question." To avoid the principal question, in English's mind, would be "as if a man prostrate, and bleeding under a lion whose teeth and claws were infixed in his throat, should tear a handful of hairs out of the animal's mane, and hold them up as proofs of victory."[25] Everett accepted English's challenge and replied with his own publication. Both works were widely read, especially in the Boston area.

Everett published *A Defence of Christianity against the Work of George Bethune English* in 1814. Everett dedicated his response to the president of Harvard, John Thornton Kirkland. Before beginning his response, Everett addressed allegations of plagiarism against English. Everett dismissed the allegations but continued, "He would needs tell us in his preface something about the sources from whence his arguments were derived. . . . Mr. English tells us that a considerable portion of his arguments are from Jews, and a few more from other sources, and then immediately proceeds to transcribing the pages of an infidel writer, though he had just settled the controversy with Deists to his satisfaction!"

Everett challenged English's newly discovered sources that supposedly undermined Christ's divinity. Everett was confident that "there is not in all of Mr. English's work a single argument against Christianity, which has not repeatedly been stated" and defended by previous scholars.[26]

Needless to say, Everett's views were widely accepted as winning the argument. In fact, Everett's *Defence* contributed to his appointment as the chair of Greek literature and resident philhellene at Harvard. His task as chair would be to better "reconcile Greek literature and Biblical criticism."[27] It is important to note that while English's views were not commonly accepted, his critical analysis of Christianity was reprinted many times throughout the nineteenth century, indicating that there was at least interest in reading his work. English himself perhaps shed some light on this phenomenon in one of his responses to his many critics. He stated that he believed that "every individual in this country has a legal and rational right to avow his sentiments, and to bring when he can everything asserted to be true, and important, nolens, volens, to the test of examination."[28] Perhaps readers were curious to see if his arguments had merit. More likely, English attracted readers because he and his ideas were seen as novelties by some members of the community who believed he was deranged. English would spend the next several years traveling the world. Although he espoused religious views that were scandalous in the eyes of New Englanders, he remained a prominent member of the intellectual elite.

English's lifestyle was certainly a source of curiosity and scandal in 1820s Boston. Harvard records later noted this about English: "[He was] of an ardent mind and possessing a great thirst for knowledge, he was extremely versatile. He was constantly changing his opinions."[29] This observation reflects a sense of disbelief in how one of Harvard's top students could write a dissertation on Christ's divinity, only two years later publish a work questioning the validity of Christianity, and then later convert to Islam. Interestingly, although seeming to commit an unforgivable offense in the eyes of most New Englanders, English remained connected to Harvard society. English even published a memoir about his adventures in Mohammad Ali Pasha's army and gave a copy to Harvard's president in 1825. This was the same person to whom Everett dedicated his response to English's denunciation of Christianity.[30]

English's surprising ability to remain connected and relevant within widely disparate social circles proved to be invaluable in his eventually obtaining a high-profile position in the government. George Bethune English became perhaps the most well-known and influential American philo-Turk of the 1820s and made significant contributions to U.S. diplomacy with the Ottoman Empire despite popular support for the Greeks.[31]

English came to know the political and commercial climate within the Ottoman Empire intimately, making him a prime candidate to serve as agent. Previous agents and current merchants in the Levant had a steep learning curve with regard to understanding the politics and manners of the Sublime Porte. Both David Offley and Luther Bradish had already discovered that the United States stood a chance at securing trade negotiations with the Sublime Porte because of its status as being an outsider to European affairs. Bradish relayed home the surprise Ottoman officials expressed when he announced that rather than placing himself under the protection of a European power, he "reposed himself upon the hospitality" of the Sublime Porte entirely and "felt assured that here I should need no other."[32] Ottoman officials had become accustomed to the interventionist designs European powers had within the Ottoman Empire. Bradish's initial approach to the negotiation process with such deference to the Ottoman government and without bringing in the interests of a European government must have been refreshing to Ottoman officials.

In contrast to Americans, Europeans were thought to yield "their individual views and interests to the support of a general system."[33] Since the United States was not part of a Holy Alliance or a "Tutelary Congress of Sovereigns" as were its European counterparts, it could more readily enter into commercial agreements with the Ottoman provinces or engage in negotiation directly with the Ottoman government. American diplomats and politicians perceived this advantage and endeavored to play to this strength by negotiating directly with Ottoman officials. They emphasized that U.S. commercial independence would prove more advantageous to the Ottoman Empire than a similar agreement with a European power. George Bethune English also understood this political climate. He had served as an officer in the Egyptian army and was familiar with Koca Husrev Mehmed Pasha, the *kapudan pasha*, the sultan's grand admiral of the Ottoman navy. This background would later help him in receiving a government appointment as American agent to the Sublime Porte.

In many ways, the ideas of George Bethune English and Edward Everett capture some of the nuances in the debate over Greek independence and the future of U.S. relations with the Ottomans. Everett represented the majority opinion, that the United States shared a common intellectual and political heritage with ancient Greece and that this sensibility was reason enough for the United States to adopt a corresponding foreign policy. English represented the other side of the debate and believed that the United States should cultivate a lasting relationship with the powerful Ottoman Empire in spite of the perceived despotism found within its borders. English understood that the United States would benefit from a commercial alliance with the Ottoman Empire, and his views aligned with those of many American merchants and procommercial politicians. Merchants and politicians recognized that a commercial treaty would mean increased opportunity for business and trade for the United States in a part of the world that had many riches to offer.

Both English and Everett vied for the job as special agent to the Mediterranean, but with very different goals in mind. Everett's star rose in the 1820s as he became a widely known and respected scholar, classicist, and philhellene. He strongly appealed to Webster and the president himself to become an agent with the intent of openly supporting the Greeks in their revolution. Because he was viewed as a partisan on the Greek question, if Everett had been given this appointment, it would have at the least upset the sultan and his government. English, on the other hand, desired to continue commercial negotiations with the Sublime Porte in hopes of opening trade in the Black Sea to the United States. If the United States could acquire such a commercial treaty, this would place it on equal footing in the Black Sea with other European powers. For Everett, to cultivate a relationship with the Ottoman Empire at the expense of Greece was to forsake the country's classical and religious traditions. For English, a commercial treaty with the Ottoman Empire would greatly assist the economic development and prosperity of the United States.

President Monroe and especially Secretary of State John Quincy Adams ultimately sided with English's point of view. Even though Adams wanted Greece to achieve independence from the Ottoman Empire, he did not wish to sacrifice the interests of the United States by aiding the Greek cause. Adams recalled that in one cabinet meeting in August 1823, Monroe proposed the question of aiding the Greek cause. John C. Calhoun and William H. Crawford spoke in support of the Greeks. Adams observed in his diary, "Their enthusiasm for the Greeks is all sentiment, and the standard of this is the prevailing popular feeling. . . . I told the President I thought not quite so lightly of a war with Turkey."[34]

Though he favored a commercial treaty, English sympathized with the plight of the Greeks. Both the Monroe administration and English saw the struggle between the Greeks and the Turks as one of "Right against Might."[35] Despite this, American officials came to support American commercial interests in the eastern Mediterranean over the desire to support Greek independence. English held that the United States had already succeeded in establishing a free society. In his mind one of the greatest American achievements was the freedom of religion, a point he made to Ottoman officials as a reason for why they should enter into a commercial treaty with the United States. This freedom had allowed for him to publish his criticisms of Christianity, endure criticism and gossip regarding his conversion to Islam, and still he was able to have a career in international diplomacy. Pressing forward with current American economic interests instead of dwelling on perceived ancient cultural ties was foremost in English's efforts as diplomat during the 1820s.

Negotiating a Trade Treaty

At the insistence of John Quincy Adams, the Monroe administration decided to renew efforts at negotiating a treaty in 1823 despite mounting popular support for Greek independence. Honing his knowledge of and experience with leaders and political officials within the Ottoman Empire, George Bethune English wrote to Adams in March 1823 expressing his outlook on the cultivation of American trade with the Ottoman Empire. English listed several reasons why the United States should continue to pursue such a treaty. "It is known to the undersigned," he said, "that the [Sublime] Porte has been long disposed to extend their relations with this country; having experienced the advantages resulting from our commerce with Smyrna, and imbibed from the events of the last war between this country and Great Britain, a very high idea of the growing power and importance of 'The New Nation' as they denominate the U.S." English continued that the Ottomans "are the more disposed to have a good understanding with us having been informed that our government have no religious animosities against them and that by our institutions a mussulmen would be on the same footing in our country as a Christian."[36] In other words, English was confident he could convince Ottoman officials that the United States, by virtue of its governing principles, was in a better position to respect Ottoman interests than their European counterparts were.

At this point in his letters, English offered his services in negotiating such a treaty. He claimed that his experiences "of the last six years of his life give him advantages over every other American citizen as a medium of obtaining such a privilege from the Ottoman government." In addition to having lived within Egypt and traveled in the Mediterranean, English also had known many Ottoman officials, and had served in the Egyptian army where he had "contributed essentially to the glory of their arms."[37] If appointed to the post, English proposed that he would first communicate with Husrev, the kapudan pasha and an acquaintance of his, upon his arrival at Constantinople and would urge him to help bring about a treaty between the two governments. English insisted that he "would gain for his country the good will of a people destined to become one day the most powerful of all the nations of the west, and whose amity might hereafter be a value to himself."

One month later, in April 1823, the Monroe administration named English as a special American agent to negotiate the preliminary stages of a commercial treaty with the Sublime Porte. Like his predecessors, English was informed that he should pretend to be a tourist and conceal his true purpose from European officials in the Levant. The philo-Turk first made his way to Marseille, where he was able to network with French seamen familiar with the Mediterranean trade. Through these connections he came to possess copies of various agreements and trade regulations between France and the Sublime Porte. He desired as much information as possible before traveling to Constantinople, and this stop proved to be advantageous. When English acquired translations of these important documents, he prepared himself for the work ahead of him in Constantinople.[38]

After arriving in Constantinople in November 1823, English discovered that the kapudan pasha was indeed the same individual with whom he had become acquainted six years earlier. English wrote to Adams in a private letter that this discovery was "very fortunate, as I shall have occasion to call upon him to pay my respects, and to request his countenance and protection during my stay at Constantinople. The first visit will probably lead to others." The American agent was correct in this assumption.

English began to execute his plan for negotiations with the kapudan pasha using his knowledge of Turkish social practices. One way in which he was able to mingle with Ottoman society in Constantinople was by dressing as an "American Mussulman" traveling throughout the East as a tourist. In the midst of the Greek Revolution, however, he found his situation "full of danger and disquietude and nothing but my determination not to disappoint by my fault your expectations with regard to me is able to countervail the anxiety the singular task I have imposed upon myself occasions me." English believed himself to be in the midst of a dangerous performance in which one misstep could call unwanted attention to his motives for traveling to the Ottoman Empire. For idle seekers wondering why the American was in Turkey, English replied that he was on holiday from the United States. Suspicious Europeans and Ottoman officials, however, speculated he was "a Greek spy in disguise" and that his presence in the region was to further American efforts at "furnishing the Greeks with the means of resistance."[39]

Aside from avoiding suspicion as a spy, English had other worries. The secret agent later conveyed that he had to be as careful as possible not to alert

European diplomats or merchants that his purpose was to negotiate a treaty. He explained that because "the superiority of the American ships and sailors would give them a great advantage over most of their competitors; and it is the apprehension of this which makes most of the European powers so jealous of our obtaining a participation in the carrying trade of the Ottoman empire, of which the British, French, and Imperialists, have at present the entire monopoly."[40] English's observations reflect some of the procommercial sentiments many American merchants had shared for decades. In English's judgment, a treaty would not only be beneficial for American commerce but also would boost American fortunes with the Ottoman Empire. Like the development of American commercial trade in the world at this time, the competitive and political climate in the Mediterranean made negotiations difficult.

The philo-Turk's efforts were not in vain, however. Early in 1824, English was invited for an audience with the kapudan pasha. English explained that the audience went well: "[Husrev] received me cordially, and made me sit down by his side on the sofa, and participated in the coffee, which was brought to me in ceremony." English described the meeting in detail to Adams perhaps to convince him of the appropriateness of his selection of secret agent. English certainly meant to indicate that his already knowing the kapudan pasha had helped him to gain an audience with such a high-ranking Ottoman official.

Interestingly, English concealed his position as a secret agent from the Husrev. He chose instead to present himself as a tourist who was requested, if an opportunity arose, to discover the general attitude the Ottoman Empire had for the United States, especially with regard to commercial relations. The reason for English's deception was perhaps due to the fact that English was not following proper channels of Ottoman protocol. Rather than speaking with the kapudan pasha, diplomats typically would present themselves to Ottoman court officials. Doing this, however, would draw attention from other powers present at the Porte. Instead, English hoped his connection would help expedite negotiations with the Porte. English reported to Adams that he attempted to persuade Husrev to favorably convey the intention of the United States to the Sublime Porte. He noted that the Ottoman Empire had relations with several European nations that had proven to be their enemies on various occasions. In contrast, English pointed out that the United States "was so far from bearing towards them any political or religious prejudices, that, by the laws of the country, a Mussulman citizen of the United States would have precisely the same privileges as a Christian; a great and powerful nation, that was rapidly advancing in the path of prosperity, aggrandizing continually its population, its riches, and its strength."[41]

Because of his own experiences, English knew better than any other American that it was possible to be a Muslim in the United States. He understood that emphasizing the religious freedom of the United States offered him his best chance at opening a dialogue with the Sublime Porte in a treaty negotiation. Husrev was impressed enough with what English had to say that he revealed that "he had always been the friend of the Americans, as was well known at Smyrna; that he had respected the nation, and esteemed highly some individuals belonging to it," but he could not provide "the opinion [English] had asked, till he had ascertained what were the causes that prevented the success of Mr. Bradish in his attempt to negotiation with the Porte some years ago."[42] Husrev requested time to discover the answer to this and asked to meet with English four days later to again take up the subject of a treaty.

The kapudan pasha had good reason to be cautious. Husrev was being pulled in several different directions at this time, perhaps explaining why negotiations on a commercial treaty stalled. On the one hand, he was preoccupied with his duties in suppressing the Greek rebellion; on the other, he had to keep his eye on the demands and ambitions of other European powers. In the midst of this, Husrev also wanted to keep his place within the Ottoman navy and not lose the favor of the sultan. Despite this, he favored relations with the United States, though the sultan did not, and was willing to speak on its behalf at the Sublime Porte. English discovered later that in so doing Husrev could potentially place himself in danger within Ottoman political circles.[43]

Meeting again as promised four days later, Husrev related the reason why Bradish had been unable to secure a treaty a few years earlier. The failure was due to "the influence of a certain European ambassador, (whom he did not name;) that it was his opinion that it would be difficult for the United States to negotiate a treaty at Constantinople."[44] The kapudan pasha believed there to be a small chance to broach the subject of a treaty again, however, if the U.S. government authorized the commander of the Mediterranean Squadron to meet him in the Greek Archipelago with instructions as to what the United States wished to obtain from the Sublime Porte. Then he would "communicate this overture to the Sultan himself, who will decide as he thinks proper, either to encourage or refuse the advances of the United States." Husrev warned English that if an American agent were to travel instead to Constantinople to negotiate with the Divan (the privy council of the Ottoman Empire), then he would "probably find himself embarrassed by intrigues which he could neither discover nor control."[45] As a result, English was led to believe that the only chance the United States had at securing a treaty rested with retaining favor with the kapudan pasha.

In part because of the kapudan pasha's advice, English determined that he must proceed cautiously and seek counsel with Adams. English was once again in Washington by early May 1824 and met with Adams on several occasions to discuss how to continue the negotiation process effectively. English and Adams exchanged letters during his stay in Washington in which they essentially rehashed what they had discussed in their meetings and proposed ideas on how to negotiate a treaty with the Sublime Porte. English repeated to Adams that displaying proper respect for the kapudan pasha would persuade him to advocate before the sultan for a commercial treaty. English further suggested that Adams include in his letter to the kapudan pasha a reminder: "From his own observation he may have been aware of the high advantages which might result to the Ottoman Empire from a free commercial intercourse between it and the U.S." In addition, there was no basis for excluding the U.S. as a trade partner, especially given that it had "no prejudices or enmities political or religious against the Ottomans from the same commercial intercourse accorded by the Sultan to European nations who have been so frequently the enemies of the Empire."[46] If Ottoman officials came to understand that, unlike their European competition, the United States would respect the Ottoman Empire as an equal nation and would only concern itself with the cultivation of free trade, they would be more likely to accept a treaty with the United States. Such an alliance, in English's mind, would be beneficial to both nations. The United States as a new nation, however, struggled to assert its maritime and commercial rights throughout the world and had more to gain from a stable commercial arrangement. For American merchants and other pro-treaty Americans, however, the development of American trade rested upon securing a commercial agreement with the Ottomans, and the Greek War of Independence posed a major obstacle to the negotiation process.

The Persistence of Popular Philhellenism

George Bethune English provided John Quincy Adams and James Monroe with updates on the Greek Revolution throughout his tenure as agent to Constantinople. All of these individuals realized that the outpouring of popular support at home for the Greeks potentially threatened their efforts at acquiring a treaty with the Sublime Porte. In January 1824, Daniel Webster and other philhellenes in Congress continued to lobby for support for the Greeks and favored naming Edward Everett as an American agent to Greece. Adams wrote in his journal on January 4 that he had called on Joel Poinsett, who brought up the subject of Webster's Greek resolution in Congress. At first, Poinsett was inclined to support Webster's resolution on account of the broad popular support for the Greek cause. Adams, nonetheless, was able to persuade him to instead represent the administration and speak against the resolution during debate.[47] Adams told Poinsett that "there was a person probably now at Constantinople upon an errand which might suffer by these movements in Congress." When Poinsett stated that Webster would be satisfied with Everett's appointment as agent, Adams again emphasized that to do this "would destroy all possibility of our doing anything at Constantinople, and Everett was already too much committed as a partisan."[48]

Indeed, in order to block the public from discovering that the U.S. government was entertaining the prospect of negotiation with the Sublime Porte, most of the correspondence Adams sent and received on the subject of the treaty was marked "secret" or "confidential."[49] English repeatedly wrote to both men that it was widely known by the Turks that the American people supported the Greeks and had dispatched aid to their shores. English relayed various conversations he had with Ottoman officials who asked him, "Why are the U.S. disposed to assist our enemies against us? Have we shown any enmity towards their United States?"[50] English found that part of his job as agent required the constant repairing of personal relations with the Ottomans, continually assuring them that despite popular support for the Greeks, the U.S. government would not recognize Greece as an independent nation and was dedicated to cultivating a treaty with the Sublime Porte.

While Adams had long supported a treaty and did not require convincing on that front, Monroe did. During English's brief return to Washington during the summer of 1824, Monroe, was still seriously considering support for the Greeks in response to the prevalent popular sentiment. English pleaded with the president that such an endeavor was futile, citing that Russia, Britain, and France were employed in "transporting for the Turks the military means of terminating a struggle against kings which Providence it seems refuses to favour—except in our own chosen country." Both Adams and English hastened to convince the president that the United States stood to gain nothing from openly supporting the Greeks, especially if it meant losing an opportunity to seal a commercial alliance with the Ottoman Empire. English continued to counsel the president:

> In this actual state of things it is obvious that the U.S. have now to take measures to preserve uninjured and uncompromised their own interests in the Levant. I flatter myself that the explanations given by me, (and I believe by

Mr. Offley also) at Constantinople, as to what would be the character of the aid the Greeks would receive from the U.S. viz. that it would be not national, but individual, will have some influence to preserve our fellow citizens and their property at Smyrna in safety as before until the receipt of the overture from the government of the U.S. suggested and expected by the Capudan Pasha.[51]

English bluntly stated to Monroe that formally recognizing and supporting the Greeks would prove detrimental not only to the proposed treaty but also to the commerce already established by Americans at Smyrna. While English could explain away donations provided by individual Americans, he would be unable to account for official government support for the Greek Revolution. Monroe therefore had to set aside his own pro-Greek sentiments in favor of a more strategic foreign policy.

English's suggestion that Monroe urge Americans to provide support to the suffering Greeks as individuals rather than offer an official response was critical. This perhaps in part led to an important shift in the philhellenic movement by 1826. Leaders such as Everett and Carey renewed their efforts for the Greek cause but emphasized the importance of private support for the victims of war rather than official government efforts to aid the Greek War of Independence. The intentional recruitment of benevolent groups and especially the assistance of women surged at this point in the movement as well. Monroe had at last come to see the advantages of a commercial treaty over heroic interventions on behalf of an independent Greek nation.

English was not the only American to point out that it was in the government's best interest to pursue a treaty in order to protect American merchants in the Mediterranean instead of officially supporting Greek independence. Due to the chaotic political arena in Greece and the provisional government's need to direct its attention toward the war with the Turks, incidents of Greek piracy increasingly became an issue for both European and American ships cruising the Mediterranean.[52] A Charleston paper reported in 1826, "The Archipelago is now swarming with Greek pirates, that plunder every vessel they meet with, no matter the nation to which they belong: every vessel coming here should have at least four guns on board."[53] A letter from a merchant in Smyrna printed in the same paper also pointed to Greek depredations. The merchant stated that Greece was devoid of true patriots and that "the people now suffer so much from Greek tyranny, that they desire nothing more ardently than to return to their allegiance, under their Turkish oppressors." Such a report was not enough to change the minds of ardent philhellenic supporters

11

in the United States. In fact, many newspapers that did report on incidents of Greek piracy also observed that the pirates "do not appear to respect the power of the Greek Senate."[54] These reports do, however, reveal the ongoing turmoil in which merchants found themselves during the Greek Revolution and suggest the perilous climate for American commercial interests and philanthropic ventures in that part of the world.

As incidents of piracy increased, merchants put additional pressure on U.S. government officials to negotiate a treaty with the Ottoman Empire and reject popular pleas for aiding the Greek rebels. Soon after he became president, John Quincy Adams wrote in his diary, "All the commanders of our armed vessels in the Mediterranean, have great abhorrence and contempt for the Greeks."[55] The public, however, disassociated Greek pirates from Greek patriots. This phenomenon posed additional problems for government officials who hoped to improve the U.S. situation abroad while also maintaining public support for the Greek cause at home.

In December 1825, President Adams gave a public speech arguing in favor of the continued maintenance of the Mediterranean Squadron. Adams pointed out that American vessels were subject to attacks made by "pirates wearing the Grecian flag." European powers, including the British, also struggled with Greek piracy. Despite Britain's trade connections with the Sublime Porte and the strength of its navy, British ambassador Stratford Canning wrote to Prime Minister George Canning in April 1826 that "cases of Piracy have multiplied so rapidly within the last month that His Majesty's officers have found it indispensable to resort to vigorous and decisive measures."[56] American commercial interests in the Levant were all the more vulnerable, which made Adams more determined to see a treaty with the Sublime Porte come to fruition. Instead of revealing his true sentiments on this matter as he had confided in his diary, Adams maintained publicly that these Greek pirates were "without real authority from the Greek or any other Government." He continued: "The heroic struggles of the Greeks themselves, in which our warmest sympathies as Freemen and Christians have been engaged, have continued to be maintained with vicissitudes of success adverse and favorable."[57] Adams hoped to save public face by paying lip service to the Greek cause while still pursuing a treaty with the Ottomans.

Once again on official assignment in the Levant, English relayed news of the revolution and the prevalence of Greek pirates in the Mediterranean. In August 1825, he told Adams that the Greeks were turning against one another. "The celebrated Greek Chief Odysseus has been strangled by his own countrymen," wrote English, and "Bobolina [i.e., Bouboulina] the distinguished heroine . . . has been shot by them. . . . The General Vicetas is dead." The commander at the time was the same man "who some time ago endeavoured to seize by military force the whole body of the Greek Government."[58] The secret agent reflected upon this grisly state of Greek affairs and concluded, "As might be expected in such a state of things, the Greeks have committed several acts of Piracy upon European vessels, and two at least on vessels of our own country." The portrait English conveyed to both Monroe and Adams was of a chaotic struggle, not a glorious exercise in which liberty would triumph over tyranny. To sacrifice a commercial treaty with a valuable trading partner in favor of supporting a losing cause in Greece was not, in English's mind, worth the risk.

Interestingly, English privately had some sympathy for the Greek cause. Like so many Americans who supported the Greeks in the 1820s, he thought of their plight as an "unequal struggle of Right against Might." This admission to President Adams, however, was quickly followed by an equally strong assertion of American commercial interests: "I hope some influence towards satisfying the executive, that, where the national sympathy and compassion is unavailing to change the fate of those whose destiny we cannot mend, it is at perfect liberty to push forward the interests of the United States in the Levant by bringing to a successful issue what has been commenced."[59]

English understood both sides of the debate. He understood the patriotic and philhellenic rhetoric espoused by pro-Greek proponents and even sympathized to some extent with those who shared this outlook. Though English believed the Greek cause to be a losing one, the pro-Greek argument advocated for an independent Greece and the creation of, hopefully, a republican government, a goal English supported at least in theory. The philo-Turk, however, ardently argued to both James Monroe and John Quincy Adams that the future strength and stability of the United States lay in forming commercial alliances. Although English understood why some Americans might support the Greeks, those sentiments were far less important to him than developing a strategic commercial bond that would promote American prosperity.

Education and Evangelization

Even though George Bethune English's arguments were convincing, neither President Monroe nor President Adams had an easy time making decisions for a treaty between the United States and the Ottoman Empire. In addition to pressure from merchants wanting a commercial treaty with the Ottomans and from philhellenes wanting to support Greek independence, there were also Americans traveling to the Mediterranean for evangelical and philanthropic purposes. Just as American merchants hoped to export goods to the Mediterranean, American missionaries desired to export American religious sensibilities to the far reaches of the world. The Muslim world especially drew the attention of the American Board of Commissioners for Foreign Missions (AB-CFM).[60] After arriving in the Levant in 1819, Levi Parsons and Pliny Fisk busied themselves with spreading the gospel and visiting some of the ancient Greek sites in the region. A couple of years later they made plans to temporarily part company in order to pursue different tasks just as conflict between the Greeks and the Ottomans began to escalate.

Not realizing how tense the conflict in the region would be, Parsons traveled to Jerusalem in 1821, leaving Fisk in Smyrna. Fisk's daily routine centered upon teaching the English language as well as reading and preaching the gospel to any locals interested in sharing his company. Fisk wrote in his journal that throughout his time in Smyrna he educated mostly Greek Christians but also encountered Turkish Muslims and Jews. Parsons's efforts in Jerusalem as well as his partner's teaching in Smyrna were cut short, however, as the Greek revolt sent shock waves throughout the Ottoman Empire, placing the missionaries in a potentially dangerous situation.

Fisk took refuge in the home of a friend in Smyrna during the first months of the rebellion. As a general rule, Christian missionaries could reside in any part of the Ottoman Empire "so far as appears without the least apprehension of interference from the government."[61] Fisk worried that because many of his students were Greek, he might be suspected of being connected to the revolt.[62] In July 1821, Fisk wrote to a friend in Vermont that, "murders and assassinations have taken place almost daily in this town for three or four months."[63] Fisk also reported back to the ABCFM that both the Greeks and the Ottomans had committed atrocities against one another and that "all of the selfish, revengeful, cruel and licentious passions of which human nature is capable are indulged without restraint."[64]

Parsons observed how the Greek war also affected life in Jerusalem. Under the authority of the Ottoman Empire, there were many groups of people with different ethnic backgrounds living in Jerusalem, including Greeks. In 1821, the conflict between the Greek and Ottoman populations in Jerusalem began to reach a fever pitch. At that point, Parsons abandoned the mission in Jerusalem and returned to Smyrna. After arriving quite ill, Parsons, joined by Fisk, decided to leave for Alexandria, Egypt, in the hopes of improving Parsons's health. This was not to be.[65]

Levi Parsons died in February 1822. Fisk then traveled to Malta to join the Reverend Daniel Temple, who had arrived from Boston with a printing press intended for missionary use in the Mediterranean. Interestingly, Fisk crossed paths with George Bethune English on the ship en route for Malta. English was bound for the United States having completed service with the Egyptian army and would soon receive his post as secret agent to the Sublime Porte. Fisk labored in vain to reconvert English to Christianity, and the two parted ways.[66] Later, English and Fisk would work at cross-purposes. English would assist the U.S. government in cultivating improved relations with the Ottoman Empire, and Fisk would assist Greek refugees, recommending to the ABCFM that Greece was a prime missionary target due to the upheavals of war.

The Greek Revolution shaped Fisk's actions in the years that followed, and he aided in distributing religious literature as well as inspired the need for American-sponsored education for the Greeks. During his travels, Fisk was able to distribute a large number of Christian texts printed on the new press to Greeks throughout the Mediterranean. Fisk reported to the ABCFM, "We have printed many thousand Tracts in Greek: they have been received with pleasure. . . . To the schools and convents we have free access for the distribution of Scriptures and Tracts, and do not often meet with Greeks who oppose our work." Fisk also explained to the ABCFM why Greece was ripe for missionary efforts, asserting, "The nation is roused—the elements of national and individual character are all in motion." The Greek Revolution helped the missionary in his work as American support for the Greek cause had led many Greeks to believe that "all [Americans] are in [Greece's] favor."[67] In addition to distributing religious tracts, Fisk was also committed to education. His encounters with war-torn Greece influenced him to take intelligent Greek boys under his wing as both a missionary and a humanitarian gesture.[68]

In 1817 the ABCFM opened a missionary school in Cornwall, Connecticut, known as the Foreign Mission School. The school admitted "youths of our own country . . . at their own expense, and at the discretion" of school officials, but the primary focus of the school was to provide education for "Heathen Youths." Some of the first students were Native American and Hawaiian, who had been recruited by missions managed by the ABCFM. The school recruited promising children from foreign lands so that they could be trained in American religious ideas, foreign languages (including English), and medicine. Once they completed their education they could return to their native lands as "useful missionaries." Potential students were required to be "of suitable age, of docile dispositions, and of promising talents."[69]

Recruiting children for the Cornwall school was part of the extended missionary process Fisk was to accomplish as head of the Palestine Mission. Traveling to Malta and the Turkish cities of Smyrna and Aleppo, Fisk endeavored to secure the trust of locals, especially Greek families. He reported to his superiors in the United States that their "Bible Society" was "known to all" in the regions where they had established a presence.[70] Although Fisk noted Ottoman suspicion, he commented that Greek families who needed assistance sought out the Palestine Mission. Once trust was established, Fisk began to recruit young foreign boys for the Cornwall school.

The American missionary received permission in 1822 for the first Greek recruit to be educated in the United States. The child, twelve-year old Photius Kavasales, had lost most of his family in a plague that had struck Smyrna in 1814.[71] His oldest brother was serving in the Greek army when young Photius departed for America. Photius never again saw his brother, who was later killed at the front.[72]

According to Photius's recollections of the event later in life, Fisk first recruited the Greek youth for a Sunday school program for local boys. After it became clear that Photius was not only bright but also possessed knowledge of modern Greek, Italian, and Arabic as well as mathematics, Fisk's interest in the child grew. With Photius's enthusiasm for receiving an education in the United States established, Fisk asked the boy's uncle to allow Photius to travel to the United States for additional education. Once the uncle was satisfied that Fisk's intentions were trustworthy, he penned a letter formally accepting the offer for Photius to be placed under the direction and care of the ABCFM. In his letter to Fisk, the uncle noted that his permission rested on his belief that the United States was an "enlightened" and "illustrious" country.[73]

The young Photius traveled to Connecticut with all expenses paid by the ABCFM and was enrolled in the organization's school in Cornwall. Upon arriving in the United States, Photius took Fisk's last name and acquired an extensive education. Photius's uncle had been an ardent supporter of the Greek uprising and had instilled ideals of liberty in his young nephew. These ideals made a deep impression on the boy, which persisted into adulthood. He eventually became an ardent supporter of the abolitionist movement in the United States. After he became a pastor himself, Photius Fisk compared the position of the Greeks in the Ottoman Empire to that of African American slaves.[74]

Photius was not the only Greek student newly admitted to the Cornwall school. A Greek priest in Malta requested that his son, Anastasius Karavelles, be sent there as well. The priest stated that if his son could not receive a proper education under Ottoman rule, he preferred that he go to the United States because it was "more enlightened than any other nation" and because it possessed a "benevolent disposition" toward the Greek nation.[75] By the end of the Greek Revolution, the ABCFM had recruited forty Greek orphans for the Foreign Mission School. Other educational institutions also sponsored the education of Greek youths at New England colleges, including Yale, Amherst, and Monson.[76]

Education and American support for the Greek cause became an important tool by which foreign locals encountered early America. Many Greeks believed that Americans sympathized with their cause and were therefore willing to send their children to be educated in the United States. In addition, the ABCFM's interest in education was similar to the philhellenic interest in educating the Greeks on their ancient roots. Both philhellenes and missionaries believed that through the attainment of knowledge, a society could be lifted up from ignorance and achieve greatness. In the case of the ABCFM, "the design would be, that these youths might return to their countrymen, with their minds cultivated, enlarged and matured, and their hearts inclined to promote the evangelical exertions of the present day." Philhellenes and the ABCFM also shared the perception that Greeks, due to their understood connection to antiquity, possessed "active and inquisitive dispositions" and that they were "hereafter to exert a powerful influence upon the state of society where they live."[77]

Although many Greek students did indeed return to their homeland, some did not. One Greek orphan named Gregory Perdicari continued his studies beyond the mission school, pursuing a classical education at Amherst College in Massachusetts. Perdicari became well-known among the philhellenic Boston community. In a letter written in 1828 while studying at Amherst, he publicly thanked the women of Boston for ardently supporting the Greek cause in an insert to the book *Turkish Barbarity: An Affecting Narrative of the Unparalleled Sufferings of Mrs. Sophia Mazro, a Greek Lady of Missolonghi.* The title alone explains its subject, a tale resembling that of the popular captive stories genre with the Greek Revolution as the backdrop.

American philhellenes in Greece also aided Greek youths, in some cases even adopting them into their families. Samuel Gridley Howe and Jonathan P. Miller both transported Greek children to the United States to give them an American upbringing. Some of these Greek immigrants later recalled the horrors of war, such as Christophoros Plato Castanis, who had been hired as an aide to Howe when he was in serving the Greek army. The young refugee came to identify America and Greece as "the children of Democracy" and that they "are one and indivisible wherever they go."[78] In the United States,

Castanis wrote, the Greek finds "traces of his ancestral spirit and fresh mementoes of the indissoluble connexion, he might almost say identity, of the Greek and American character. A Greek here beholds home-like objects, crowding about his path; the government is democratic; the architecture is classic; the people are inquisitive; the society is unprejudiced; and the literature of the country, even some of the highest models of oratory and poetry, are grounded on Greek subjects."[79] Castanis found the United States to be like a "second homeland."

The success of these young Greeks and the stories they told about their homeland inspired American philhellenes and missionaries alike, reinforcing popular support for the Greek cause. For the philhellenes, these refugees were proof that modern Greeks could become successful, freedom-loving, educated individuals who could recapture the glories of the ancient Greeks. For the missionaries, the Greek youths proved that there were many deserving and willing "foreign heathens" in the Mediterranean who would welcome American missionaries in their homeland. The Greek Revolution nurtured the goals of both philhellenes and missionaries, leading them to conclude that American ideals would inspire foreign peoples to transform themselves into an American likeness. In the years that followed, missionaries and philhellenes continued to make their way to the Levant and became especially successful in establishing schools in the region. Nonetheless, merchants and the U.S. government continued to see a commercial treaty with the Ottoman Empire as the country's paramount concern, producing ongoing domestic social tension.

The Military and the Acquisition of a Treaty

Though the United States did not have an official trade agreement with the Sublime Porte, it did have an official military presence in the Mediterranean. The purpose of the U.S. Mediterranean Squadron was to protect American merchants and commercial interests from foreign powers and marauding pirates.[80] By the 1820s, the U.S. naval presence had developed into a formidable force, escorting merchants and philhellenes into the region.[81] For the duration of the Greek Revolution, the Mediterranean Squadron played an intermediary role between the U.S. government and the merchants who desired commercial trade with the Ottoman Empire and the American philhellenes who supported Greek independence. That the squadron transported merchants and diplomats to the Sublime Porte and philhellenes to Greece jeopardized the treaty's success.

In August 1825, President John Quincy Adams gave George Bethune English his instructions.[82] English was required to travel to Norfolk, Virginia, where he would embark on the *North Carolina*. There he would meet the new commander of the Mediterranean Squadron, the fifty-three-year-old naval veteran from Maryland, Commodore John Rodgers. English was to offer his services to him for the duration of his employment as an agent for the United States. His duties would include serving as an interpreter for Rodgers as well as performing any other services that the newly named commodore deemed "expedient and proper."[83] With English's assistance, Commodore Rodgers was ordered to assist in facilitating negotiations with the Sublime Porte.

Like English, Commodore John Rodgers had extensive experience with affairs in the Mediterranean. Rodgers served in the U.S. Navy as one of the first commanders of the Mediterranean Squadron during both the First and Second Barbary Wars. He was eventually appointed secretary of the navy under President Monroe in early 1823. Renamed the commander of the Mediterranean Squadron in late 1824, Rodgers would play an important role in the United States' efforts to maintain a stable commercial presence in the Ottoman Empire.[84]

English left Washington for Norfolk in February 1825 and arrived with the squadron in Smyrna late in August. The squadron reached the Levant after spending two months at Gibraltar and the Island of Paros in the Aegean Sea. During this voyage, English busied himself with gathering as much information as he could about affairs in the eastern Mediterranean, including the current status of the Greek Revolution. English discovered that while the Greeks had won a number of battles, the provisional Greek government was mired in tension, leading to confusion among the citizens and mismanagement of the war. English came to believe that an imminent victory for the Ottomans would expedite the negotiation process.[85]

The mission to establish contact with the Sublime Porte was not the only one for which Rodgers was responsible. Another passenger onboard the *North Carolina* was an eager philhellene who had gained renown among pro-Greek political circles for his willingness to travel as agent for the philhellenic cause. Estwick Evans, a resident of New Hampshire, left his wife and four children and sailed for the unknown in Greece. As secretary of state, John Quincy Adams had successfully dissuaded President Monroe from naming Edward Everett as an agent to Greece. Adams was unable, however, to prevent Monroe from sending the less well-known Evans. Though Evans was not given any official responsibilities, Monroe's interest in Greece prompted him to provide Evans with permission to travel with the squadron in order to collect information on the Greek war effort. Evans carried with him letters written by Edward Everett and the Greek Committee of Boston, which were intended for various Greek officials, including Greek statesman Alexandros Mavrokordatos. In addition to letters of introduction, the Greek Committee of Boston also provided monetary aid for Evans's travel.[86]

Evans's journey to Greece was illustrative of the disconnect between the philhellenic movement and American commercialists in the early years of the war. If Evans's status as an agent was meant to be kept a secret, that was no longer the case before he even departed his home state. In December 1824, the New Hampshire state legislature sent Evans off with its best wishes and a letter for the Greek provisional government. Evans even gave a farewell address wherein he swore to his fellow philhellenes that his role as agent to Greece would "endeavour to infuse into her councils the wise, moderate and progressive nature of our own happy institutions; and to guard her from anarchy on one hand, and from the subtle and corrupt influences of neighboring aristocracies on the other." Evans went on to pledge that it was his "determination never to leave the soil of Greece until her liberties are achieved;—or at least, whilst one Greek banner remains unfurled."[87]

Evans's enthusiasm and the comparable support he received from philhellenic organizations was out of touch with the reality of the war and placed the efforts at negotiating a treaty in jeopardy. Though Adams and English had expressed this concern to Monroe, evidently one of Monroe's last decisions as president was to at least give his blessing to an agent supported by the Greek Committee of Boston. This would receive popular support, and with Evans's journey financed by private individuals, Monroe could also avoid upsetting American merchants and Ottoman officials by not providing official monetary assistance to Evans. Adams must have been relieved that at least Monroe had not decided to send the more famous Edward Everett. In addition, given that they knew each other personally and by reputation, if English and Everett had found themselves on the same ship bound for the Mediterranean, English's secret mission would have at least attracted suspicion.

After arriving in Greece, Evans managed to ingratiate himself to neither his own countrymen serving in the Greek army nor the Greek officials he swore he so admired. Evans expected the Greeks to cover his expenses and had no intention of assisting them in a military capacity. To the Greeks, Evans seemed useless. Samuel Gridley Howe's journal entry from July 18, 1825, summed up the general feeling toward Evans: "Yesterday came from Napoli Jervis in company with Mr. Estwick Evans, an American Philhellene just arrived. . . . He is a lawyer—a theoretical genius who will not be able to do much good to Greece, much as he desires it."[88] Howe's sentiments proved more correct than he could have imagined. Evans, who promised to serve Greece until independence was won, lasted a little more than one month in war-torn Greece before he insisted upon returning to the United States.

Despite Evans's short stay, his mission reveals an interesting dichotomy in American foreign policy. Rodgers's mission to the Mediterranean was to protect American merchants and, with George Bethune English's assistance, establish negotiations with the kapudan pasha for a treaty with the Sublime Porte. Simultaneously, however, the Monroe administration dispatched an agent whose purpose was to continue friendly relations with the rebel Greek government. Monroe expected Rodgers to transport both men and did not seem to recognize that by doing so the United States appeared insincere in its intentions on both fronts.

Upon the departure of the *North Carolina*, both English and Evans were reported as sailing to join the Greek forces.[89] Neither the American public nor Evans knew that English had been dispatched to cultivate friendly diplomatic ties with the Ottomans. Indeed, given the public expression of enthusiasm for Evans's departure, it is likely that if English's mission had also been publicized there would have been a public outcry against both Monroe and Adams. Though philhellenes had changed the target of their fund-raising from the army to Greek civilians, it was impossible to suppress popular support for the Greeks. That the United States had transported one agent to Greece and another to communicate with the Sublime Porte created additional confusion in the Mediterranean. These muddled signals attracted European as well as Ottoman attention. British officials in particular tried to convince the Ottomans that the Americans were demonstrably against the rule of the Ottomans—an opinion upon which they were inclined to agree with given the conflicting evidence.

This conflicting message did not dramatically change in the months that followed. Despite the fact John Quincy Adams had been elected president, the U.S. government continued to pursue both a treaty with the Sublime Porte and contact with the Greeks. The new secretary of state, Henry Clay, gave secret instructions to Evans's successor, William Clarke Somerville, to assure the provisional Greek government that the United States supported independence and that indifference should not be inferred "from the neutrality which they have hitherto prescribed, and probably will continue to prescribe, to themselves."[90] Somerville and other American philhellenes continued to travel to Greece with large amounts of supplies for the Greek army and Greek civilians; this was done with tacit approval from the government.[91] The Mediterranean Squadron's mission continued with conveying these agents to Greece and providing protection to American vessels when needed.

When Rodgers was not protecting American philhellenes, he was fulfilling other duties. One of the first issues he addressed upon his arrival in the Aegean Sea was that of Greek piracy. English wrote to President Adams that Rodgers had decided it was the squadron's immediate duty to "afford protection to the commerce of the U.S. in this sea [the Aegean], whose safety is jeopardized through the desperation of the Greeks."[92] Indeed, Greek pirates proved to be an ongoing problem throughout the duration of the Greek Revolution not only for the United States but for other European powers conducting business in the region as well.[93] While the squadron labored to protect American vessels, the commodore also prepared for the next steps in gaining an audience with the kapudan pasha. One way in which Rodgers endeavored to do this was through diplomatic hospitality. He made plans for an exposition using the squadron's warships.

Upon the arrival of the squadron in Smyrna, Rodgers believed that he had an opportunity to impress locals with "such a fine specimen of the American Navy." He opened the *North Carolina* to visitors. The ship on which English sailed to Smyrna first achieved notoriety from "both sexes" of a variety of nationalities including Europeans, Ottomans, Greeks, Armenians, and Jews. English observed that "the Great Ship that came from the New World," as the locals called it, so captivated "the irresistible cravings of female curiosity" that "even the vigour of Oriental reserve has in this instance yielded" to the interest of the fairer sex. After the commodore's open house, English explained, "Every attention has been lavished upon the Commodore by the Ottoman Authorities, and there can be no doubt that the appearance of the Squadron here has contributed in no small degree to aggrandize the national character among the people of the Levant."[94] Not only had Rodgers attracted local attention, but European diplomats and merchants in the region had taken notice and immediately began to speculate on the purpose of the American arrival.[95]

Rodgers hoped to establish immediate communications with the kapudan pasha. At least initially, however, the commodore was disappointed. On August 31, 1825, Rodgers wrote a private letter to Secretary of State Henry Clay that the kapudan pasha and his entire fleet were at "Missolonghi, at the entrance of the gulf of Patrasso, engaged in besieging that place by sea." Realizing the kapudan pasha was otherwise engaged, Rodgers determined it would be "impolitic to attempt an interview so long as he continued thus employed."

Rodgers would instead remain at Smyrna "until a more favorable moment presented itself of communicating with him."[96] Several months later, the Ottomans would achieve victory in this siege, much to the dismay of the American public.

Once again, the Greek Revolution stood at the center of a mixed diplomatic message. As Rodgers ostensibly aided the Greek cause by delivering American agents to the Greek shores, he realized that only through a careful stance of neutrality could he hope to gain an audience with the kapudan pasha. The commodore put this point plainly to the secretary of state. If Americans continued to display confidence and strength through the squadron's presence in the Mediterranean and exercised "strict neutrality," then he had "reason to believe" that the United States would eventually prevail in achieving its objective with the Sublime Porte.[97]

The negotiation process was not solely left to Commodore Rodgers and George Bethune English. David Offley also continued to exert influence over the negotiation process. Offley was an invaluable asset to the U.S. government who had long established trade connections at Smyrna. Rodgers observed that for the greater part of fourteen years since Offley had arrived in the region, "he has discharged the duties of consul; and in a manner, too, judging from the estimation in which he appears to be held by the public authorities of that place and the different European consuls as well as American merchants residing there, not only creditable to himself, but beneficially to the commercial interests of his country."[98] Through the combined efforts of David Offley, Commodore Rodgers, and George Bethune English, a treaty between the United States and the Ottoman Empire at last seemed possible.

A meeting between the Americans and the kapudan pasha did not take place, however, until after the fall of Missolonghi the following year (1826). The meeting had been delayed for a number of reasons, including pressure from European powers such as England and France who already enjoyed a commercial agreement with the Ottoman Empire and did not want competition from the United States. Rodgers tried to expedite a meeting with the kapudan pasha by writing a letter to Husrev Mehmed Pasha in September 1825. In the letter, Rodgers wrote, "It is believed in America, that nothing but the opposition and jealousy of certain European diplomatists at Constantinople, more friendly to their own interests than to those of the Ottoman Empire, have hitherto impeded the accomplishment of the wishes of the Government of the United States to enter into friendly relations with the Porte, the perfecting of which would so obviously be the means of benefitting both countries."[99] Pressure from European powers, however, was only part of the problem.

The ongoing conflict in Greece also occupied much of Husrev's time. When the meeting at last took place, Rodgers observed that from the "distinguished manner" in which he was received, there should be no doubt that the meeting would eventually lead to the desired treaty.

Along with David Offley and George Bethune English, the commodore told the kapudan pasha the United States would like to negotiate a treaty that would permit American ships to gain access to the Black Sea. The kapudan pasha assured the American envoy that "not only his own personal feelings were peculiarly friendly towards the Government and people of the United States, but that he could confidently add, that, on this subject, his sovereign, (the Sultan,) entertained sentiments similar to these he had just expressed."[100] Whether the sultan indeed felt this way is unclear; however, the kapudan pasha seemed devoted to assisting the United States in its commercial interests.

Rodgers reassured the kapudan pasha of his country's commitment to neutrality in European affairs: "Our Government would regret to take any measures which might possibly tend to disturb the friendly relations at present subsisting." The kapudan pasha was evidently satisfied with the Americans' pledge of respect. He assured them that because of his successful campaign against the Greeks at Missolonghi, he was now "a greater favorite than ever with the Grand Seignor" and that he expected to be appointed grand vizier upon his return to Constantinople. In four months' time, the kapudan pasha assured them, an answer would be conveyed to the commander of the squadron.[101]

Despite Rodgers's optimism in the summer of 1826, the favorable word he waited for from Constantinople did not arrive. In February, Rodgers wrote to Clay expressing dismay that the squadron had still received no contact from the kapudan pasha. Rodgers offered what he believed to be the primary reason for the delay: European agents had been intentionally circulating information concerning the Greek frigate controversy in order to sour relations with the Porte. In order to resolve an embarrassing situation in which an American shipbuilding company had mismanaged the construction of two ships for the provisional Greek government and billed the Greeks for an amount they could not afford, the federal government had stepped in and purchased one of the ships. Even though the ship was purchased for the U.S. Navy, this had given the impression that the United States officially sympathized and supported Greek independence.[102]

The *Hope* (renamed *Hellas*), the American-built ship purchased by the Greeks, set sail for Greece in August 1826, roughly the same time Rodgers was attempting to settle plans for negotiating the treaty with the Sublime Porte.

An enthusiastic American crew was recruited to deliver the ship to Greece. One Philadelphia newspaper reported there was so much enthusiasm in acquiring these positions that "two hundred persons have applied for the office of Captain's clerk."[103] When the *Hope* arrived at Nafplio, seat of the provisional Greek government, it was rumored that the captain had been sent to offer his services on behalf of the United States. Both the captain and the crew had a difficult time convincing the grateful Greeks that no such arrangement had been made.

Rodgers, Offley, and English worked to reassure Ottoman officials that the United States had no intention of officially supporting the Greeks nor had plans to recognize Greece as an independent nation. Thanks to European reports, Ottoman officials had come to believe that the frigate *Hope* contained a cargo consisting of "large quantities of arms, and naval and military stores." In addition, European authorities had informed the Ottomans that the United States had transmitted the supplies "to Greece for the use of their enemies, and that this had been done with the knowledge and sanction of our Government."[104]

Offley and English wrote to Adams and Clay on several occasions that it was difficult to convey to Ottoman officials the political complexities of American society. Ottoman officials could not be persuaded that any support provided to the Greeks was done without the sanction of the American government. This was probably all the more difficult to believe given the rumors circulating that the Mediterranean Squadron had indeed provided support and transportation for American philhellenes. Rodgers explained to Clay that he had done everything asked of him but that despite his best efforts, philhellenic activity and the confusing actions of the national government now threatened commercial negotiation. Rodgers wrote to Clay of his frustration about the Greek frigate controversy: "In justice to myself, permit me, sir, to say that, if I should fail, before my return, in executing the business which led to my communication with the Capudan Pasha, it will not be my fault."[105]

Despite the fact no letter had been received from the Sublime Porte, Rodgers continued to hope for the long-awaited negotiations. He continued in his letter to Clay that the kapudan pasha was more popular than ever; in fact, if promoted to grand vizier he would have increased access to the sultan. In addition, the pasha of Smyrna, someone David Offley would have interacted with as merchant, was to be appointed as the new kapudan pasha. If this intelligence proved to be correct and Rodgers could successfully distance the U.S. government from the frigate *Hope*, all of these political developments within the Ottoman court would only buttress American hopes for a treaty.

Yet back at home, it would have been almost impossible for the national government to discourage popular support for the Greeks. The fall of Missolonghi combined with the Greek frigate controversy increased public enthusiasm for the Greeks to a fever pitch. Donations for Greece poured into Greek relief societies in New York, Philadelphia, and Boston from all corners of the country. Many communities worked in conjunction with others in the hope that such a gesture "would open to them, and to us, a common channel of communication with Greece."[106] National solidarity in support of the Greeks energized the movement, giving it a life of its own.

Around the same time, however, the major thrust of American philhellenic relief shifted from the embattled Greek army toward providing more aid for Greek civilians. George Bethune English may have encouraged this shift. He hoped that the United States would appear less sympathetic to the enemies of the Sublime Porte. With an emphasis now on aiding noncombatant Greeks— primarily women, children, and the elderly—public aid came primarily in the form of clothing and food instead of weapons and supplies for the army.[107] This humanitarian shift, however, did not quickly convince the Porte of the United States' intentions in the region.

Plans for negotiating a treaty had stalled for a number of other reasons that were outside of the United States' control. With the dissolution of the janissaries, ongoing problems with suppressing the Greeks, the threat of war with the new pro-Greek Tsar Nicholas I, all the while confronting European efforts to intervene in Ottoman affairs, Sultan Mahmud II and his trusted advisers were less concerned with an American treaty. In addition, instead of becoming grand vizier, Koca Husrev Pasha was reassigned as the *serasker*, or commander, of the Ottoman army, with orders to help modernize its forces after the massacre of the janissaries.[108] As a result, Husrev would be unable to advance the American proposal as Rodgers and the other American agents had hoped. Yet another envoy to the Levant returned without a definite commitment to acquiring a treaty with the Sublime Porte. In 1828 Commodore Rodgers relinquished command of the squadron, with William Crane replacing him. George Bethune English died suddenly, not long before he was to leave Washington on his third mission to the Levant. David Offley would be the only familiar face if negotiations indeed went forward. By spring 1828, however, these negotiations were on hold once again due to Ottoman conflict with Russian and British intervention on Greece's behalf in settling terms for the end of the rebellion.

Commodore Rodgers and his staff were demoralized by popular support for the Greeks in the United States. John Quincy Adams wrote in his diary in

March 1828 that he had met with Commodore Rodgers, who had recently returned from the Mediterranean. The commodore informed the president of his "bitter contempt of the Greeks, whom he represents as a mere nest of pirates" and conveyed "severe ridicule of the contributions levied in this country to sustain the Greek cause." Rodgers's sentiments were in part understandable given that he had spent over a year in the Mediterranean working toward a commercial treaty for the United States, only to be denied his objective because of blatant popular American support for Greek independence. Adding insult to injury was Rodgers's incessant encounters with Greek pirates. President Adams, while thanking him for his service, informed him that "the prejudice in favor of the Greeks in this country was so warm that even the attempt to negotiation with the Turks would meet with censure."[109]

That by 1828 there was still no treaty with the Sublime Porte frustrated American merchants. Merchants who had been waiting anxiously for more than ten years for improved commercial relations in the Mediterranean knew that the widespread support for the Greek War of Independence at home was a major reason for why a treaty had not yet been signed. Merchants and sailors alike were also plagued consistently by Greek piracy. Labeled "mishellenes" by Henry A. V. Post, an American agent of the Greek Committee of New York, this group of anti-Greeks consisted of naval officers, captains of merchant vessels, and any other person "whose duties call them to the Levant." According to Post, these individuals had limited contact with the "most vicious and degraded portion of the Greek nation" and therefore "pronounced a sweeping renunciation against all who bear the name."[110] The mishellenes longed for a treaty with the Sublime Porte and grew tired of the delays in favor of popular sentiment for the Greeks. To the mishellenes, the Greeks did not deserve the widespread American support.

These mishellenes faced a difficult situation because they did not profess sentimental views on restoring modern Greeks to their alleged ancient glory but nevertheless were entangled in the Greek cause because the American government hesitated to go against popular opinion at home. Many of these men, including Commodore Rodgers and David Offley, saw openly siding with the Turks as being far more advantageous than supporting a rebellion with which they had little connection and from which they stood to gain little commercial advantage.

Some of these mishellenes took matters into their own hands. Reports made by American diplomats in the region indicated that there were several incidents where American merchants in the Mediterranean actively supported the Ottoman army in Greece. William Shaler, American diplomat to Algiers, informed Secretary of State Henry Clay in the summer of 1825 that an American ship had reportedly assisted in transporting an Egyptian flotilla under the command of Ibrahim Pasha (the general who led the Ottomans to a victory at Missolonghi) to the Morea on two separate occasions. There were also reports that one or two American merchants had served in the Ottoman service in Greece as well. Speaking from the philhellenic perspective, Shaler observed to Clay that such action "obviously tends to tarnish the purity of our Flags and to injure the national character in this part of the world."[111]

John Quincy Adams and Henry Clay agreed with Shaler. Though the United States would not formally support the Greek Revolution, actively supporting the Ottoman suppression of the rebellion was also not an option. Clay instructed William C. Somerville, the new agent to Greece, "If any such instances should fall within your observation, you will acquaint the parties concerned with the high displeasure of the President as conduct so unworthy of American Citizens, and so contrary to their duty, as well as their honour; and that if they should bring themselves, in consequence of such misconduct, into any difficulties, they will have no right to expect the interposition of their Government in their behalf."[112] The United States trod a thin line of neutrality during the 1820s. While appeasement of the American public was important to the Monroe, Adams, and Jackson administrations given that various forms of aid were permitted to be dispatched to Greece, government officials also did not lose sight of what many of them saw as the most important means of advancing the fledgling nation: foreign commerce with the Ottoman Empire.

With the end of the Greek Revolution came a new opportunity for negotiating a treaty. President Andrew Jackson appointed David Offley in 1829 to take on the role as American agent. Accompanying him would be James Biddle, the new U.S. Navy commodore, and New York merchant Charles Rhind.[113] David Offley wanted nothing more than to be successful in his commission, but he also wanted to be certain that any treaty he secured would give the United States the same privileges and advantages as European nations. While locked in negotiations with Pertev Efendi, the reis efendi, Offley informed him that "my Government would not consent to purchase the friendship of any nation." Not convinced a commercial treaty with the United States would be advantageous, the reis efendi replied, "It was not a question of selling or purchasing friendship, but one of obtaining advantages in exchange for those required."[114] As the foreign minister, Pertev was all too accustomed to the fact that Ottoman politics and commerce were frequently dominated by European interests and any treaty with the United States would have to hold some advantage for the Sublime Porte, either diplomatically or commercially.[115]

Concerned that the Sublime Porte would require a large sum of money or gifts to essentially bribe Ottoman officials into securing a treaty, Offley proceeded cautiously. In addition to this, Offley also desired that any tariff the United States paid to the Ottoman Empire would have to be "the same as paid by other nations in treaty with the Porte."[116] After more than a year of negotiations that included British attempts to again quash the treaty, and having to start discussions all over again after the deposition of Pertev, David Offley and the other American negotiators finally secured a treaty with the new reis efendi, Mohammed Hamid, in 1830.[117]

★   ★   ★

At last, after more than ten years of anticipation, American merchants were permitted access to the Black Sea and were guaranteed equal treatment to that of other European powers who already enjoyed access to this trade network. The goal had always been to advance an American perspective of commerce that, as one treaty advocate wrote in 1819, was to overcome "those odious monopolies and impolitic restrictions, which have generally been deemed necessary by other nations." The advocate continued: "Those political impediments which prevent our mercantile fleets from navigating the Black Sea, and preclude them from participating with those of Europe, in the trade of the Ottoman empire, can only be removed by national intervention."[118] National intervention had indeed secured a treaty, but popular intervention on the part of the philhellenes as well as European politics had prolonged the process. American officials not only had to navigate a geopolitical landscape then dominated by less than friendly empires and monarchies, but they also struggled to explain to their Ottoman counterparts the nature of a republican society: some members of the American public may have supported Greek independence, but the United States government desired a friendly and lucrative relationship with the Sublime Porte. By the end of negotiations, the Greek Revolution had served as the backdrop for early American efforts at communicating their political identities to a larger world.

Chapter 5

Abolitionism, Reform,
and Philhellenic Rhetoric

In a hot and crowded exhibition room at the National Academy of Design in New York in August 1847, a reporter for the *National Era* clamored for his chance to view the American artist Hiram Powers's *Greek Slave*. Writing under the pseudonym, "John Smith the Younger," the reporter spent an hour at the exhibit, gazing upon the great work of art and taking in the public reaction to the first nude statue placed on display in the United States. "It is a marvellous image of grace and purity," wrote the reporter. "Every line and lineament of the figure conveys ideas of loveliness and beauty which impress themselves upon the soul forever." Eager to gauge the thoughts of those in the room around him, the reporter looked to the faces of "the fairer sex" especially, wondering if they were as inspired by the statue as he. "I rejoiced to perceive," John Smith the Younger reported, "evidence of the great progress which has been made in the scale of social refinement." Noting only "one prude in the room," the reporter concluded that *The Greek Slave* had enjoyed a successful opening in the United States. "But, alas!" he realized, "in the midst of the pleasing emotions excited by this admirable work of art," the sad thoughts brought to the minds of the onlookers was for the likeness of "a helpless virgin chained in the market place of brutal lust" on a Turkish auction block, and not for the "awful story of the American slave!"[1]

Anticipated for two years, Hiram Powers's statue *The Greek Slave* finally arrived in New York in August 1847. Displayed throughout the country, the sculpture provoked immense controversy wherever it was shown. The statue combined classical artistry and appreciation for ancient Greece with the modern

Figure 5.1. This engraving depicts *The Greek Slave* at the center of the Dusseldorf Gallery in New York in January 1858. The display of this statue was especially momentous, as it was the first female nude statue created by an American artist put on public display in the United States. That *The Greek Slave* was associated with the Greek cause, a philhellenic as well as charitable cause, made the display of a nude statue socially acceptable for women and children to view. R. Thew, *The Greek Slave*, 1858, in *Cosmopolitan Art Journal*, vol. 2, December 1858. Library of Congress, Prints and Photographs Division, LC-USZ62-50519.

Figure 5.2. This statue is one of five marble copies of *The Greek Slave* produced by Powers's studio from a clay model. These five statues were eventually sold to private European and American art collectors. The statue depicts a young Greek maiden about to be sold on a Turkish auction block. Powers intentionally played up the subject's religion and youth through the cross she holds in her shackled hands, and her modesty, which is indicated by her attempts to cover her nudity. It was the reference to the Greek Revolution, the subject's religion, and her modesty that made the statue palatable to a traditionally conservative American audience. Hiram Powers, *The Greek Slave*, marble, 1846. National Gallery of Art, Corcoran Collection (gift of William Wilson Corcoran).

disgust for slavery in the Ottoman Empire.[2] Although the Greek War of Independence had ended almost twenty years earlier, Powers's statue resonated with the American public, evoking for some Americans a disdain for slavery in the Muslim world while reminding others that even in their own country, women—both black and white—were systematically oppressed.

As the reaction to the Powers statue suggests, American men and women castigated the Ottoman Empire for its treatment of both slaves and women. In poems, books, plays, and public speeches, they repeatedly pointed out that the Ottomans' customs regarding women and slaves revealed the empire's truly barbarous and tyrannical nature. As public interest in the abolition of slavery grew, some abolitionists compared slavery in the United States with that in the Ottoman Empire, calling the South the "Barbary States of America."[3] The Ottomans came to represent the ultimate symbols of tyranny as the oppressors of women and enslavers of people within their borders.

Just as women had played an important role in raising funds for the Greek cause, women continued to play an important role in reform in the years that followed.[4] In the early years of the war, male organizers, such as Mathew Carey and Edward Everett, actively sought out female membership and support. The condition of women and children in Greece, whom they claimed had been debased by tyranny for centuries and massacred by "Mahometans," was particularly persuasive in gathering this female support.[5] Female reformers often emphasized the condition of the newly freed Greek women. The lack of education among the Greeks became a focal point for American education advocates such as Emma Willard and Almira Phelps who sought to rescue their Greek sisters from an oppressive life under tyranny.

Public support for the Greek cause contributed to the creation of the early antislavery societies and women's rights organizations. When the Greek cause first emerged, it was supported by local community-based charity organizations. The cause brought Americans together and became intertwined with popular notions of early American patriotic identity. By the end of the 1820s, however, the issue of slavery inspired some American men and women to draw connections between the condition of women and slaves in their own country and the condition of those in the far distant Ottoman Empire. Appropriating the critique of slavery and the degradation of Greek women from the philhellenes, antislavery supporters and women's rights advocates employed similar rhetoric to develop their own causes. By the end of the 1820s, American advocates for abolition and women's rights such as David Walker, William Lloyd Garrison, and Emma Willard invoked references to the Greek War of Independence and Ottoman slavery in arguing for slavery's eradication and improvement in the status of women in the United States. Long after the Greek War of Independence had ended in 1830, the American abolitionists employed the ideas and tactics of the philhellenic movement, engaging new audiences on the question of slavery and spurring interest in the notion of women's rights.

Slavery Abroad

Long before abolitionism and women's rights became organized movements within the United States, many Americans viewed slavery as it existed in the Muslim world to be abhorrent. The popularity of captivity tales, which described the experiences Westerners had as captives in the Muslim world, informed and sustained negative feelings toward the Ottoman Empire and Muslims in general. Authors of the captive tales contrasted American ideals with those of Muslim slave masters, providing a rich commentary on American knowledge of slavery in the Muslim world. By the end of the Second Barbary War, a discernable shift began to take place within the captivity genre. Some American authors had begun to question the condemnation of slavery within the Ottoman Empire at the same time that slavery persisted within the United States. Did it occur to Americans at home and abroad that their condemnation of Ottoman slavery was hypocritical given that African slavery persisted in a nation they termed as the freest in the world? The answer to this question is both yes and no. While captivity tales provide perspective on how early Americans viewed the Muslim world, they also provide insight into how early Americans viewed themselves in comparison.

Antislavery literature of the late eighteenth and early nineteenth centuries often claimed that slavery undermined the social and economic potential of a republic rather than promoting it. Noah Webster, a prolific author and lexicographer from New England, was also an early supporter of abolition. In a 1793 pamphlet titled *Effects of Slavery, on Morals and Industry*, Webster referenced the "pernicious effects of Slavery, on the moral character, the industry and prosperity of nations" as the reason for why the modern Greeks were, in his view, lazy, dispirited, and debased at the hands of the "lazy Turks."[6] According to Webster, slavery was a reflection of environment rather than of racial inferiority. Slavery was a corrupting force in society and thus should be abolished, especially if it meant that American society might come to be so degraded, in Webster's estimation, as to resemble Ottoman society.[7]

Even before the Barbary Wars, Benjamin Franklin criticized American slavery by juxtaposing the enslavement of Americans in Algiers with that of Africans in the United States.[8] In 1790, Franklin anonymously published an article in the *Federal Gazette* that not only criticized a proslavery speech made in Congress but also suggested that slavery in the United States was no better than slavery in the Ottoman Empire.[9] Franklin parodied a proslavery speech made by Congressman James Jackson of Georgia by putting Jackson's words into the mouth of a proslavery Muslim, Sidi Mehemet Ibrahim, a fictional member of the Divan, an assembly of court officials in Algiers. Franklin compared Ibrahim to Jackson by observing that the two possessed "surprising similarity." To prove it, Franklin provided his readers with a mock letter written from the point of view of the proslavery Muslim. Ibrahim stated that if Algiers did not continue to enslave Christian sailors, "Who in this hot climate, are to cultivate our lands? Who are to perform the common labours of our city, and in our families? Must we not then be our own slaves?" Ibrahim went on to argue, "If then we cease taking and plundering the Infidel ships, and making slaves of the seamen and passengers, our lands will become of no value for want of cultivation; the rents of houses in the city will sink one half; And the revenues of government arising from his share of prizes must be totally destroyed. And for what? To gratify the whim of a whimsical sect! who would have us not only forbear making more slaves, but even to manumit those we have."[10] This was Congressman Jackson's argument in defense of slavery in the United States turned on its head.

Franklin's biting article satirically suggested that economic and biblical evidence supported the use of American sailors as slaves in the Barbary States. Franklin's use of the Oriental tale transports his readers into the mind of a Turk, an exercise that probably shocked his audience. To early Americans, the Turks were the mysterious "other" in literature, a foil to the heroic and free American citizen found in contemporary literature. Casting Americans as Turkish slaveholders was specifically intended to be a troubling image.[11] A more commonplace late eighteenth-century perspective toward slavery would have referred to it as regrettable but necessary in order to maintain social and economic order. The racially ordered social hierarchy of the United States would have made it difficult for even the American captives in the Barbary States to identify their situation with those of African slaves at home.[12]

Most captivity tales of this period did not make the connection to slavery in the United States as Franklin had. In 1798, American captive John Foss viewed the biggest difference between Americans and the Turks as based in the different types of governments the two nations employed. Foss argued that even his own captors were impressed with the American efforts to free their citizens from the Algerian captors and that if liberty were instituted in Algiers, such cruel atrocities against the different people residing there would no longer exist. Foss's sentiments on this subject are best summed up with his description of the reactions from his captors when he and his fellow Americans were finally freed: "The Republican government of the United States have set an example of humanity to all the governments of the world.—Our relief was a matter of admiration to merciless barbarians. They viewed the character of Americans from this time in the most exalted light. They exclaimed, that 'Though we were slaves, we were gentlemen'; that 'the American people must be the best in the world to be so humane and generous to their countrymen in slavery.'"[13] Foss does not, however, make mention of the persistence of slavery in the United States when discussing the people of Algiers. In his mind, he is a citizen of the United States and therefore guaranteed liberty by his country. For him, slaves in the United States were not citizens and therefore lay outside of this guarantee.

Foss's failure to draw connections between his experience as a captive and that of African slaves did not necessarily reflect larger attitudes. The historian Lawrence Peskin has observed that Foss lifted a significant amount of text for his own captivity tale from a popular history of the time, *A Short History of Algiers* by Mathew Carey, first published in 1794.[14] Carey observed, "We are not entitled to charge the Algerines with any exclusive degree of barbarity. The Christians of Europe and America carry on this commerce an hundred times more extensively than the Algerines." Carey continued by admonishing his fellow Philadelphians: "Nobody seems even to be surprised by a diabolical kind of advertisements, which, for some months past, have frequently adorned the newspapers of Philadelphia."[15]

Although Carey was in the minority for his time in making such a connection, Foss undoubtedly read Carey's work and would have at least been exposed to this sentiment. Nonetheless, in his own work Foss did not pursue the meaning of Carey's insight about slavery in the two regions. It is also important to note that Carey's views on slavery were more complicated than he suggested in his history of Algiers, given that he would later support the domestic institution of slavery during and after the Missouri Crisis.[16]

Royall Tyler's 1797 tale *The Algerine Captive* made an observation similar to Carey's 1794 assessment. Employed to inspect the bodies of the newly enslaved to determine whether they were suitable for sale, Tyler's fictional character Dr. Underhill lamented that the inspection was "transacted with all that un-

feeling insolence, which wanton barbarity can inflict upon defenceless wretchedness."[17] After he was taken as a slave by Algerian pirates, Underhill was
comforted by one of the Africans whom he had just days before examined
and sold as a slave. Underhill was humbled by the gesture. Later he was confronted by a Muslim cleric who attempted to convert him to Islam. Underhill
could not deny the cleric's observation that although the "Christians of your
southern Plantations . . . baptized the unfortunate African into your faith," they
then use their brother Christians "as brutes of the desert." In contrast, under
Islamic law, one could not keep fellow Muslims as slaves, and minority groups
living within the Ottoman Empire, such as the Greeks, were protected and
could not be enslaved unless they were in rebellion.[18] Through his experiences,
Underhill was forced to recognize that the United States, though he loved it
and held it to be the freest country in the world, was flawed. Tyler concluded
his tale with Underhill pledging that if he is ever freed he "will fly to our fellow citizens in the southern states; I will, on my knees, conjure them, in the
name of humanity, to abolish a traffic, which causes it to bleed in every pore."[19]

While most captivity tales of the late eighteenth and early nineteenth centuries did not draw connections between American slaves held captive in the
Barbary States and African slaves held captive in the United States, one narrative published at the conclusion of the Barbary Wars did. This overwhelmingly popular and influential tale was by James Riley. Born in Connecticut
during the American Revolution, Riley came to be the captain of the brig
Commerce in 1815. After the brig was shipwrecked off the coast of present-day
Western Sahara, Riley and his crew wandered for quite some time before they
eventually made contact with a group of Arabs, who immediately enslaved
them. After two years, Riley escaped slavery and returned to the United States.
He published his story in 1817, which was an immediate success in both the
United States and England. Riley's reflection upon his captivity and the persistence of slavery in the United States make his story stand out from earlier
captivity tales.[20]

Aided by an Arab who sympathized with Riley, both of whom were fathers
of a young family, Riley was delivered into the protection of a British consul
in the port city Mogadore in Morocco. Riley's ordeal was finally at an end,
but he had gained a changed perspective on slavery in general. In his memoir
he wrote, "I have drunk deep of the bitter cup of sufferings and woe; have
been dragged down to the lowest depths of human degradation and wretchedness . . . enduring the most excruciating torments, and groaning, a wretched
slave . . . of barbarous monsters."[21] Riley deviated from the usual captivity genre
formula. Instead of ending his story there, he continued with observing that

even though he had been restored to his family and "the comforts of civilized life" where citizens are guaranteed "the greatest share of personal liberty, protection, and happiness," he realized that his "proud-spirited and free countrymen still hold a million of the human species in the most cruel bonds of slavery, who are kept at hard labour and smarting under the savage lash of inhuman, mercenary drivers." He continued: "I have now learned to look with compassion on my enslaved and oppressed fellow creatures, and my future life shall be devoted to their cause: I will exert all my remaining faculties to redeem the enslaved, and to shiver in pieces the rod of oppression." As a result of this declaration, Riley transformed his narrative into an antislavery tract.

Unlike Royall Tyler's fictional character who made a similar declaration, Riley had in reality been a slave in northern Africa, providing weight to his conclusion concerning slavery in America. In fact, his captivity was reported widely in newspapers beginning in January 1816.[22] Riley himself had written the reports, which also detailed some of his and the crew's sufferings under slavery. Even before his memoir was made available, there was a rising interest in Riley's story. Shortly after its publication, some readers accused the author of being a fraud, arguing that the story was filled with "falsehoods and misrepresentations."[23] These accusations were quickly quashed as members of the crew came to their captain's defense by writing and printing reviews of the narrative. Riley himself seemed to be aware that his conclusion would be controversial. He argued that while he was not in favor of immediate emancipation, he did "desire that such a plan should be devised, founded on the firm basis and the eternal principles of justice and humanity, and developed and enforced by the general government, as will gradually, but not less effectually, wither and extirpate the accursed tree of slavery, that has been suffered to take such deep root in our otherwise highly-favoured soil."[24] In the years after his release, Riley became an active member of the colonization movement.

Captain James Riley's book did not immediately ignite an awakening among his fellow countrymen regarding the parallels between their own institution of slavery and that of the Ottoman Empire. Yet Riley's narrative enjoyed popularity in both Northern and Southern states. At the same time, the narrative was not viewed as a threatening piece of literature. It did, however, inspire animosity toward Arabs and anger at their enslavement of Riley and his crew.

Jared Sparks, editor of the *North American Review* in Boston, suggested why Riley's narrative did not generate as much attention to his conclusion as did his wanderings as a slave in Morocco. In his review, Sparks stated that "the eye of criticism should pass gently over the pages of the traveler" and then went on to define the purpose and use of a travel narrative, The facts of a travel narrative usually could not be proven and were often not written by scholars to begin with. Thus, Sparks dismissed Riley's reflection on slavery in America by suggesting that authors of travel narratives should "keep in the humbler walks of plain narrative and simple description, and venture to leave the more weighty and less obvious concerns of governments, national character, and historical disquisitions, to statesmen, civilians, and philosophers."[25]

The philhellenic movement in part benefited from the popularity of the captivity tale genre and also laid the rhetorical groundwork for self-reflection. In many ways, the philhellenic movement in the United States represented a transition between the charitable movements of the first decades of the early nineteenth century and the antislavery and women's rights movements of the late 1820s. Philhellenic enthusiasm and the popularity of American captivity tales composed the general attitude Americans had toward the Ottoman Empire at the beginning of the Greek Revolution, but few Americans connected African slavery in America to the subjugated condition of the modern Greeks. After a few years, there was a distinctive shift in which antislavery and women's rights advocates began to use American support for the Greek Revolution to point out the lack of interest in supporting such causes at home.

Women were at the center of this shift. Philhellenes Edward Everett and Mathew Carey and many others had relied on the involvement of women, effectively extending benevolence onto an international stage. Moreover, once the movement focused more on humanitarian goals, such as aiding and educating Greek women and children, women were more likely to support the cause. By becoming involved in such a movement, these women, like their male counterparts, held that they were extending the benefits of the American Revolution to the most deserving of nations. Philhellenic literature frequently referred to female civilians caught in war-torn Greece who were destined for an Ottoman auction block—an image that played on the sympathies of many benevolence activists. Through involvement in the Greek cause, women began to believe their work in Greece would not be complete when the war was over.

Ongoing female involvement in the philhellenic movement in America developed into an independent philanthropic cause that advocated for the education of Greek women and children. Women began to establish the first American-run schools in Greece in 1828. Education efforts in Greece were focused on moving "towards the emancipation of the minds of Greece from their long bondage."[26] The ABCFM worked with Greek aid societies, including the Ladies' Greek Committee of New York, toward the establishment of schools in Greece. Individuals such as Emma Willard, the founder of the first female institution for higher learning in the United States, and her sister Almira Phelps also participated. One Greek refugee later singled out Willard and Phelps in his memoir. Christophoros Castanis recognized that women had provided crucial support for education of the Greeks.[27] The primary goal for the new schools in Athens and elsewhere was to bring intellectual freedom to all parts of the civilized world, an extension of the secularized missionary spirit born from the philhellenic movement.[28] The Greek cause proved to be an important expansion of female benevolence, making it possible for American women to make a difference for the uneducated and exploited both at home and abroad.

American Liberty and Philhellenism Questioned

The Greek cause had inspired domestic unity behind a foreign cause aimed toward ending the perceived enslavement of the modern Greeks. Northerners and Southerners agreed upon the importance of this cause despite the fact that the issue of slavery within the United States had become a major topic of debate. Although slavery had been controversial since the time of the American Revolution, sectional tensions between North and South as well as the development of the Market Revolution had further solidified the institution of slavery within the American South, and industry in the North increasingly depended upon it.[29]

Northerners and Southerners could talk about Greek liberty without a thought of hypocrisy because of their cultural and intellectual link to ancient Greece, because the modern Greeks were Christian and the Ottomans were Muslim, and because they saw the Greeks as white and the Ottomans as anything but. The Greek cause remained separate from the debates over the domestic issue of slavery until the late 1820s, when the abolitionist movement shifted with the emergence of the immediatism movement. Sectional tensions proved to be so volatile that even the unity Northerners and Southerners shared in their affection for the ancient Greeks and their modern descendants would not last.[30]

The Greek cause itself did not form a new part of the abolitionist movement. The leaders of the American philhellenic movement did not become members of the abolitionist movement either. Although Mathew Carey had condemned slavery both at home and abroad in his *Short History of Algiers*, he embraced a different attitude in the aftermath of the War of 1812 and the Panic of 1819. Concluding that the United States needed to pursue a more diverse domestic economy, which he believed Henry Clay's American System would do, he also necessarily had to embrace slavery as part of that economy. Slavery would be a necessary component of a diverse economy that included agriculture, commerce, and manufacturing. As a result, Carey came to support slavery as not necessarily a "positive good," but also not "infinitely wretched."[31]

Edward Everett also would not be a major figure in the abolitionist movement, though he had argued for Greek independence. As Matthew Mason has noted, Everett did not move in "one direction or in a predictable way" on the subject of slavery. As a lifelong supporter of Atlantic reform movements Everett did not condemn the abolitionist movement out of hand, understanding the reformist impulse. Everett's conservatism, however, informed his thoughts toward slavery in the United States. In a speech he gave in 1826, Everett stated that slavery was "sanctioned by religion, morality, and law," and therefore emancipation must take place gradually in order to avoid a race war. Since the new wave of abolitionism that emerged in the late 1820s and early 1830s was centered upon the principle of immediatism, Everett certainly would not support the abolitionist cause.[32] Instead, the role the American philhellenic movement played in American reform movements of the antebellum era was through its proven effective rhetoric and public appeal.

Since philhellenic efforts had proven so successful, more marginally popular causes of the time began to draw from the rhetoric of the Greek cause for their own purposes. Beginning in the mid-1820s, abolitionists and women's rights advocates drew comparisons between their cause and that of Greece. Pamphlets on these topics especially began to emerge by 1825 when the Greek cause enjoyed renewed interest after Byron's death and the fall of Missolonghi. Authors identified the paradox of seeking to free the Greeks from Ottoman slavery while enslaving African Americans in their own country. Using similar rhetoric as the philhellenes, abolitionists and women's rights advocates managed to raise awareness and increase support for their own movements, a phenomenon that continued well after the Greek War of Independence concluded.

With enthusiasm for the Greek cause at an all-time high in the late 1820s, abolitionists began to see the value in using philhellenic rhetoric for their own purposes. African American publications referenced the Greek Revolution with frustration and appealed to their readers to recognize the similarities between the life of a Greek under Ottoman rule and the life of an African slave under a Southern master's rule. Several articles were published in the first African American newspaper, *Freedom's Journal*, at the height of the Greek cause's popularity. One author pointed out, "We had many exhibitions of its [slavery's] character, during the late ardour in behalf of the Greeks. It would be instructive to take any of the addresses, speeches, or resolutions made on that occasion, and to see how many of the most odious features of Turkish slavery may be fairly matched in this free and enlightened country." The author continued at length to compare Greek servitude under the Ottomans and concluded based on the author's understanding of slavery in the Ottoman Empire and the amount of attention the Greeks had enjoyed from early Americans, "What generous mind would not rather be the Greek than the black?"[33] Another article written more than a year later similarly referred to the widespread interest in the Greek cause and the lack of public fervor with regard to slavery within the United States. "In the midst of these nations who call themselves the friends of liberty and humanity," wrote an author from *Freedom's Journal*, "involuntary servitude is justified while it is even a problem whether the understanding of Negroes be of the same species with that of white men."[34]

Still another example of an African American abolitionist using the Greek cause as a rhetorical tool was David Walker. Printed in 1829, Walker's radical pamphlet, *Appeal to the Coloured Citizens of the World*, rallied both free and enslaved African Americans to stand up to the institution of slavery. As others of similar mind had done, Walker contrasted the Greek Revolution and the widespread support for it in the United States with the lack of interest in eradicating slavery from American society. Walker poignantly observed that while reading a South Carolina newspaper, he came across an article stating, "The Turks are the most barbarous people in the world—they treat the Greeks more like brutes than human beings." Alongside this article was an advertisement that said, "Eight well built Virginia and Maryland Negro fellows and four wenches will positively be sold this day to the highest bidder!"[35] For Walker, the disconnect between a foreign institution of slavery and a domestic one was unpalatable. Walker concluded by warning white Americans that even though "[they] can hide it from the rest of the world, by sending out missionaries, and by [their] charitable deeds to the Greeks," they could not hide their hypocrisy from God.[36]

Contrasting popular interest in Greece with the lack of interest in the issue of American slavery proved to be powerful.[37] If the Turks were indeed barbaric for holding slaves, what made American slaveholders different? For Walker and others, racial differences did not provide sufficient justification. If Americans could see the similarity between the Greeks and African slaves, then it would be clear that the institution itself was the problem, not the racial characteristics of the slaves. Americans might come to see that both groups were part of the human race and therefore deserving of the freedom and liberty enjoyed by white Americans.

Perhaps the most famous white abolitionist of the antebellum era almost made his humanitarian debut as an American philhellenic soldier. William Lloyd Garrison was just twenty years old when the Greek cause in America was at its height of popularity. Caught up in the midst of the pro-Greek fervor, Garrison, like many other youths of the time, aspired to defend the Greeks by joining the Greek army. Garrison probably read about fellow Massachusetts-born Samuel Gridley Howe and his adventures in Greece in local newspapers. After completing his apprenticeship with the *Herald* newspaper, Garrison seriously considered a military education at West Point in order to "join the forces of the revolutionists against Turkish tyranny."[38] Whether discouraged by the warnings printed in newspapers that life in the Greek army was an arduous ordeal or that his financial and professional situation did not allow for it, the budding abolitionist ultimately decided not to join the Greek forces. He did go on to write for a newspaper called the *Free Press* and played a small role in the spread of philhellenic literature, as the newspaper printed many articles on the Greek war effort.[39]

Philhellenic rhetoric stayed with Garrison throughout his life, however, and made many appearances in his abolitionist writing. For example, in 1828 Garrison participated in a Fourth of July celebration in his hometown of Newburyport, Massachusetts, where he read the Declaration of Independence and also recited an ode he had written for the occasion. The ode focused upon the colonists' successful efforts to cast off British tyranny and referenced the ongoing disagreement on American slavery between the North and South: Despite "plots of division, though artfully done, / Will fail on a people whose hearts are but one!" Garrison acknowledged the need to eradicate "tyranny" from American soil, undoubtedly a reference to the persistence of slavery. "Our march" he continued, "must keep pace with the march of the mind, / Progressing in grandeur for ever and ever; / Our deeds and example are laws to mankind, / And *Onward to Glory*! Shall be our endeavor . . . / For the reign of free thoughts and free acts has begun."[40]

On this occasion Garrison made only one specific reference to tyranny outside of the United States, and this was to Greek subjugation under the Turks: "A prayer and a tear for the suffering brave— / For Greece in this day of her terrible anguish! / May the Turkish oppressor be hurled in the grave . . . And punish the shedders of innocent blood; then peace, hope, and love, like a river shall run, / And dwell with a people whose hearts are but one!" Garrison's ode compared the Greek and American Revolutions and speculated that once the Turks were defeated Greece would establish its own nation, as the patriots of 1776 had over fifty years previously. In Garrison's mind, his desire for freedom and abolition for slaves in the United States was the same as the Greeks'.

A few years later, Garrison continued to adroitly use philhellenic rhetoric as part of his antislavery arguments. In 1831 he openly accused his country-men of being hypocrites for supporting the Greeks while forsaking African slaves. In a piece titled "The Insurrection," which was printed in Garrison's publication the *Liberator*, Garrison reprimanded his contemporaries who feared slave insurrection and flatly stated that African slaves did not need to be pushed into insurrection by abolitionist influence. Instead, they could find incentive "in their stripes—in their emaciated bodies—in their ceaseless toil." Garrison continued his accusation of hypocrisy by pointing out that most Americans had applauded the Greek insurrection and observed that African slaves "de-serve no more censure than the Greeks."[41]

In an article written for the New England Anti-Slavery Society, Garrison pushed the Greek comparison further by pointing out that American tyranny was much more inexcusable than Turkish tyranny, given that the United States was supposed to be a nation of freedom and liberty. Referring to the philhel-lenic movement, Garrison observed, "At that time Daniel Webster and Henry Clay denounced Turkish tyranny in terms as severe and indignant as any that we have used in respect to American tyranny, which . . . is much more inex-cusable than Turkish [slavery]." Attempting to turn this argument around on his readers, Garrison reminded them that all had applauded the Greek insur-rection against the Ottomans, but then he asked, "Where is the difference be-tween such a case and our own?"[42] Garrison's persistent use of the Greek Revolution as a comparison to African slavery in America indicates that it was rhetorically effective. For ten years American philhellenes had asked the Amer-ican public to reflect on their intellectual origins and support Greece based on this sentimental connection to a people and nation to which most had never—and would never—travel. If Americans could be so engaged in sup-porting a faraway revolution, perhaps they could be made to see that slavery in the United States was equally tyrannical.

Garrison's writing, especially his "Insurrection" article, created controversy wherever it was reprinted, in both the North and South. One Portsmouth, Maine, newspaper reported that North Carolinians were especially up in arms, demanding in 1831 that anyone who circulated the *Liberator* "ought to be bar-becued."[43] The *Portsmouth Journal* made a similar historical connection as Garrison had with the Greek Revolution, pointing out that if the *Liberator* would incite insurrection in the South, then the *North Carolina Free Press* should also stop publishing pieces about liberty and equality and "rejoicing at the suc-cess of the Greeks."

Something had changed. When the Greek Revolution first began in 1821, Americans had seldom connected the abolition of "Greek slavery" with the condition of slavery in the United States. African slaves were not the descendants of the ancient Greeks, and the Greeks were certainly not of African descent. Citizens of the American South rejected any link between the plight of the Greeks and that of their own slaves. The spreading desire for freedom "which will not stop—*which cannot be stopped*" would eventually come to the American South, predicted the *Portsmouth Journal*, and African slaves would, like their Greek counterparts, revolt.[44]

In response to Garrison's paper and his "Insurrection" article, Georgetown, for example, passed an ordinance mandating that any "free negro or mulatto person . . ." found in possession of a copy of the *Liberator* would be fined and jailed.[45] Although whites were not included in this ordinance, the sentiments expressed by the *North Carolina Free Press* as reprinted in the *Portsmouth Journal* clearly indicated Southern attitudes toward abolitionists, even if they did use philhellenic rhetoric to engage their audience. The national consensus behind supporting the Greek cause was becoming a distant memory by the 1830s and was instead joining with the divisive political rhetoric of the antebellum era. The diverging perspective in the North and South on Turkish slavery versus the institution in the United States would become clearer by the 1850s. The outrage over white slavery versus African slavery became especially apparent with the unveiling of Powers's *Greek Slave*.

Aside from the literature published by Garrison, the Greek Revolution, as part of the antislavery argument, also emerged in more mainstream publishing outlets by the mid-1820s. For example, one article, signed with the pseudonym "Acacius," was printed in the *Columbian Centinel* in 1825. This article pointed out the hypocrisy of widespread support for the Greeks while the plight of the African slave was ignored. The article was accompanied by a printer's note that suggested the abolitionist sentiments professed in the article were not yet common in the North. "The following communication has been under consideration for several days," explained the printer. "We are aware how restive some of our southern fellow citizens are whenever the subject of it is discussed, but we cannot believe they can wish to suppress remarks on it." The printer continued by vouching for the character of the author while also withholding his name, explaining that he was an honorable and good man and thus despite the controversial subject matter, the editor had determined to print the article.

Acacius's article was a response to a recent address made by Daniel Webster at the dedication of the Bunker Hill Monument on June 17, 1825. Webster spoke about the American Revolution and the Battle of Bunker Hill in particular, but he also made reference to the Greek Revolution. Drawing a connection between the two revolutions, Webster called on the United States to directly intervene in the conflict. In response, Acacius emphatically pointed out that "I have not observed any expression of sympathy for the millions of slaves in our own country or a word of regret that this land is emphatically a land of slavery as well as a land of freedom."[46]

The author focused much of his writing on explaining what he viewed as particularly hypocritical in Webster's speech with reference to Turkish tyranny. "Prior to a resort to arms," explained the author, "the condition of the Greeks was far less deplorable and degraded than that of the slaves of our country; and the Negroes have far more cause of complaint against our government than the Greeks had against the Turkish despotism. Why then, should we feel more for the Greeks of Europe than for the Negroes of America?" Acacius continued to scold Webster and others who had not given a thought to the servitude of the African race in the United States. He concluded that if the new Bunker Hill Monument should accurately convey to future generations the contemporary feeling toward freedom for Americans, it should read, "In A.D. 1825, Fifty years subsequent to the Battle for Liberty, The Inhabitants of the United States were a FREE PEOPLE, Excepting TWO MILLIONS of Slaves, Whose condition had excited but little sympathy."

This indictment against Webster's Bunker Hill Monument speech provided further controversy. One editor wrote that the article by Acacius was more "likely to produce mischief."[47] Another response was printed in the *Portsmouth Journal of Literature and Politics* and questioned printing the article at all. Criticizing the *Columbian Centinel* as well as the author of the scathing editorial, the author of the *Portsmouth Journal* article wrote that articles such as the one authored by Acacius "tend merely to produce bitter feelings without pretending to show that the evil can be removed, they certainly do not extend the spirit of benevolence from which they probably spring."[48] Acacius penned a response to his critics in October and defended his reasons for writing with such inflammatory language. "It is not my wish," the abolitionist wrote, "'to excite unpleasant feelings between the people of different sections of the country," but rather to see the execution of plans to remove "from the nation the reproach of being a FREE—but *slave holding people!*"[49]

Many other antislavery reformers began to challenge American support for the liberation of the Greeks while pointing out their comparative silence and inaction on the subject of slavery in the United States. Addressing the success of the philhellenic movement, they pointed to the huge amounts of aid that had been raised by communities throughout the country, especially in Boston and Philadelphia. At the same time, they noted Americans' failure to devote as much attention to the injustices caused by slavery in their own country. Missionary and abolitionist Samuel Worcester rhetorically quizzed his readers: "Should such gallant spirits as the lamented Bozzaris [hero of the Greek Revolution] fall a sacrifice to the bow-string of the Grand Seignior, would you dress your countenances with smiles of joy? No—your hearts would wring with agonized emotion for the martyrs of liberty. . . . And now you have no tear for the poor slave?"[50] A minister in Philadelphia similarly used the Greek cause to make his argument for colonization by pointing out, "When Greece, whose sons we had never enslaved, called on us for aid, who refused to contribute, or rather who did not rejoice to contribute? And shall we hold back from Africa, when this society would send home her sons, whom we have stolen away?"[51]

Some refugees from Greece made the case themselves for comparing the plight of the Greeks with that of American slaves. At least two active members of the abolitionist movement, Photius Fisk and John Zachos, were Greek orphans who had been rescued by American philhellenes and brought to the United States to be educated. Joseph Stephanini was another Greek refugee who came to the United States through the financial assistance of the Greek Committee of New York. At the age of twenty-six, Stephanini wrote a memoir in which he condemned American slavery and encouraged Americans to see the similarity between the institution of slavery and the conflict that persisted within the Ottoman Empire.

The author believed he had a unique perspective on the subject given that he had experienced Ottoman slavery firsthand. Ottoman soldiers captured Stephanini while his village was under attack early on in the war. For several years he lived as a captive, not knowing whether he would ever see his family again. Through a series of fortunate events, Stephanini managed to escape his captors and gained passage on an American ship bound for New York. Upon arriving in New York, Stephanini was taken under the wing of the Greek Committee of New York. The group granted him passage on a ship it was sending back to the Mediterranean stocked with relief items for the suffering Greeks. Stephanini became a Greek committee representative of sorts. Almost immediately he returned to the United States on another American ship carrying correspondence for the Greek Committee of Boston.[52]

On this second visit to the United States, Stephanini remained for several years, visiting supporters of the Greek cause in Charleston, South Carolina. It was on this visit to a Southern, slaveholding state that Stephanini saw for himself the American institution of slavery. The former Greek slave attempted to keep his language uncontroversial by observing how much he admired the United States for its assistance to the Greek cause. He concluded his memoir, however, by referring to African slavery: "The emancipation of a family from the miseries of slavery,—a slavery of whose horrors I can speak from bitter experience, is an enterprise which such a people, I confidently trust, will not refuse to aid."[53] Stephanini's memoir, written and sold specifically to raise money to help him return to Greece to find his enslaved family, concluded on an abolitionist note. Given his understanding of Americans and their dedication to Greek freedom, he believed that the American people would be moved to eradicate slavery from their borders.

Stephanini was a young, poor refugee who just a few years earlier had not been able to speak a word of English.[54] There are questions about how much of his memoir he wrote himself. Nonetheless, the young Greek achieved national fame. Through the help of philhellenes in Boston, New York, and Philadelphia, he traveled throughout the United States. Several newspapers reported on his travels. The *Vermont Gazette* printed that while unwilling to accept charity, Stephanini intended to publish a memoir that would help to raise ransom money to free his mother and sisters. The whole effort would be done in Charleston with the assistance of an unnamed South Carolinian.[55] Published in 1829, Stephanini's memoir was advertised as being a true story, which no doubt was intended to aid in selling more copies. To say the memoir was a true story was not enough, however. Following the preface, letters of introduction penned by several well-known American men appeared. The only South Carolinian who wrote a letter for the book, or who was thanked by Stephanini in his conclusion, was Thomas S. Grimké.

Thomas S. Grimké was the son of a wealthy South Carolina slaveholder and the brother of Sarah and Angelina Grimké, both of whom would emerge as outspoken advocates of the antislavery movement in the 1830s. Thomas Grimké was a respected lawyer as well as philanthropist, serving as a member of the American Colonization Society and the American Peace Society.[56] Grimké was not specifically named as the South Carolinian who assisted Stephanini in editing his manuscript for publication. However, Grimké had at least some input: his letter of introduction for the memoir stated that he had examined Stephanini's letters and therefore recommended him "with great pleasure to all who feel a sympathy for his personal misfortunes."[57]

Joseph Stephanini managed to collect enough proceeds from his memoir to leave the United States and return home to Greece.[58] Other Greek refugees who arrived in the United States claimed it as their new home. These Greek refugees were mere children when they came to America to receive an education sponsored by local Greek committees. Photius Fisk and John Zachos were educated in the United States and carried their experiences from the Greek Revolution into adulthood.

Photius Fisk came to the United States under the sponsorship of the American Board of Missions as well as philhellenic Americans. With a brother in the Greek army, biographer Lyman Hodge noted, Fisk "was imbued in childhood with that ardent love of liberty, and that undying detestation of every form of slavery, which impelled him in his active manhood to persistent and efficient effort to advance the anti-slavery cause in the United States. He was an Abolitionist before he saw America."[59] Fisk became an ordained minister and was named a chaplain in the U.S. Navy in 1841, where he frequently worked and conversed with officers who owned slaves. Photius eventually decided to join the antislavery cause even though he knew that "social ostracism was the penalty of holding anti-slavery views."[60]

Through Fisk's work for the abolition of slavery and other philanthropic causes, admirers recognized the connection between his devotion to the antislavery movement and his experiences with "the wrongs imposed upon the people of his country by the Turkish tyrants."[61] Fisk became well acquainted with William Lloyd Garrison, Wendell Phillips, Frederick Douglass, and many other members of the antislavery movement. Perhaps the most noteworthy member of the abolitionist movement with whom Fisk became associated was John Brown. Garrison introduced Fisk to John Brown in Boston in 1859 while Brown was making secret arrangements for his raid on Harpers Ferry. Holding Brown to be a "true friend of the anti-slavery cause," Fisk contributed one hundred dollars to Brown's mission.[62]

John Zachos also became an ardent abolitionist. John (Joannes) Celivergos Zachos was ten years old when he came to the United States under Samuel Gridley Howe's care. Zachos was born into an affluent and educated Greek family and to a father who supported and participated in the Greek Revolution. When his father died early in the revolution, his mother was left to look after two small children in a war-torn country. Zachos spent the early years of his childhood fleeing from "a bloody enemy and a lawless soldiery."[63] One of the young Greek's earliest memories was of playing on the beach with his younger sister. Their nurse discovered them striking white balls with large white clubs. To the nurse's horror, the white clubs were the "dried and bleached bones of some poor victims of the war." At the end of the war, Zachos's mother was remarried to a man who was acquainted with Howe. Fearing her new husband was not astute with their finances, Zachos's mother agreed to allow Howe to take young Zachos to the United States to be educated. American philhellenic patrons paid for the young boy's education and living expenses. Zachos graduated in 1840 and became an educator and school principal. During the American Civil War, Zachos volunteered to serve on the Educational Commission of Boston and New York, a group organized to send teachers to the South in order to educate the newly freed slaves.[64]

Zachos penned various pamphlets that revealed his interests in education as well as abolition. He wrote several instructional pamphlets, including a reader published in 1855 titled *The New American Speaker*, a title advertised by booksellers throughout the country. This work included a number of literary excerpts on the subject of Greek independence.[65] In 1864, Zachos published a pamphlet entitled *An Appeal to the Friends of Education for the Immigrant, and the Freed-People of the South*, which was intended to raise money for the printing of the Bible into phonetic English for distribution. Zachos's own experience as a foreigner and his professional experience of educating freed slaves in South Carolina during the war compelled him to believe that "all these ought to be taught to read as the first step towards the higher and broader life of American institutions."[66]

Through his affiliation with the Educational Commission of Boston and New York, Zachos traveled to South Carolina in 1862 as part of the Union presence in the region. Zachos would assist with providing education to the newly freed slaves, a venture not dissimilar from the efforts made by benevolent groups for Greek education in the years that followed the revolution. A report printed in a New York newspaper related the arrival of the Union forces as well as the presence of "three to four thousand" freed slaves who had assembled to celebrate emancipation day.[67] The "plentiful supply of abolition speeches" included an ode written by John C. Zachos declaring the African slaves finally free.

These Greek refugees made an impression on the American public in different ways, but their common identity as Greeks who had fled Ottoman tyranny was the basis for public interest in their thoughts and lives. Their voices, like those of former African slaves such as Frederick Douglass, Harriet Jacobs, and Harriet Tubman, were similar in that what they had in common was the loss of their liberty and families at the hands of servitude. Greek refugees who began life under Ottoman rule demonstrated that they too were a valuable asset to the abolitionist cause.

Education for Women

In addition to abolitionism, the cause of women's rights also benefited from the philhellenic movement. American women came to be involved in the

Greek war effort as an extension of other benevolent organizations of the period. Women connected the ideals of the philhellenic movement to other female-led reform efforts such as temperance, antiprostitution, and religious movements. The organizations they led built upon women's domestic and familial roles within society and extended women's reach beyond the home.[68] As noted earlier, aiding Greek women and children was an important way in which women came to be involved in the Greek war effort. Unlike previous benevolent causes, female participation in the Greek cause grew into an international movement, expanding female participation in the public sphere to include not only American women but Greek women. Through their participation, American women were able to expand their influence within civil society well beyond individual towns and communities.[69]

Female access to education in the United States was a movement that had developed simultaneously with the American philhellenic movement. First gaining momentum in the post-Revolutionary era, female education reform in the United States had extensive popular support by the 1820s. As early as the 1780s, Benjamin Rush had advocated for education reform for American women and had founded the Young Ladies' Academy of Philadelphia. In Rush's view, women's influence over children as well as their husbands made female education an important reform to cultivate.[70] European reformers also influenced ideas on female education. Mary Wollstonecraft's *Vindication of the Rights of Woman* provided some of the intellectual framework for education reform, stating that educating young girls was important in order to "render women truly useful members of society" while also improving society as a whole.[71] With the rise of the "middling classes" by the 1820s, more young girls were able to receive an education at female academies and were educated with curricula similar to those of their male counterparts.[72]

Female education by 1820 was associated with uplifting and preserving feminine virtue, and women began to connect education with benevolence. Historian Mary Kelley has linked organized benevolent societies from 1797 to 1820 to the first generation of women who acquired advanced education at female academies. She also has noted that these women legitimized their involvement in benevolent organizations through an emphasis upon a female moral superiority.[73] This first generation of educated women influenced the next generation of young girls, who would incorporate this sense of feminine moral superiority into the emerging interest in aiding the poor and spreading moral reform.[74]

By the 1820s, interest in providing access to education for women in the United States came to include an international dimension. Female interest in the Greek War of Independence had become increasingly concentrated toward aiding Greek women and children through sending aid and supplies. There is evidence indicating that women from communities large and small, especially in the Northern states, organized sewing circles and donation drives to aid the Greeks. In the town of Utica, New York, for example, women made over five hundred garments with the help of their sisters from neighboring villages, then sent the garments to Greece along with gifts and other donations.[75] By the end of the 1820s, some women began to direct their attention toward assisting Greek women by raising money and dispatching teachers to Greece. American women believed that by providing education to Greek women, they were helping to uplift Greek families and eventually Greek society as a whole. The woman perhaps most involved in advocating the importance of female education reform on a global scale was Emma Willard.[76]

Born in 1787 in Connecticut, Emma Willard became devoted to the advancement of women's education in the United States early in life. As the founder of the Troy Female Seminary in Troy, New York, Willard wrote to the New York State legislature in 1819 arguing that the ladies of America "have the charge of the whole mass of individuals, who are to compose the succeeding generation. . . . How important a power is given by this charge! Yet, little do too many of my sex know how, either to appreciate or improve it." Willard pointed out that "civilized nations have long since been convinced, that education, as it respects males, will not, like trade, regulate itself . . . but female education has been left to the mercy of private adventurers."[77] Willard believed that the status of female education in any nation reflected how civilized the society was as a whole.[78] Ten years later, with the Greek Revolution drawing to a close, Willard took particular interest in extending this perspective toward female education reform in Greece. Willard expressed concern for the immediate and long-term success of Greece as a stable nation and applied these notions to organizing a charitable venture, which she called the Troy Society, that would provide education to the Greeks.

Willard's devotion to establishing a school at Athens was piqued after meeting a young Greek refugee. This individual had been so moved by Willard's dedication to education that he wept "to see these American ladies and think of my own countrywomen. Yet nature has made them equal. Would that they too could be instructed!"[79] Willard entered into negotiations with members of the ABCFM, and she persuaded some of her former pupils to journey to Greece to establish a school. Willard observed, "In ancient story we are told that one of our sex remaining in Troy wrought harm to the Greeks. In modern recital may it be said, that women of *American* Troy have done them lasting good."[80]

Willard connected the issue of female education in Greece with her interest to spread female education not only throughout the United States but throughout the world. Willard argued that it was imperative to establish schools in Greece while it was still a new nation in order to establish the roots of a successful and free society where "half of these are females." Advocates for female education in America had long argued that the success of the American republic depended upon virtuous and enlightened mothers; Willard sought to extend this concept to other parts of the world. Through female education, Willard actively extended women's influence abroad into a realm previously reserved for men only.[81]

While Emma Willard was perhaps the most well-known female advocate for female education in Greece, many ladies' benevolent organizations, especially in Northern states, also supported education reform for Greek women and children. Women from communities such as New Haven, Connecticut; New York City; Boston; and Philadelphia continued the work they had already begun in supporting Greek civilians during the war and transitioned this humanitarian outreach into building schools in Greece. Women followed these reform efforts through newspapers and ladies' magazines, sending donations to advance the cause.

One Philadelphia magazine reported that both men and women had organized a committee for the advancement of education in Greece. Appealing to the community for "Money, Books, Globes, Maps, Mathematical Instruments, Slates, &c.," a public notice read, "Now is the time—they are leaving the manners of the East, and adopting those of Europe. . . . If America does nothing now to form the character of this interesting people, the time for exertion will soon be past."[82] The committee proposed raising $2,500 for the purpose of building a new school in Athens, which would be led by two American missionaries.

The Troy Society frequently worked cooperatively with local organizations in order to more effectively raise funds and supplies. When the Troy Society raised revenue to enlarge the building occupied by the Episcopalian Mission School at Athens, a Boston women's committee "formed themselves into a society co-operative with the Society in Troy for the 'Advancement of Female Education in Greece.'"[83] In New Haven, Connecticut, men and women organized an association that would raise funds and work with "similar benevolent institutions" in Greece to establish a school for Greek females. The New Haven Ladies' Greek Association joined forces with a local mission, sending a Miss Mary Reynolds under the care of the Reverend Josiah Brewer in December 1829 to commence "their benevolent labours on one of the Grecian islands." This school was ultimately established at Smyrna and became one of the first such schools founded in the Ottoman Empire. The success of the society's goal in educating Greek women and youths depended upon the aid of "those ladies who have heretofore taken an active interest in relieving the wants of the distressed families of Grecian patriots."[84] A combination of missionary and philhellenic zeal provided funding and general interest in sustaining such schools in Greece and the Ottoman Empire for some years.

With their focus on education reform in Greece, some reformers could not help but connect the status of women denied an education to the status of slaves. One organization appealed for support on the basis that Greek civilians had formerly been slaves under the Turks and now must be aided in establishing a free society. Recalling the previous success of the American philhellenes, a public address printed in Philadelphia stated, "While they were slaves, we did much to feed and clothe the body; now they are becoming freemen, shall we do nothing for the immortal mind?"[85]

Believing they had assisted with removing Turkish chains, education reformers also imagined that only an American education could help the Greeks fully embrace their independence. The Greek School Committee of New York, chaired by Albert Gallatin, former secretary of the treasury and minister to France and Britain, expressed this sentiment. In the committee's 1829 plan for building elementary and high schools in Greece for both boys and girls, Gallatin explained, "Our common school system is more perfect than even that of the enlightened country whence we derive our lineage. Education here [in the United States] . . . is well suited to a people just emerging from revolution, and among whom equal rights are acknowledged." Gallatin concluded by requesting support for the plan: "Shall we not then, help the Greek boy to the best spelling and ciphering book? And the Greek girl to the best thoughts of our writers on Female Education?" For this committee and many others, transplanting American schools onto Greek soil was the only way of helping the Greeks to nurture their newfound independence.[86]

Samuel Gridley Howe also promoted American-sponsored schools in Greece, and specifically supported Willard's efforts. In 1834, an exchange of letters between Willard and supporters such as Howe appeared in the *American Ladies' Magazine*, then edited by Sarah Josepha Hale, also an advocate for female education. In writing to Emma Willard, he expressed his thoughts on the effect an American-style education would have on the Greek population. Emphasizing the importance of Willard's efforts, Howe referred to his own experiences in Greece, stating that there were many things that could prevent the advancement of women to their proper place in the new Greek nation.

"The national traditions show that she has been the humble servant, or the petted slave of man from the remotest antiquity," Howe explained. "During the last four centuries the country has been ruled by the Turks, who deny to woman a participation in human nature."[87] Willard shared these sentiments. In her 1833 report on the Troy Society's efforts at raising funds, she stated that female education in Greece was especially important because the Greeks had been slaves under Ottoman rule for so long. It was necessary, argued Willard, for "others to resuscitate the principle of life within her. When this is once effected, she will walk abroad in her own strength and provide for herself and her children."[88]

Willard's sister, Almira Phelps, also spoke about the establishment of schools in Greece and played an important role in their fund-raising and organization. With the assistance of the ABCFM, Phelps helped to oversee the education and training of female teachers to be sent to Greece to establish and maintain schools. In an address in which she outlined efforts at continuing to staff these schools, Phelps outlined both her philhellenic and missionary interests in Greece. "When we reflect on these abuses of the virtuous of our sex, holding them in intellectual bondage," Phelps explained, "and at the same time paying unbounded homage to the unblushing females of ancient Greece—when we consider what they have since endured from the licentiousness of Turkish soldiers and of Turkish princes, or from the servitude to which they have been condemned, can we but feel our hearts burn within us with the wish to elevate the Greek female in the scale of being, and to impart to her some of the blessings of improvement, so richly bestowed upon us?"[89]

While clearly philhellenism helped shape the reasons for organizing these schools, a missionary spirit also helped fuel Phelps's enthusiasm. One feature of the Troy Society, observed Phelps, that "especially commends it the approbation of Christians" was that "it has sprung up from the root of Christian benevolence, unobstructed by sectarian feelings; and its members ardently desire that it may grow and enlarge." Phelps went on to report that the Troy Society had especially enjoyed support from individuals in New York, Connecticut, Massachusetts, and Maine. There was also reason to believe, Phelps observed, that their efforts at raising funds might be taken up in the South. At the moment, she admitted, "benevolent effort has been checked by opposition, which, as it was founded on misapprehension of the views of the Society, it is to be hoped will cease, when they shall be understood."[90]

Although Emma Willard never explicitly connected the lack of education to the status of slaves in the United States, other education reformers, including Phelps, did. Though Phelps's address on Greek education did not explicitly state why efforts at raising funds in the South had been stalled, it is possible that Phelps's views on education and slavery contributed to the trouble. In 1833, the same year Phelps penned her address on female education in Greece, she compared those who denied education to women to Southern slaveholders. She noted that a bill for the endowment of a female seminary "was defeated through the influence of those [who thought] . . . of the evils which might result, from the enlightening the minds of those, who were destined to a limited and subordinate sphere."[91]

Applying her thoughts of education as being the ultimate method of enlightening any group of people, Phelps observed, "As respects the slave, this reasoning is undoubtedly correct; let the black population of the south be taught that they in fact possess the greater physical power; let their minds be opened to the truths of man's equality by nature and of the unjust tenure" of their bondage.[92] Phelps more subtly made the same comparison in her address on Greek education during the same year, declaring that through missionary and education reform the enslaved might have freedom: "For what is it to the humiliated, the broken spirited slave, that he lives in the boasted land of liberty?—liberty which exists for all, but not for him. . . . Woe must be to him who dares to anoint the intellectual eye of the negro."[93]

Emma Willard was more vocal in her support of women's rights than in her support of abolition. In an address advocating for female education in Greece, she spoke about the long battle before her to spread female education from the United States to the rest of the world: "But I wish not to exhaust the subject of female education. . . . Justice will yet be done. Woman will have her rights. I see it in the course of events. Though it may not come till I am in my grave."[94] Willard's sentiments proved truer than she perhaps imagined. Female activism in the American philhellenic movement did open doors, however small, for American women, as well as for women and girls in Greece who benefited from the establishment of American schools. Through activism in Greek aid societies, women were able to extend their domestic domain to a public and political cause that included an international dimension.

Working alongside their male counterparts, the ladies of America successfully formed female organizations and engaged other women throughout the country in the same pursuit. Their efforts were so successful that even a population of people thousands of miles away marveled at American women's devotion to the Greek cause during and after the Greek Revolution. American women believed they were helping to advance their sex by aiding their sisters living under Ottoman rule, while simultaneously, participation in the Greek cause heightened women's receptivity to the larger question of women's rights at home and in the larger world. The rhetoric of the Greek cause became fused with reformist rhetoric for decades to come.

The Greek Slave, Abolitionism, and Women's Rights

Born in 1805 in Vermont, Hiram Powers grew up in Ohio and from a young age demonstrated natural artistic talents in sculpture. Powers's flair for the neo-classical earned him notoriety in the United States, as he completed a number of commissions for classically inspired busts of contemporary public figures including John C. Calhoun and Andrew Jackson. Powers traveled to Florence, Italy, in 1837 in order to study among the great European artists of his day. It was while in Florence that Powers created *The Greek Slave*. In a pamphlet writ-ten to promote the statue, Miner K. Kellogg, Powers's close friend and patron, wrote that *The Greek Slave* was not "merely a Grecian maiden, made captive by the Turks and exposed at Constantinople, for sale"; rather, she also was meant to represent "a being superior to suffering, and raised above degradation, by inward purity and force of character."[95] Powers evidently did not intend his work to be an indictment against slavery in his home country, or at least he did not articulate this intention. Abolitionists, however, drew parallels between Greek slavery and African slavery in the United States.

In many ways, the philhellenic movement and its reformist rhetoric were transformed by the rising tensions of the antebellum era. Powers's *Greek Slave* represented the collision of these factors. Many American men and women who viewed the 1847 unveiling of *The Greek Slave* linked philhellenic senti-ments with the impulses of abolitionism and women's rights in a shocking yet powerful and persuasive new way. *The Greek Slave* was the first nude statue to be accepted by the American public, in part because of the subject matter: a young Christian Greek girl on a Turkish auction block.[96] The statue toured the United States and was viewed by thousands of Americans, both male and female, stimulating social debate wherever it went. The work compelled many Americans to recall their support for the Greek Revolution, their disdain for Ottoman slavery, and the status of women both at home and abroad. The im-age of *The Greek Slave* could no longer inspire unity as the American philhel-lenic movement had in the 1820s; rather, it represented the feelings of political and sectional division that plagued antebellum America.

Although the Greek Revolution had long since ended, the discourse de-nouncing Ottoman enslavement of the Greeks had not disappeared. Ameri-can newspapers reported the public reaction to *The Greek Slave*.[97] While there were some critics of the statue, including one writer for the *Liberator*, who commented that the statue was "too white for their philanthropy," most reacted as Powers intended—that is was not the Greek *slave*'s nudity but her spirit that was on display, revealing a steadfast trust in divine providence even though she stood "exposed to be sold to the highest bidders."[98] Even religious leaders of the day could not find fault with the nude statue. Unitarian minister Orville Dewey of Boston wrote a review of the statue that was printed in a number of newspapers, including the *Alexandria Gazette*. He criticized classical statues in general for their nudity and pagan symbolism, but for Hiram Powers and his *Greek Slave* Dewey had nothing but praise. "The Greek Slave is clothed all over with sentiment; sheltered, protected by it from every profane eye," explained Dewey. "Brocade, cloth of gold, could not be a more complete protection than the vesture of holiness in which she stands.—For what does she stand there? To be sold; to be sold to a Turkish harem!"[99]

For many Americans, however, *The Greek Slave* did not merely conjure images of the Greek Revolution and the struggles of innocent civilians. *The Greek Slave* stood as an idealized symbol of freedom, an image that highlighted the degree to which American society fell short of the ideal.[100] Frederick Douglass's newspaper, the *North Star*, captured this sentiment best. In a review, the author described the statue in great detail and offered an emotional reaction to seeing the innocent young girl in chains. "How heart and brain burn with hatred for the cruel Turk who does thus violate the sacred rights of human nature," condemned the reviewer. "And to this feeling heart and discerning eye *all slave girls* are GREEK, and *all slave mungers Turks* . . . their country Algiers or Alabama, Congo or Carolina the same." The review concluded that such was the power of viewing *The Greek Slave* that "had Congress appropriated ten millions of dollars to buy this silent moral mentor, and given it a place in the halls where so much crime has been legalized and connived at, ours would have been a wiser and better nation."[101] Many Americans saw in the statue not just the plight of a young Greek but a larger injustice. If the owner of this young Greek girl was cruel and despotic, then so too was any individual who stole away the innocence and freedom of another.

Many other reviews of *The Greek Slave* echoed similar sentiments. Another antislavery publication reviewed Powers's statue and observed that in so doing, "a yet deeper moral is there, for Americans . . . It is an impersonation of SLAVERY. This creature, exhibited for sale in the slave market, is a counterpart of thousands of living women. Every day does our own sister city of New Orleans witness similar exposures, with a similar purpose." The author of the article concluded with this hope: "Would that the Greek Slave as she passes through various portions of our country, might be endowed with power to teach, to arouse, to purify public opinion."[102] Yet another publication printed in its review of the statue that while Powers's image "enchants the world . . . there were fair breasts that heaved with genuine sympathy beneath the magic power of the great artist, that have never yet breathed a sigh for the sable sisterhood of the South! . . . May many a mother and daughter of the Republic be awakened to a sense of the enormity of slavery, as it exists in our midst!"[103] These reviews clearly indicate that for many Americans who flocked to see *The Greek Slave* they saw the statue not only as a beautiful work of art or as a political statement against slavery within the Ottoman Empire but also as an indictment against slavery within Powers's own home country.

Some antislavery advocates in the United States even argued that a slave's condition was better within the Ottoman Empire than in their own country. It is important to note that by the time the statue was unveiled in the United States, parts of the Ottoman Empire had begun to limit and even outlaw the enslavement of certain groups of people.[104] Americans were aware of this and condemned the United States for not taking similar measures. One newspaper commented on this irony given the popularity of *The Greek Slave*, stating, "It brings home to us the foulest feature of our National Sin . . . and the still more humiliating fact that while the accursed system from which it springs has well nigh ceased in Mahomdedan countries, it still taints a portion of our Christian soil, and is at this very moment clamoring that it may pollute yet more."[105] Like abolitionists of the late 1820s using popular philhellenic rhetoric to advance their arguments, Powers's statue now served a similar purpose. What is clear is that midcentury abolitionists recognized that after several years of national notoriety and fame, *The Greek Slave* could serve as a powerful point of contrast and comparison between the United States and the Ottoman Empire.

Most American Southerners, however, did not see the relevance of connecting *The Greek Slave* with slavery as it existed within the United States. Many Southern newspapers reported to their readers the progression of *The Greek Slave*'s travels through the United States, the reactions the statue inspired from locals, and the hope for its continued success. The *Southern Patriot* printed a series of articles beginning with the statue's arrival in New York in August 1847, each declaring that the statue had safely arrived somewhere in the United States and that it was to be put on public display immediately. Yet another Southern newspaper reported on the reception Powers's statue had enjoyed, regarding it as "a splendid specimen of American art."[106] The *Mississippi Free Trader* reported on the arrival of the statue in Natchez in 1851, expressing confidence that locals would "crowd the rooms to see the life-size form of the manacled maiden, so intense in passion and apparent mental suffering, as to make the cold marble appeal to the human heart, as forcibly as if her tears and voice were palpable to the senses."[107] In October 1847, at the request of a New Orleans doctor, *The Greek Slave*, which was owned at the time by Powers's close friend Miner A. Kellogg, was used as a means for raising funds to benefit "the sufferers by the pestilence in New Orleans."[108] That many Southerners saw *The Greek Slave* as a beacon of hope and an example of unparalleled art by an American artist is undeniable. Whether they saw a connection to Powers's statue and slavery as it existed within the South is doubtful; at least, any reviews printed in Southern newspapers and magazines remained silent on the subject.

Some reviews printed by abolitionist publications declared their hope that when the statue traveled through the American South it would change the hearts of slaveholders who looked upon the statue. One such article printed by the *National Era* speculated on the impression *The Greek Slave* might have on a slaveholder in St. Louis. "I am gazing upon an image as white as the driven snow," says the fictional slaveholder who had come to see Powers's masterpiece,

> and in view of the wrongs of the kind she represents, contemplating the complete emancipation of all the white people of the earth, under the genial influence of Christianity; and I cannot have my thoughts perturbed by the intrusion of such black and thick-lipped images as these I see flitting before my eye of imagination. Away! Away! I came not to think of ebony maidens or men, or what humanity requires for them, but to be regaled with the elevating and humanizing sentiments which I dreamed this image should inspire me with.

The reviewer fantasized that *The Greek Slave* might turn on its pedestal to the slaveholder and say in response,

> "Why limit your sympathies? . . . I was carved from Parian, rather than from Ebony, that I might more effectually appeal to perverted justice and partial sympathy; but I am the representation of the captive and the forsaken everywhere, and whatever sympathy I may secure for my enslaved sisters in Turkey, are due to my sisters of another hue in the land throughout which I am making my pilgrimage."[109]

As is made clear by the *National Era* review, the connection between *The Greek Slave* and slavery within the United States was obvious. The connection was an invalid one in the Southern mind, however. The defense of slavery in the American South was part of a long-standing tradition that had become solidified by the Missouri Crisis and was a foundational part of the Southern way of life. Proslavery arguments only become more intense by the 1830s as Northern abolitionist societies increasingly began publishing indictments against slavery in publications such as William Lloyd Garrison's *Liberator*. In addition, the figure portrayed in *The Greek Slave* was thought of as a white woman about to be sold into slavery to, presumably, a nonwhite male. By condemning the enslavement of whites in the world, Southerners could simultaneously defend a global concept of freedom while still defending black slavery at home. This "racial hellenism" must also therefore be understood when considering Southern reaction to Powers's *Greek Slave*. From the Southern perspective, white Americans shared not only a cultural link to antiquity with the modern Greeks, but a link to whiteness itself. Greek enslavement was therefore unnatural. Rather than change the hearts and minds of slaveholders, as was hoped by the *National Era* reporter, the article would have only been viewed as a challenge to Southern liberty and an insult to their honor.[110]

British subjects also speculated on the impact *The Greek Slave* might have on the persistence of slavery in the United States, or at least they noted the hypocrisy of its continuation. In 1851 a copy of *The Greek Slave* was sent to England to appear in the Crystal Palace Exhibition. *The Greek Slave* influenced a cartoon by John Tenniel printed in the British periodical *Punch*. Titled *The Virginian Slave*, it depicted a nude African woman standing in a similar way to the Greek woman in Powers's work of art.

Draped over the post to which the Virginia slave was chained was an American flag. At the base of the statue, the words "E pluribus unum" were clearly chiseled. The caption for the cartoon read, "Intended as a Companion to Power's [*sic*] 'Greek Slave.'"[111] Tenniel's critique received even more notoriety when a fugitive American slave attended the exhibition with the purpose of making an antislavery demonstration in the presence of *The Greek Slave*. When he arrived, the fugitive placed a copy of *The Virginian Slave* near *The Greek Slave*, stating, "As an American fugitive slave, I place this Virginia Slave by the side of the Greek Slave as its most fitting companion."[112]

British antislavery society circles, like their American counterparts, criticized American enthusiasm for Powers's statue. Members of the Anti-Slavery Society of London who viewed *The Greek Slave* at the Crystal Palace were especially disgusted. One member, the Reverend Thomas Bloney, observed that the Americans who visited the exhibit must have been struck "with a sort of judicial blindness in the selection." Choosing *The Greek Slave* to represent

THE VIRGINIAN SLAVE.

INTENDED AS A COMPANION TO POWER'S "GREEK SLAVE."

Figure 5.3. Now famous for his *Alice in Wonderland* illustrations, John Tenniel satirized Powers's *Greek Slave* and its popularity in the United States with his *Virginian Slave* illustration printed in *Punch* magazine. One of the copies of *The Greek Slave* was put on display in the American exhibit at the Crystal Palace in London. Chosen as an example of excellence in American art, abolitionist critics in Britain found the statue's symbolism less palatable than did its American audience. Tenniel's illustration references the American institution of slavery through the use of the American flag draped over the auction block and the traditional motto of the United States, "E pluribus unum" (Out of many, one) chiseled into the base of the statue. John Tenniel, *The Virginian Slave*, wood engraving, in *Punch*, 1851, Library of Congress Prints and Photographs Division, LC-USZ62-98525.

the United States and American artists "exhibited the worst taste possible," especially given that in addition to this, the Americans also had placed "a man with a stick to turn [*The Greek Slave*] round, precisely as they would do were they trafficking in human sinew and bone."[113] As was the case when Northerners critiqued Southerners, when the British brought up slavery and its persistence in the United States, it usually only further entrenched slavery as a supposedly peculiar aspect to life in the American South.[114] While *The Greek Slave* did not change Southern minds toward abolition, it was adopted into abolitionist rhetoric and aided in the intensification of their arguments.

Though not all women who participated in the philhellenic movement joined radical antebellum reform movements, philhellenism did influence subsequent reformers. The display of *The Greek Slave*, for example, inspired conversations concerning a woman's place in American society. Female abolitionists, such as Lucy Stone Blackwell, Lucretia Mott, and Elizabeth Cady Stanton, had increasingly come to see the similarity between the plight of enslaved people and their own status as disenfranchised women. What these reform groups had in common was the use of philhellenic rhetoric for their own purposes.

In many ways, Powers's statue brought together ideas from abolitionist and women's reform groups. For female reformers, *The Greek Slave* resonated with their own legal status as well as the status of African slaves. The image of the slave as a symbol of lost personhood was especially powerful for women who lacked legal control over their bodies.[115] Historian Karen Sanchez-Eppler argues, "Feminists and abolitionists were acutely aware of the dependence of personhood on the condition of the human body, since the political and legal subordination of both women and slaves was predicated upon biology."[116] That *The Greek Slave* depicted a nude Christian female with no control over her body, let alone her future, was an association not lost on American women.

When in 1851 *The Greek Slave* was on exhibition in Boston, Lucy Stone (Blackwell), a budding abolitionist at the time, visited it. Upon seeing the statue, Stone was struck by how "emblematic of women" the statue was, with its "fettered hands and half-averted face." Stone claimed that viewing Powers's statue was one of the most momentous events in her life. In contemplating the meaning of the statue, Stone recalled that "hot tears came to my eyes at the thought of millions of women who must be freed."[117]

Viewing *The Greek Slave* inspired Stone to speak about women's rights as well as abolition. After Lucy Stone spoke at a Massachusetts Anti-Slavery Society meeting and conveyed her newfound passion for freeing all women from the ways in which they were subjugated, one of the event organizers criticized her speech, reminding her that "the people came to hear anti-slavery, and not woman's rights." Stone responded, "I was a woman before I was an abolitionist," and insisted that she would speak about women or resign from speaking further for the Anti-Slavery Society. Unwilling to lose an increasingly popular speaker, the Anti-Slavery Society ultimately decided to permit Stone to speak on both subjects, but she could only speak about women's rights at her own expense.[118]

Other women also responded to Powers's statue by intensifying their public commitment to women's rights. A contemporary of Hiram Powers was Harriet Hosmer, an American sculptor who endeavored to convey a message of antislavery and pro–women's rights through her art. Born in 1830, Hosmer's talents were recognized from a young age. Hosmer's family sent her to Rome to train with some of the top sculptors of the time, which helped her cultivate an interest in classical artistic themes especially focused on female subjects.[119] As Hosmer's notoriety as an artist rose, she attracted the attention of female abolitionists and women's rights advocates such as Lydia Maria Child and Lucy Stone.[120] Only in her early twenties at the time, Hosmer critiqued Powers's *Greek Slave* by producing her own sculpture of a female slave. With the encouragement of both Child and Stone, she had set to work on a sculpture of a woman that, unlike *The Greek Slave*, depicted a resolute defiance in the face of male oppression. Hosmer's statue depicted Zenobia, the queen of Palmyra (in present-day Syria), who was enslaved by the Romans in 274 CE.

With Powers's *Greek Slave* as inspiration and motivation, Hosmer diligently gathered the advice of her female supporters and created a statue that combined women's rights and abolitionism.[121] One of Hosmer's most famous supporters of the period was English poet Elizabeth Barrett Browning, who saw *The Greek Slave* while it was on display at the Crystal Palace in London. After viewing the statue, Browning penned a well-known poem detailing her reaction:

> On the threshold stands
> An alien Image with enshackled hands,
> Called the Greek Slave!
> . . . .
> To so confront man's crimes in different lands
> With man's ideal sense. Pierce to the centre,
> Art's fiery finger, and break up ere long
> The serfdom of this world. Appeal, fair stone,
> From God's pure heights of beauty against man's wrong!
> Catch up in thy divine face, not alone
> East griefs but west, and strike and shame the strong,
> By thunders of white silence, overthrown.[122]

Figure 5.4. Harriet Hosmer's *Zenobia in Chains* was in part a response to Hiram Powers's *Greek Slave*. Known for her use of the classical style, Hosmer endeavored to depict a strong and defiant woman though enslaved by her Roman captors. The stance of Hosmer's statue was a critique of the modest and demure *Greek Slave*. Harriet Goodhue Hosmer, *Zenobia in Chains*, marble, 1859. © Courtesy of the Huntington Art Collections, San Marino, California. Photograph © 2014 Fredrik Nilsen.

Hosmer visited Browning while in Florence and made her initial plans for her Zenobia statue at that time. Browning criticized Powers's statue as being too passive and likely influenced Hosmer to create a female statue that would "imbue Zenobia with the sense of dynamic action that many observers would later comment on."[123] Instead of a demure and vulnerable maiden, Hosmer's *Zenobia in Chains* depicts a fully clothed, strong, and determined woman with almost a sense of impatience at her captivity in chains. Hosmer herself said that this was "most strongly expressed in the hand which is grasping the chain" as if ready to break it in two.[124]

Lydia Maria Child, abolitionist and women's rights advocate from Massachusetts, also provided suggestions on how Zenobia should appear, emphasizing that Hosmer's statue should portray a strong rather than a weak woman. Child wrote many laudatory reviews of Hosmer's work. Her review of *Zenobia in Chains* reflects her interest in Hosmer's statue and highlights its differences from Powers's: "The expression of the beautiful face is admirably conceived. It is sad, but calm, and very proud; the expression of a great soul, whose regal majesty no misfortune could dethrone."[125] Like Browning, Child disagreed with Powers's depiction of a subdued, weak, and demure woman suffering under male oppression and rather preferred that such a female figure should stand resolute and determined. Hosmer wrote Child specifically addressing this aspect of the statue, explaining, "I have tried to make her too proud to exhibit passion or emotion of any kind; not subdued, though a prisoner; but calm, grand, and strong within herself." Child concluded her review by observing: "Are you not glad a woman has done this? I know you are; or I would not have written to you of my own delight in this great performance of our gifted countrywoman."

Abolitionist and women's rights advocate Frances Dana Barker Gage was equally impressed with Hosmer's abilities as a sculptor of female subjects, further associating Hosmer's work with the antislavery and early feminist movements. In an article written for the *Liberator* titled "Masculine Women," Gage wrote a biting critique of an article that had suggested that any female achievement was an exhibition of a masculine trait rather than a feminine one. "Is it any more masculine to be able to paint the beauties of a horse, than to be able to see one and admire it with womanly eyes?" Gage demanded. "The triumphant claim to masculinity of genius made by this gifted woman [i.e., Hosmer] is no where to be found, except in the fact that she has excelled even man himself." Gage continued: "The mad-dog cry of masculinity has wellnigh spent its force. The world will recognize talent and power; and the wise ones are fast coming to the conclusion, that 'it will not pay' to let one half the genius and worth of a holy humanity lie undeveloped and unemployed, because the possessors, by an accident of birth, are women."[126]

Hosmer's *Zenobia in Chains* did not obtain the same fame and notoriety as Powers's *Greek Slave*. Female advocates for abolition and women's rights, however, rallied around Hosmer and her work. They saw *Zenobia in Chains* as a visual critique of Powers's statue and by extension their society's expectations of respectable women. Whereas Powers's statue represented a philhellenic and abolitionist icon by portraying a powerless woman in need of rescue, Hosmer's statue represented the aspirations of the women's rights movement. For the women who admired, endorsed, collaborated on, and created *Zenobia in Chains*, such an artistic symbol of women's rights should not passively accept subjugation and slavery like Powers's *Greek Slave*, but rather should defy it.[127]

The more radical feminists of the time translated this critique into fashion. An easily recognized symbol of Eastern exoticism in nineteenth-century America, Turkish trousers, turned the despotic Turkish paradigm on its head and came to represent the pursuit of female freedom rather than its oppression. Three years after Hiram Powers's *Greek Slave* made its tour through the United States, women's rights advocates promoted a new fashion trend driven toward displacing social restrictions on women.[128] Named after Amelia Jenks Bloomer, who first wore it in the United States, "the Bloomer costume" was a fashion sensation in the 1850s, with newspapers reporting throughout the country a multitude of sightings of women wearing them.

The Bloomer costume was inspired by Turkish trousers that included a shorter overskirt. The trousers, or pantaloons, were made from "the same materials as the dress," which extended "from the waist to the instep, [and] are gathered around the ankle, and allowed to fall over the gaiter."[129] Discussed by women and the American public from New England to Texas, the Bloomer costume was worn without a bodice and included yards of fabric composing the necessary petticoats and skirts typically worn by women of the nineteenth century.[130]

This was not the first time Turkish-inspired trousers were adopted by women as a symbol of female independence. The use of Turkish trousers can be traced to the eighteenth century with the printing of Lady Mary Wortley Montagu's letters from the Turkish embassy. Based on her experiences in the Ottoman Empire as the wife of an English diplomat, Lady Montagu's letters conveyed that women in Turkish harems, in some ways, had more rights than she did as an Englishwoman.[131] Lady Montagu's observations of the Turkish female fashions were greatly altered after a visit to a Turkish bath. Lady Montagu arrived at the bath and discovered that only women were there, all bathing nude and

Figure 5.5. This lithograph by Currier and Ives illustrates the short skirt and pantaloons iconic of the Bloomer costume. The woman depicted modeling the costume is portrayed as a fashionable yet respectable woman through her demure pose and accompanying handkerchief. N. Currier, *The Bloomer Costume*, lithograph, 1851, Library of Congress Prints and Photographs Division, LC-USZ62-970.

openly discussing the news of the day. "In short," she commented, "'tis the women's coffee house, where all the news of the town is told, scandal invented etc." When Lady Montagu attempted to excuse herself, she was persuaded not only to stay but also to loosen her stays. This, she wrote, "satisfied them very well, for I saw they believed I was so locked up in that machine, that it was not in my own power to open it, which contrivance they attributed to my husband."[132] Upon her return to England, she wore Turkish-inspired attire as an outward display of admiration for the Ottomans and of the greater freedom the fashion gave her as a woman.[133]

By the late 1820s, some Americans also began to question the tendency their countrymen had to cast themselves as culturally superior to the Ottomans. Lydia Maria Child went so far as to print in her publication for young people, "We ought to respect what is good, wherever we find it, and rather seek to imitate the virtues of others, than to excuse faults of our own." Speaking specifically on the American tendency to cast Turks as cruel and wicked characters in stories, Child enumerated at length examples of Turkish virtue and honesty, concluding that Americans "and all the civilized world" should "imitate the Turks."[134] In donning the Bloomer costume, American women made not only a fashion statement but a cultural one as well, suggesting there were aspects of the Ottoman Empire that were preferable to those commonly practiced in the United States.

Women who favored the Bloomer costume made a political statement with the fashion by intentionally organizing processions in the Turkish-inspired costume in Fourth of July celebrations. One article printed in a medical journal reported that such a celebration had taken place in Springfield, Massachusetts, in 1851 where women came together to celebrate "an invention which will save thousands from a premature grave." The article continued with a public address: "Ladies and Gentlemen—We congratulate ourselves, and one another, this day, not for deliverance from the British yoke, but from the despotism of a pampered and vitiated appetite, and from the death-grip of the corset string."[135] Still other examples of women wearing the Bloomer costume intentionally on the Fourth of July included a group of ladies from Lowell, Massachusetts. Calling themselves the "Legion," these ladies made arrangements a full month in advance to process on the Fourth "in white and in the Bloomer costume."[136] And in Hartford, Connecticut, a Fourth of July procession of "thirty-one young ladies in the Bloomer costume" emerged to "represent the several States of the Union."[137]

Well-known feminists of the day promoted the costume to female audiences. Elizabeth Cady Stanton did so in an article printed in the *Lily*, a temperance and abolitionist newspaper edited by Amelia Bloomer, which was subsequently reprinted in the *Liberator*. Stanton asked readers, "A long, full, flowing skirt, certainly hangs more gracefully than a short one; but does woman crave no higher destiny than to be a mere frame-work on which to hang rich fabrics to show them off to the best advantage?"[138] Though, as Stanton believed, the Bloomer costume was not "generally becoming" on all women, the freedom of movement the fashion allowed was at least momentarily popular.[139]

The fashion, of course, proved to be controversial. While the women who wore the fashion did so primarily for health and freedom, the general public perceived the Bloomer costume as representing a number of taboos. For some, it represented a demand for political equality, as "some of those who advocated the right of suffrage wore the dress." Those who wore the fashion were thought to be "strong-minded" and advocates of "free love" and "easy divorce."[140] Even though the Bloomer costume had disappeared by 1860, its brief popularity represented a surge in female independence and the assertion of women's rights. By donning a style that was associated with Turkish despotism and female oppression, women's rights advocates signaled that their reform efforts would not be demure and accepting of their condition as Powers had depicted in his *Greek Slave*. Rather, women's rights advocates would "insist that they have immediate admission to all the rights and privileges which belong to them as citizens of the United States."[141] Ironically, women's rights advocates had transformed Turkish oppression into a form of women's liberation.

★ ★ ★

The Greek Slave was in many ways an embodiment of the anxiety and frustration that dominated antebellum culture and politics. The statue reminded Americans in both the North and South of the shared experience they had in advocating for independence for the Greeks twenty years earlier. Both Northerners and Southerners had expressed outrage over Turkish enslavement of the Greeks on the basis of religion, history, and even race. *The Greek Slave* also elicited controversy. It was this controversy that lay bare the growing sectionalism in the United States.

Though not all Northerners supported abolition in 1850, the subject of slavery, discussed through any medium however innocent, revealed the differences between North and South. Where *The Greek Slave* stimulated conversation concerning African versus white slavery, the topic was met by silence in the American South. To Southerners, white slavery was an abomination and a subject they enthusiastically took up under the mantle of freedom. African slavery, however, was an entirely different subject.

The philhellenic movement in the United States had taken on a life of its own. First inspired by the European movement, American philhellenism became an expression of American identity and charity. Philhellenes embarked on efforts to spread American reform not only on the basis that the United States shared the legacy of ancient Greece, but also that they uniquely under-

ABOLITIONISM, REFORM, AND PHILHELLENIC RHETORIC   193

stood the hardships a revolution would impose on its populace. The Greek Revolution as an international event drew American reformers onto a global stage, extending their ideas regarding education and religion beyond the borders of the United States.

The American philhellenic movement forever changed domestic reform as well. Philhellenism in part informed early Americans of their superiority, both on the basis of their own revolution and because of how they connected their own history to that of ancient Greece. Reformers took notice of the public enthusiasm for freeing the Greeks and began to make similar references to the Turks and Turkish slavery as the epitome of global despotism. These references were applied to domestic reform. For some American women, *The Greek Slave* represented not only the subjugation of women within the Ottoman Empire, but also within the United states where women did not enjoy the same rights as white male citizens. Abolitionists applied philhellenic rhetoric to the condemnation of slavery within the United States. Southern reactions to this revealed that the enslavement of the Greeks within the Ottoman Empire and the enslavement of Africans within the United States were not seen in the same light south of the Mason-Dixon line. When the unity the Greek Fire had inspired began to deteriorate in the antebellum era, the rhetorical fragments of the movement were taken up by different groups and used as weapons to advance their own separate causes.

Conclusion

The Legacy of American Philhellenism

Franklin Benjamin Sanborn, abolitionist and friend of Samuel Gridley Howe, offered perhaps the best synthesis of the importance of the Greek cause within antebellum reform. Sanborn was a schoolteacher from Concord in 1857 when he joined a small radical abolitionist group devoted to raising funds in support of John Brown and other antislavery residents of Kansas. The group included Howe. Later renamed "The Secret Six," the group began to provide assistance in February 1858 for Brown's next great effort to end slavery in the United States. Brown's plan was to incite an armed slave insurrection, which would begin at Harpers Ferry, Virginia, the following year.[1] Though Brown's slave insurrection was suppressed almost immediately, the event further exacerbated sectional tensions between the North and South. Sanborn was forever associated with this climactic event, which ultimately paved the way toward civil war.

Years later, Sanborn wrote the preface and notes for Howe's collected letters and journals. In the preface, Sanborn praised his friend for his dedication to the emancipation of Greece and of the slaves within the United States. Howe was "a born philanthropist," observed Sanborn, "and well aware that the service of mankind often requires political revolutions." Sanborn went on to state that Howe's devotion to the antislavery cause in the nineteenth century had "begun in Greece" and culminated "in our American Civil War."[2] Reflecting on the legacy of the Greek Revolution and the aftermath of the Civil War from the vantage point of the early twentieth century, Sanborn viewed the progress toward abolition in the United States from a more global perspective. To Sanborn at least, the abolition of slavery in the United States could not have been accomplished without the influence of the Greek War of Independence.

Early Americans of the 1820s believed they were imparting wisdom and humanitarian relief to the Greek population. At the same time, their experiences in the Greek War of Independence had a profound impact on American culture that reverberated within politics and reform for decades to come. Henry A. V. Post, Greek Committee of New York agent, traveled to Greece on committee business in 1827. Post wrote a memoir of his travels and characterized the Greek Revolution as a battle between liberty and tyranny, Christianity and Islam.[3] American philhellenes and missionaries alike shared a common outlook on the potential redemption of the Greek people. These ideals brought both groups to the shores of Greece in the 1820s. Fueled by American nationalism and an imagined connection between the United States and Greece, these Americans endeavored to build an empire of ideas wherein they believed they could assist the embattled Greeks in establishing a free society. They could educate them, convert them to an American Protestant perspective, and help them realize the full potential of their ancient heritage. By bringing knowledge and American Christianity to Greece, pro-Greek enthusiasts believed they could extend American freedoms to foreigners abroad. It was a way of giving back to the land that had given birth to their own political principles.

Opposing the philhellenes and missionaries were those who favored the expansion of American commerce. Even though many of these procommercial Americans intellectually sympathized with the Greek cause, they viewed diplomacy and commerce with the Ottoman Empire as being the best means for securing the stability and continued economic growth of the United States. Though these merchants pledged support for neutrality in European affairs, they did desire to participate in European markets. For merchants, their sense of American identity depended upon the ability to conduct business abroad. As they understood it, vanquishing pirates, keeping the seas free, and clearing the way for a prosperous trade with the Ottomans would produce far more lasting results for the country than a romanticized quest to share American revolutionary ideals with the Greeks.

The U.S. government stood at the center of this conflict. Early American diplomacy has been frequently couched in terms of neutrality, with the Monroe Doctrine playing a pivotal role in the argument. While the U.S. government tried to pursue a neutral stance on European affairs, it was nevertheless drawn into foreign conflict through the will of the people at home as well as sailors and merchants abroad. This complicated the image each presidential administration of the 1820s wished to project to the rest of the world.

In the years that followed the Greek Revolution, philhellenes and missionaries reaped an unexpected benefit from the U.S. government's improved relations with the Ottoman Empire. Many of those who had supported the Greek cause traveled in increasing numbers to the Mediterranean and journeyed more safely as a result. For many of these travelers, Greece and the surrounding region was their destination. The missionary spirit of spreading American ideals through education as well as religion fed the desire to assist Greece and its citizens as a developing independent nation. How these missionaries imagined the identity of the United States as a free and Christian nation played an important role in their mission work.

By 1830, both reformers and merchants had achieved a certain amount of success. A venture reformers and missionaries shared was the establishment of schools in Greece. Emma Willard, with the assistance of many other American female reformers, including Lydia Sigourney and Sarah Josepha Hale, raised funds throughout the 1830s and sent female teachers to Greece to help establish schools in Athens.[4] American merchants also benefited from access to the Levant. Now able to freely come and go, they conducted business under their own nation's flag as promised by the navigational treaty between the United States and the Sublime Porte of 1832.[5] American reformers, missionaries, and merchants now had the freedom to travel to the Levant with their own divergent visions of how to spread American liberty.

Popular efforts in support of the Greek War of Independence also led to new movements and new ways of thinking. Greek relief efforts in the United States helped shape the discourse of antebellum slavery and women's rights movements, drawing new participants into the public sphere. Women, for example, played an active and publicly visible role in the Greek war effort, which provided them with additional access to reform and politics. They reacted to the Greek Revolution from the perspective of benevolence. These women, like their male counterparts, condemned the perceived despotism of the Ottomans, believing that their rule prevented Greek women from assuming the same roles as American women held in their homes and communities. Women therefore became especially involved in the relief of Greek civilians and refugees. By aiding Greek mothers and their children with relief and education, American women believed that they would play as important a role in establishing a free Greek nation.

In multiple ways, philhellenism and antebellum reform converged to create a powerful new synthesis in social reform movements. Turkish despotism as a common archetype associated with the Ottoman Empire remained a constant throughout early America and persisted into the antebellum era. The tense years of the Barbary Wars magnified by the Greek Fire solidified this perception. By the 1830s, to recall the tyranny of the Turks was to summon the ultimate definition of despotism in the contemporary world. The Greek cause became part of a reformist legacy linking the progression of these antebellum reform movements to a global story rather than just a domestic one.

Perhaps the best example of this literary device was Senator Charles Sumner's *White Slavery in the Barbary States*, published in 1853. While the title indicates the work was intended to be a history of slavery in the Barbary States, the antislavery sympathizer repeatedly used Turkish slavery as a comparison to slavery in the American South. By referring to the South as the Barbary States of America, Sumner offered a multitude of points of comparison to the Barbary States—for example, that "Virginia, Carolina, Mississippi, and Texas should be the American complement to Morocco, Algiers, Tripoli, and Tunis." In addition, wrote Sumner, the Barbary States occupy "nearly the same parallels with the Slave States of our Union."[6] With the slaves' "long catalogue of humiliation and woes" not yet complete, Sumner's history of the Barbary States illustrated that the system of slavery philhellenes had so reviled decades earlier was really not dissimilar to the system they themselves allowed to continue within their own borders.

At the same time, the unveiling of Hiram Powers's *Greek Slave* proved to be a pivotal symbol of women's involvement in the Greek cause that later stimulated interest in the abolitionist and women's rights movements. Widespread activism in the philhellenic movement made way for female efforts at reform in women's education in the United States and Greece. Viewing the denial of education to women as not dissimilar to the denial of education to African slaves, the women's rights and abolitionist movements shared many of the same members. Drawing on philhellenic rhetoric that pleaded with women to "depart from that retired circle" within which women of early America were bound, women mobilized female interest in saving the defenseless Greek matron and maiden from the hands of the cruel Turk. As time went on, however, and women increasingly enjoyed access to reformist organizations, members of both abolitionist and women's rights circles became more outspoken.

The legacy of the philhellenic movement also continued with the suffrage movement. In their history of the woman's suffrage movement in the 1880s, authors Elizabeth Cady Stanton, Susan B. Anthony, and Matilda Joslyn Gage quipped in the preface that their object in writing their history was to "make it an arsenal of facts for those who are beginning to inquire into the demands and arguments of the leaders of this reform." Among these facts throughout their three-volume work include comparisons of slavery elsewhere in the world to the condition of women in the United States. "American men may quiet their consciences with the delusion that no such injustice exists in this country as in Eastern nations," scoffed the suffragettes, "yet the same principle that degrades her in Turkey, *insults* her in this republic." Qualifying this statement, Stanton continued: "Custom forbids a woman there to enter a mosque, or call the hour of prayers; here it forbids her a voice in Church Councils or State Legislatures. The same taint of her primitive state of slavery affects both latitudes."[7]

The relevance of global events in early American society and politics come into focus by evaluating the origins of the abolitionist and women's rights causes in terms of the Greek Revolution. Historians have studied the origins and development of these reform movements from a national and internal perspective, but when the focus expands to include an international perspective, these movements assume an added dimension of complexity. Even though early Americans condemned Ottoman culture and politics, they were influenced by them. Knowledge of a broader world and activism in the Greek War of Independence informed nineteenth-century perspectives on issues of reform. Antebellum reform movements absorbed some of the rhetoric philhellenes employed, especially in regard to Ottoman slavery and the alleged subjugation of women under the Ottoman Empire in order to build a more powerful and influential argument for their cause.

Although the Greek Fire initially aimed at helping the Greeks as an extension of philanthropic relief abroad, ironically, in the end, it transformed American society. Both the rhetoric of the Greek cause and participation in the movement influenced the participants, inspiring them to bring attention to abolition and women's rights through a global lens. Though the consensus among philhellenic organizations of the early 1820s was short-lived and not all supporters went on to became radical advocates of abolition and women's rights, the memory of the Greek cause continued to play a pivotal role in American reform through the nineteenth and into the early twentieth centuries.

Notes

Introduction

1. Although the Ottoman Turks conquered Constantinople in 1453, the city was still commonly referred to as Constantinople by Europeans for the next several hundred years. The Ottomans referred to the city as Konstaniniyye, which uses the Arabic suffix meaning "place" instead of the Greek. The name Istanbul came into common use at the beginning of the twentieth century. I refer to the city as Constantinople because this is the name used by early Americans in nineteenth-century sources. See Quataert, *Ottoman Empire*, 4.

2. I use "American" and "United States" interchangeably. One reason for this is due to the prevalent use of the term "American" within primary source material of the period.

3. "The Greek Cause," *Columbian Centinel*, December 20, 1823. The *New-York Commercial Advertiser* article was reprinted in several newspapers in New York, Massachusetts, and Rhode Island; the *Columbian Centinel* was one of the earliest reprintings of this article. "The Greeks," *Salem Gazette*, December 23, 1823; "Greek Meeting," *Saratoga Sentinel*, January 20, 1824; "Town Meeting. Petersburg, Feb. 6," *Richmond Enquirer*, February 10, 1824; "Periclean Society of Alexandria, Virginia, 1821–1824," Library of Alexandria, Local History and Special Collections. I refer to the "Greek Revolution" and the "Greek War of Independence" interchangeably. Both are accepted by the academic world. Ilicak, "Radical Rethinking of Empire, 2n2."

4. The modern Greeks were not slaves within the Ottoman Empire, but rather were classified as *reaya*, or subjects. Under Ottoman law, insurgents could lose this classification and instead could be treated as war captives and sold into slavery. Examples of Greek enslavement tend to be drawn from the period covering the Greek Revolution rather than from before. There is also evidence to suggest that the potential enslavement of Greek insurgents was decided at the local level rather than sanctioned by the sultan. Early Americans, however, described Greek subjugation under the Ottomans before the revolution as slavery. See Erdem, *Slavery in the Ottoman Empire*, 26, 29–30, 32; Dragonas and Birtek, *Citizenship and the Nation-State*; and Pizanias, *Greek Revolution of 1821*.

5. Percival, *Poems by James G. Percival*, 35. The "Franks" were Western Europeans living in the Levant.

6. "The Greeks," *Richmond Enquirer*, January 15, 1824; Repousis, "'Cause of the Greeks,'" 333; Roland, "Secrecy, Technology, and War," 655.

7. "Greek Fire," *Farmer's Cabinet*, January 10, 1824.

8. On the rise of the philhellenic movement in Europe and the United States, see Bass, *Freedom's Battle*; Dakin, *British and American Philhellenes*; Herzfeld, *Ours Once More*; Larrabee, *Hellas Observed*; Marchand, *Down from Olympus*; Pappas, "United States and the Greek War"; Repousis, "'Cause of the Greeks'"; Repousis, *Greek-American Relations*; and St. Clair, *That Greece Might Still Be Free*.

9. See Herzfeld, *Ours Once More*; Larrabee, *Hellas Observed*; Pappas, "United States and the Greek War"; Richard, *Golden Age of the Classics*; St. Clair, *That Greece Might Still Be Free*; and Winterer, *Mirror of Antiquity*.

10. Walther, *Sacred Interests*, 35–36; and Fitz, *Our Sister Republics*, 131–32.

11. Jefferson, *Notes on the State of Virginia*, 142, 143; Gordon-Reed, *Hemingses of Monticello*, 271, 343; and Coleman, "Notes on the State of Virginia," 44–45.

12. Nott, Gliddon et al., *Types of Mankind*, 40, 458–59; see also Cain, "Art and Politics of Looking White," 29–30; and Stein, "'Races of Men,'" 27–88.

13. See Bailyn, *Ideological Origins of the American Revolution*; Baron, *Crisis of the Early Italian Renaissance*; Pocock, *Machiavellian Moment*; Reinhold, *Classica Americana*; Richard, *Founders and the Classics*; Winterer, *Culture of Classicism*; and Wood, *Creation of the American Republic*.

14. Cooper, *Classical Taste in America*; and Winterer, *Mirror of Antiquity*.

15. Spellberg, "Islam in America," 28–29; and *Proceedings and Debates of the Convention of North-Carolina*, 217–18. In addition to concerns over potential Muslims serving in future public office, Henry Abbot expressed similar concerns about other religious minorities, including Catholics.

16. Several historians have addressed early American understanding of the East in their work. For further reading on this topic, see Allison, *Crescent Obscured*; Egan, *Oriental Shadows*; Field, *America and the Mediterranean World*; Lambert, *Barbary Wars*; and Marr, *Cultural Roots of American Islamicism*.

17. For works that address American support of the French Revolution, see Branson, *These Fiery Frenchified Dames*; and Waldstreicher, *In the Midst of Perpetual Fetes*.

18. Fitz, *Our Sister Republics*, 117–18, 153–54. Fitz's work provides a valuable look at American enthusiasm for revolutions in nineteenth-century South America.

19. "The Turks Have Impaled Forty-Two Christians in Servia . . . [from the] Federal Republican," *New-York Commercial Advertiser*, March 10, 1815. News of the Serbian Revolution was periodically reported in American newspapers. Few public opinion pieces or reports address the raising of funds to aid the Serbs.

20. Richard, *Golden Age of the Classics*, 181–203; Winterer, *Mirror of Antiquity*, 165–90. Both Richard's and Winterer's discussion of the contrasting takes on Athenian slavery in the North and South placed these debates primarily in the context of the antebellum era after the rise of the abolitionist movement in the late 1820s.

21. See Field, *America and the Mediterranean World*, vii.

22. Boylan, *Origins of Women's Activism*; Kelley, *Learning to Stand and Speak*, 26–33; Kierner, *Beyond the Household*, 180–85; Salerno, *Sister Societies*, 11–12; and Zagarri, *Revolutionary Backlash*, 140–46.

23. Repousis, "'Cause of the Greeks.'" Angelo Repousis has written about national popular support for the Greek cause; he argues that it represented an important episode in the history of American humanitarianism abroad. Repousis, "'Trojan Women.'" This article discusses Emma Willard's leadership efforts to establish American schools for girls in Greece at the end of the Greek Revolution.

24. Lyman, *Diplomacy of the United States*, 495.

25. Elliot, *American Diplomatic Code*, vol. 2, 653; and Field, *America and the Mediterranean World*, 136–37. Field describes American views on diplomacy and commerce in terms of the American Revolution, and notes that to early Americans the subsequent expansion of commercial interests abroad became the ultimate victory of liberty over tyranny.

26. Field, *America and the Mediterranean World*, 104.

27. Zagarri, "Significance of the 'Global Turn.'"

28. Anderson, *Imagined Communities*. In part, I examine the phenomenon of an imagined American community linked to the ancient world and the ways in which this understanding inspired many Americans to participate in supporting the Greek War of Independence. I am also interested in the ways in which this imagined community evolved and conflicted with other perceptions of the American identity.

29. Said, *Orientalism*, 4. Said's groundbreaking work argued that the United States lacked a formal empire before World War II, and thus any analysis of American relations in the Orient was focused on the twentieth century; for titles that address official and unofficial American foreign relations with the Orient during the early Republic, see Conroy-Krutz, *Christian Imperialism*; Heyrman, *American Apostles*; Makdisi, *Artillery of Heaven*; Rouleau, *With Sails Whitening Every Sea*; and Walther, *Sacred Interests*.

30. See Allison, *Crescent Obscured*; Heyrman, *American Apostles*; Makdisi, *Artillery of Heaven*; Marr, *Cultural Roots of American Islamicism*; and Rouleau, *With Sails Whitening Every Sea*.

31. Shoemaker, "Extraterritorial United States," 36–37.

32. See Conroy-Krutz, *Christian Imperialism*; Heyrman, *American Apostles*; Makdisi, *Artillery of Heaven*; and Walther, *Sacred Interests*.

33. Walther, *Sacred Interests*, 27–28. Karine Walther makes a similar caveat. See Pizanias, *Greek Revolution of 1821*. Petros Pizanias and Vasilis Panagiotopoulos provide useful discussion on identity, nationalism, and language in terms of the Greek Revolution. See Dragonas and Birtek, *Citizenship and the Nation-State*. Hakan Erdem's analysis of nationalist rhetoric as used by the Greeks and the Turkish understanding of it is especially useful (see *Slavery in the Ottoman Empire*). See also Ilicak, "Radical Rethinking of Empire."

34. Howe, *Letters and Journals*, xi. Franklin Benjamin Sanborn was a close friend of Howe's and wrote the introduction to a volume of his friend's printed journals and letters. Both Sanborn and Howe were members of the "Secret Six," a group of men who privately provided John Brown with financial support for his raid at Harpers Ferry in 1859.

1. Americans, Greeks, and Ottomans before 1821

1. Smyrna is now known as Izmir. I refer to the city as Smyrna as it was known in the nineteenth century.

2. Heyrman, *American Apostles*, 150. Early Americans frequently referred to all Muslims in the Ottoman Empire and affiliated regions as "Turks."

3. David Offley to Mary Offley, July 10, 1818, folder 1, in Offley Family Papers.

4. For further reading on the influence of Rome and Greece in early American intellectual life and culture, see Richard, *Founders and the Classics*; Richard, *Golden Age of the Classics*; Sellers, *American Republicanism*; Shalev, *Rome Reborn*; Winterer, *Culture of Classicism*; and Winterer, *Mirror of Antiquity*.

5. American Board of Commissioners for Foreign Missions, *Missionary Herald*, vol. 16, 266.

6. Quataert, *Ottoman Empire*, 2.

7. Quataert, *Ottoman Empire*, 4; Hamadeh, "Ottoman Expressions," 34; and Lambert, *Barbary Wars*, 30.

8. Quataert, *Ottoman Empire*, 38.

9. Quataert, 37.

10. Ilicak, "Radical Rethinking of Empire," 244–45; Erdem, "'Do Not Think of the Greeks,'" 68; and Erdem, "Greek Revolt."

11. Quataert, *Ottoman Empire*, 46.

12. Davison, *Turkey*, 68–70; Quataert, *Ottoman Empire*, 44–45; and Faroqhi, *Ottoman Empire*, 24–25, 100, 111–35.

13. Quataert, *Ottoman Empire*, 44; Hamadeh, "Ottoman Expressions," 33, 38–40, 43; and Zarinebaf, "Istanbul in the Tulip Age."

14. Quataert, *Ottoman Empire*, 44.

15. Erdem, *Slavery in the Ottoman Empire*, 2–3.

16. Erdem, "'Do Not Think of the Greeks,'" 68; Pizanias, "From Reaya to Greek Citizen," 12; and Faroqhi, *Ottoman Empire*, 13–15.

17. Pizanias, "From Reaya to Greek Citizen," 13–14, 20–26.

18. Anderson, *Imagined Communities*, 195.

19. One of the earliest letters in which Jefferson expressed his support for Greek independence was written while he was in Paris: Thomas Jefferson to John Page, August 20, 1785, in Jefferson, *Papers of Thomas Jefferson*.

20. Erdem, "'Do Not Think of the Greeks,'" 67–68; Larrabee, *Hellas Observed*; and Pizanias, *Greek Revolution*, 15–16.

21. St. Clair, *That Greece Might Still Be Free*, 30–31; and Davison, *Turkey*, 73.

22. Pizanias, "From Reaya to Greek Citizen: Enlightenment and Revolution" in *Greek Revolution*, 7.

23. Panagiotopoulos, "Filiki Etaireia," 101.

24. Pizanias, "From Reaya to Greek Citizen: Enlightenment and Revolution" in *Greek Revolution*, 31–32. Pizanias outlines the intellectual changes in Greek identity during the period, and Vasilis Panagiotopoulos's article ("Filiki Etaireia") directly addresses the development and role the Society of Friends played in the outbreak of the Greek Revolution.

25. Ilicak, "Revolt of Alexandros Ipsilantis," 225–26. H. Sukru Ilicak writes that Ottoman officials came to the conclusion that the Greek Revolution was brought on in part by a Russian conspiracy to pledge support to insurgents. Although some of the reasons for this conclusion reveal an atmosphere of Russophobia, the Ottoman officials' reason for drawing the conclusion is supported. Panagiotopoulos, "Filiki Etaireia," 104; St. Clair, *That Greece Might Still Be Free*, 134–35, 160.

26. Panagiotopoulos, "Filiki Etaireia," 106.

27. Panagiotopoulos, 122.

28. Panagiotopoulos, 104.

29. Goloboy, "The Early American Middle Class" 538–40; The classical tradition in America has been extensively discussed among historians of the period. See Bailyn, *Ideological Origins*, 25–27; Reinhold, *Classica Americana*; Richard, *Founders and the Classics*; and Winterer, *Culture of Classicism*.

30. Gallman, "Changes in the Level of Literacy," 567n1, 574; Perlmann and Shirley, "When Did New England Women Acquire Literacy?" 51; and Lockridge, *Literacy in Colonial New England*.

31. Warner, *Letters of the Republic*, 7.

32. Pasley, *"Tyranny of Printers,"* 403.

33. Cornell, *Other Founders*, 11, 34–50.

34. Richard, *Founders and the Classics*, 8; and Bailyn, *Ideological Origins*, 25–26.

35. The Society of the Cincinnati, a veterans organization founded at the end of the revolution, used Cincinnatus as its inspiration. Founded in 1790, Cincinnati, Ohio, took its name from the Society of the Cincinnati and, by extension, the American Cincinnatus, George Washington.

36. Zelinsky, "Classical Town Names," 472.

37. Examples include Bingham, *Columbian Orator*, and N. Webster, *American Selection of Lessons*; see also Pasley, *"Tyranny of Printers,"* 403; and Shalev, *Rome Reborn*.

38. Winterer, *Culture of Classicism*, 45–46.

39. Kerber, *Women of the Republic*, 218; and Richard, *Golden Age of the Classics*, x, 3.

40. Winterer, *Mirror of Antiquity*, 103.

41. Winterer, *Mirror of Antiquity*, 102–8.

42. Nance, *How the Arabian Nights Inspired*, 19–21.

43. Winterer, *Mirror of Antiquity*, 108.

44. Murray, *Thomas Hope*, xix.

45. Bushman, *Refinement of America*; and Richard, *Golden Age of the Classics*, 83.

46. Bushman, *Refinement of America*; Cooper, *Classical Taste in America*; Larrabee, *Hellas Observed*, 24–25; Richard, *Golden Age of the Classics*; and Winterer, *Mirror of Antiquity*.

47. Larrabee, *Hellas Observed*, 25.

48. Brackenridge, *Modern Chivalry*, 180; and Larrabee, *Hellas Observed*, 6. Larrabee discusses late eighteenth and early nineteenth century literature that might have influenced early American popular opinion with regard to Greek independence.

49. "Professorship of Greek Literature in Harvard University," *North American Review and Miscellaneous Journal 1*, no. 1 (May 1815), 129; and Winterer, *Culture of Classicism*, 51–52.

50. St. Clair, *That Greece Might Still Be Free*, 298.

51. James Madison to Thomas Jefferson, October 17, 1788, in Jefferson, *Papers of Thomas Jefferson*.

52. *Proceedings and Debates of the Convention of North-Carolina*, 220–21; Spellberg, *Thomas Jefferson's Qur'an*, 73–74. Spellberg's work addresses the extent to which Americans of the late eighteenth century considered it possible for a Muslim to serve in public office. See also Heyrman, *American Apostles*, 72–74. Heyrman illustrates that early American sentiments regarding Islam and Catholicism had not changed by the 1820s.

53. Spellberg, *Thomas Jefferson's Qur'an*, 158–95.

54. Lambert, *The Barbary Wars*, 34–36 and 38–40. Lambert describes the progression of the Ottoman Empire's interaction in global trade; by the end of the seventeenth century the English and the Dutch actively sought to decrease the threat of piracy in the Mediterranean. As a result, the naval force of Algiers, for example, was reduced by 75 percent. The Barbary powers were reduced to petty states, unable to launch more than a dozen ships.

55. Allison, *Crescent Obscured*; and Lambert, *Barbary Wars*, 42–43.

56. Lambert, *Barbary Wars*, 119.

57. Lambert, 10–11; and Peskin, *Captives and Countrymen*.

58. Washington to Lafayette, March 25, 1787, in Washington, *Papers of George Washington*.

59. Lambert, *Barbary Wars*, 121–23.

60. Jefferson to Washington, July 12, 1790, in Washington, *Papers of George Washington*.

61. Allison, *Crescent Obscured*, 181; Baepler, *White Slaves*, 9; and Lambert, *Barbary Wars*, 124–25.

62. Lambert, *Barbary Wars*, 124.

63. Jefferson to Yusuf Qaramanli, May 21, 1801, in Jefferson, *Papers of Thomas Jefferson*.

64. Lambert, *Barbary Wars*, 183–84. The British assured the dey of Algiers that they would provide support and naval protection for any action against the "enemies of Great Britain," thus pledging support against the United States in the Mediterranean.

65. Lambert, *Barbary Wars*, 193–94; and Madison, "Message from the President." The treaty specifically stipulated that the United States would not pay tribute to Algiers in any form.

66. "The Struggles of Opposition Unavailing," *Albany Argus*, November 17, 1815.

67. "United States," *Shamrock*, November 18, 1815.

68. Allison, *Crescent Obscured*, 52; and Marr, *Cultural Roots of American Islamicism*, 24–25.

69. Walther, *Sacred Interests*, 23; Lambert, *Barbary Wars*, 113; and Allison, *Crescent Obscured*, 48–52.

70. Nance, *How the Arabian Nights Inspired*, 22; see also Brown, *Knowledge Is Power*; Davidson, *Revolution and the Word*; Hall, *Cultures of Print*; and Warner, *Letters of the Republic*.

71. Egan, *Oriental Shadows*, 78.

72. Schueller, *U.S. Orientalisms*, 26.

73. *American Plays Printed 1714–1830*. This catalog indicates that many plays printed and performed in America from the 1780s through the 1830s were based on Oriental tales or reflected contemporary attitudes on the East.

74. Marr, *Cultural Roots of American Islamicism*, 44–45; Egan, *Oriental Shadows*, 99–101; and Nance, *How the Arabian Nights Inspired*, 19.

75. *Arabian Nights' Entertainments*, vol. 2, frontispiece.

76. Egan, *Oriental Shadows*, 101.

77. Nance, *How the Arabian Nights Inspired*, 20.

78. N. Webster, *American Selection of Lessons*, 261.

79. Educational Research Library and Alvina Treut Burrows Institute, *Early American Textbooks*; and Goldsmith, *Grecian History*, vol. 1, iii.

80. Goldsmith, *Grecian History*, vol. 2, 375.

81. Lambert, *Barbary Wars*, 105–22.

82. For further reading on the Barbary Wars and captivity tales, see Baepler, *White Slaves*; Allison, *Crescent Obscured*; Egan, *Oriental Shadows*; Lambert, *Barbary Wars*; Marr, *Cultural Roots of American Islamicism*; and Peskin, *Captives and Countrymen*.

83. Baepler, *White Slaves*, 87–88, 92; Foss, *Journal*, 1, 34, 47.

84. Baepler, *White Slaves*, 95; Foss, *Journal*, 55.

85. Tyler, *Algerine Captive*, 1:iii. David Humphreys served as an aide-de-camp under George Washington during the American Revolution before he went on to a career in foreign relations and diplomacy. See also Humphreys, *Life of General Washington*; Eicher, *Raising the Flag*, xiii. Eicher discusses the practice of using the title "minister" instead of "ambassador" because the former was thought to be less pretentious and more appropriate for an official from a republic.

86. Tyler, *Algerine Captive*, 2:82.

87. Tyler, *Algerine Captive*, 2:241.

88. Yothers, *Romance of the Holy Land*, 7.

89. Baepler, *White Slaves*, 147.

90. Carey, *Short History of Algiers*, 12; and Martin, *History of the Captivity*, 12.

91. Baepler, *White Slaves*, 147–58.

92. Zagarri, *Revolutionary Backlash*; and Kerber, *Women of the Republic*.

93. Akalin, "Ottoman Seraglio," 353–61; Bickerstaff, *Sultan*; Allison, *Crescent Obscured*, 69; and Marr, *Cultural Roots of American Islamicism*, 50–51. No copies of the American version of *The Sultan* survive. Copies of the unadapted version printed in the United States do, however.

94. Bickerstaff, *Sultan*, 8.

95. Bickerstaff, *Sultan*, 17, 20, 21; see also Baepler, *White Slaves*, 49; and Marr, *Cultural Roots of American Islamicism*, 50.

96. Marr, *Cultural Roots of American Islamicism*, 43–49.

97. Baepler, *White Slaves*, 18. Baepler suggests this idea especially in his discussion of Maria Martin; see also Peskin, *Captives and Countrymen*.

98. Yeazell, *Harems of the Mind*. The harem as a concept shrouded in fantasy forms the basis for Yeazell's study on Western perceptions of the harem.

99. Yeazell, *Harems of the Mind*, 76–77.

100. Marr, *Cultural Roots of American Islamicism*, 43.

101. Jehlen and Warner, *English Literatures of America*, 866.

102. Field, *America and the Mediterranean World*, 116–17.

103. Lyman, *Diplomacy of the United States*, 495.

104. Elliot, *American Diplomatic Code*, 2:653; and Field, *America and the Mediterranean World*, 136–37. Field describes American views on diplomacy and commerce in terms of the American Revolution, noting that for early Americans the subsequent expansion of commercial interests abroad became the ultimate victory of liberty over tyranny.

105. Field, *America and the Mediterranean World*, 7–24. Field examines several facets of American interest in the Atlantic World, including the expansion of self-determination among foreign societies as well as Christianity.

106. Field, 113.

107. Field, 117.

108. Field, 118; and Morison, "Forcing the Dardanelles," 223.

109. Rouleau, *With Sails Whitening Every Sea*, 10–11. In particular, Rouleau's work addresses American sailors, but David Offley fits into Rouleau's analysis of "nonstate actors."

110. David Offley to Edward Livingston, January 14, 1832, United States Senate, *Public Documents: Third Session*, doc. 200, p. 128.

111. Field, 118; Barrell, *Letters from Asia*, 13–14; and Heyrman, *American Apostles*, 88–90. Heyrman discusses Barrell's presence in the Levant and the impressions he had of the region.

112. Field, *America and the Mediterranean World*, 118. Early American spellings of this title vary. For the most part, it was written as "captain pasha," but variations include "capudan pasha" and "kapudan pasha." Unless quoted otherwise, I have chosen to use the transliteration of the Turkish spelling, "kapudan pasha."

113. Barrell, *Letters from Asia*, 14.

114. United States Congress, *House Documents*, doc. 250, p. 4.

115. United States Congress, doc. 250, p. 17.

116. First Church Cambridge, *Records of the Church of Christ*, 394; George Bethune English, in *Harvard University Biographical Files*, which further confirms this information; and Larrabee, *Hellas Observed*, 29, 45.

117. Obenzinger, "Holy Land Narrative," 257.

118. Dunn, "Americans in the Nineteenth Century Egyptian Army," 124n4. Dunn makes a convincing argument in favor of using the Turkish spelling of Mohammed Ali, pointing out that Ali never learned Arabic and thus would have preferred the Turkish version, Mehemed Ali. However, early American sources overwhelmingly use the Arabic spelling.

119. Field, *America and the Mediterranean World*, 62; and English, *Narrative of the Expedition to Donogola*. English mentions Khalil Aga on several occasions in his memoirs. Vivian, *Americans in Egypt*, 77.

120. Finnie, *Pioneers East*, 165; and Macintyre, *Man Who Would Be King*.

121. Although the early American missionary movement is not the main focus of this work, books that I have drawn from to contextualize my work include Conroy-Krutz, *Christian Imperialism*; Heyrman, *American Apostles*; and Makdisi, *Artillery of Heaven*.

122. Field, *America and the Mediterranean World*, 71; and Conroy-Krutz, *Christian Imperialism*, 1–18.

123. Field, 72–73; Hatch, *Democratization of American Christianity*, 173–74; Makdisi, *Artillery of Heaven*, 3; and Richter, *Facing East*, 182–83.

124. Field, *America and the Mediterranean World*, 74.

125. Bond, *Memoir of the Rev. Pliny Fisk*, 67; American Board of Commissioners for Foreign Missions, *Missionary Herald*, vol. 19, 66–68; for a recent analysis of the origins of early American

missionary work and its relationship with British missionary groups, see Conroy-Krutz, *Christian Imperialism*.

126. Obenzinger, "Holy Land Narrative," 242; Bond, *Memoir of the Rev. Pliny Fisk*, 87; Field, *America and the Mediterranean World*, 84–87; Hatch, *Democratization of American Christianity*, 170; and Heyrman, *American Apostles*, 72–89.

127. Pliny Fisk to Rev. Dr. Woods, January 30, 1820, in Bond, *Memoir of the Rev. Pliny Fisk*, 110.

128. Pliny Fisk to Rev. Dr. P. of Shelbourne, Massachusetts, in Bond, 112.

129. Bond, 139.

2. European Philhellenism Crosses the Atlantic

1. "Boston; Lord Byron; Poet; Greeks," *Essex Register*, June 19, 1823.

2. "Lord Byron," *Providence Gazette*, July 23, 1823.

3. "Latest from England: Lord Byron," *Times and Hartford Advertiser*, August 26, 1823; "Latest from England: Lord Byron," *City Gazette and Commercial Advertiser*, September 27, 1823. These are examples of the reprinting of the news of Lord Byron in both New England and the South. Newspapers everywhere reprinted similar news.

4. "From the NY Statesman: Cause of the Greeks," *Essex Register*, July 28, 1823.

5. Bass, *Freedom's Battle*.

6. "Grecian; Ex Arch Germanicus; Patresso; Peloponesus; Bunker Hill," *Alexandria Gazette*, August 3, 1821; "Patriot. Saturday, December 20, 1823," *Independent Chronicle and Boston Patriot*, December 20, 1823; "Connecticut Courant. Hartford, December 30. Greek Cause," *Connecticut Courant*, December 30, 1823; and "Address; Committee; Boston; Greeks," *Boston Commercial Gazette*, January 15, 1824; for analysis concerning race and slavery, see also Stein, "'Races of Men,'" 73–76.

7. Regarding foreign involvement in the Greek War of Independence, the British philhellenic movement has received more attention than the U.S. movement. For further reading, see Bass, *Freedom's Battle*; Dakin, *British and American Philhellenes*; Larrabee, *Hellas Observed*; Pappas, *Greek Revolution*; and St. Clair, *That Greece Might Still Be Free*.

8. Herzfeld, *Ours Once More*; Marchand, *Down from Olympus*; and St. Clair, *That Greece Might Still Be Free*.

9. Erdem, "'Do Not Think of the Greeks'"; Larrabee, *Hellas Observed*; and Panagiotopoulos, "Filiki Etaireia." Both Erdem and Panagiotopoulos discuss the origins of Greek nationalism and its influence on the origins of the Greek Revolution. See also St. Clair, *That Greece Might Still Be Free*, 19–20.

10. Larrabee, *Hellas Observed*, 25; Pappas, "United States and the Greek War," 57–58; and St. Clair, *That Greece Might Still Be Free*, 15–16.

11. Quoted in Larrabee, *Hellas Observed*, 31–32; see also Mason, *Apostle of Union*, 20–21.

12. Giraud de la Clape, ex-etudiant en droit, *Appel aux Francais en faveur des Grecs* (Paris, 1821), quoted in, St. Clair, *That Greece Might Still Be Free*, 56–57.

13. Gordon-Reed, *Hemingses of Monticello*, 61–62, 97; and Larrabee, *Hellas Observed*, 34–35.

14. Herzfeld, *Ours Once More*; Larrabee, *Hellas Observed*, 3–6; and St. Clair, *That Greece Might Still Be Free*, 19–20.

15. Bass, *Freedom's Battle*, 91–92.

16. Thomas Jefferson to George Wythe, September 16, 1787, in Jefferson, *Papers of Thomas Jefferson*.

17. Thomas Jefferson to Charles Thomson, September 20, 1787, in Jefferson, *Papers of Thomas Jefferson*.

18. Thomas Jefferson to Richard Henry Lee, July 12, 1785, in Jefferson, *Papers of Thomas Jefferson*.

19. Bass, *Freedom's Battle*, 55; see also Rawes, "Lord Byron"; and Roessel, *In Byron's Shadow*.

20. St. Clair, *That Greece Might Still Be Free*, 17. St. Clair's comprehensive study of the philhellenes and the Greek Revolution places Byron at the center of the larger European movement.

21. Rawes, "Lord Byron," 180; and Umunç, "In Search of Exoticism."

22. Byron, *Childe Harold's Pilgrimage*, 101–2.

23. St. Clair, *That Greece Might Still Be Free*, 17; and Umunç, "In Search of Exoticism," 328–29, 334.

24. Bass, *Freedom's Battle*, 52.

25. Bass, *Freedom's Battle*, 54; Larrabee, *Hellas Observed*, 42, 69; and St. Clair, *That Greece Might Still Be Free*, 150–54. See also Dakin, *British and American Philhellenes*.

26. Bass, *Freedom's Battle*, 55; and Larrabee, *Hellas Observed*, 31–39.

27. Both Nicholas Biddle and Edward Everett, for example, shared this sentiment.

28. For additional reading on Elgin and the Parthenon marbles, see especially St. Clair, *Lord Elgin*.

29. "Elgin Marbles," *Boston Daily Advertiser*, June 28, 1816.

30. Numerous books that cover the Elgin Marble controversy include Bass, *Freedom's Battle*, 55; St. Clair, *Lord Elgin*; Larrabee, *Hellas Observed*, 30; and Marchand, *Down from Olympus*.

31. Bass, *Freedom's Battle*, 58.

32. Bass, 63; Rodogno, *Against Massacre*, 70–71; Castlereagh quoted in Schwartzberg, "Lion and the Phoenix," 146.

33. McNeal, "Joseph Allen Smith," 64–66.

34. Larrabee, *Hellas Observed*, 11; McNeal, "Joseph Allen Smith," 66; and "We announce with pleasure, the arrival at New York, from Europe . . ." *Alexandria Daily Advertiser*, January 16, 1808, originally published in the *Charleston Courier*: "No American, we may safely say, few, if any Europeans have possessed such means and opportunities of viewing to advantage the various parts of the old world as Mr. Allen Smith. . . . With such means and advantages, it is ardently to be desired that this distinguished traveller may be persuaded by his friends to publish the result of his researches and observations."

35. McNeal, "Joseph Allen Smith," 84.

36. Biddle, *Nicholas Biddle in Greece*, 11–12.

37. Biddle, 49.

38. Biddle, 217–18.

39. Biddle, 222.

40. "N. Biddle, Esq.; Philadelphia; Greek Fund," *New Hampshire Sentinel*, December 19, 1823.

41. Baker, "Lord Byron," 64–65; and Larrabee, *Hellas Observed*, 30.

42. "Boston, Oct. 22, 1819. Panorama of Athens," *Boston Daily Advertiser*, October 22, 1819; Quoted description of the panorama found in "Harvard University; Hon. Jonathan Russell," *Boston Intelligencer and Evening Gazette*, October 23, 1819; and McNeal, "Athens and Nineteenth-Century Panoramic Art."

43. "Harvard University; Hon. Jonathan Russell," *Boston Intelligencer and Evening Gazette*. In addition to a brief description of the panorama, this article also reported with pride that while Oxford and Cambridge had desired to purchase this work, an American had instead succeeded. Barker et al., *Description of the View of Athens*. Barker's work includes sketches of the Panorama and is one of the few sources that provides an indication of what the panorama looked before it was destroyed in a fire in 1842.

44. W. A. Cooper, *Classical Taste in America*, 11.

45. Earle, "American Interest," 47.

46. Quoted in *North American Review and Miscellaneous Journal*, 1821, 433; Fitz, *Our Sister Republics*, 131–32. Fitz describes Everett's lack of interest in South America as being consistent with views commonly held by Federalist New Englanders.

47. Larrabee, *Hellas Observed*, 24.

48. Ilicak, "Radical Rethinking of Empire," 43, 90–91. The Turkish spelling of Ali Pasha of Ioannina is "Tepedeleni Ali Pasha."

49. St. Clair, *That Greece Might Still Be Free*, 9–10; see also Fleming, "Historiography, Historical Context."

50. Erdem, "Greek Revolt," 261; Ilicak, "Radical Rethinking of Empire," 68–69; Ilicak, "Revolt of Alexandros Ipsilantis," 225–26; Panagiotopoulos, "Filiki Etaireia," 121–24; and St. Clair, *That Greece Might Still Be Free*, 10–11.

51. Ilicak, "Revolt of Alexandros Ipsilantis," 225–27, 234–35; Panagiotopoulos, "Filiki Etaireia," 122–23; and St. Clair, *That Greece Might Still Be Free*, 10–12.

52. Quoted in Erdem, "'Do Not Think of the Greeks,'" 68–69; see also Ilicak, "Revolt of Alexandros Ipsilantis," 225–40.

53. Alex. Ysilanti, "Greek Insurrection," *Baltimore Patriot and Mercantile Advertiser*, May 23, 1821. Early Americans and Europeans frequently used different spellings of Ypsilantis's name.

54. Panagiotopoulos, "Filiki Etaireia," 115; and St. Clair, *That Greece Might Still Be Free*, 2–3.

55. Ilicak, "Revolt of Alexandros Ipsilantis," 226. "The Morea" was the name associated with the Peloponnese in Greece from the Middle Ages to the nineteenth century.

56. Larrabee, *Hellas Observed*, 65–66.

57. Erdem, "'Do Not Think of the Greeks,'" 73–74; Pizanias, *Greek Revolution*, 12; and St. Clair, *That Greece Might Still Be Free*, 3–4.

58. "Two Days Later from Europe," *Baltimore Patriot and Mercantile Advertiser*, May 19, 1821.

59. "Late Foreign News," *Washington Gazette*, May 24, 1821; "Miscellaneous," *Portsmouth Journal of Literature and Politics*, March 23, 1822.

60. St. Clair, *That Greece Might Still Be Free*, 44–47.

61. Alex. Ysilanti, "Greek Insurrection."

62. Larrabee, *Hellas Observed*, 55–62. Larrabee acknowledges that very few Americans were in the Mediterranean in the early 1820s, but their knowledge of the conflict did make its way back to the United States. Rouleau, *With Sails Whitening Every Sea*. Rouleau's work discusses the significance of American seafarers in the dissemination of information from abroad, especially in chapter 2, titled "Schoolhouses Afloat."

63. "Proclamation of the Messenian Senate," *Boston Daily Advertiser*, October 15, 1821; and Larrabee, *Hellas Observed*, 34–35. The ancient Greek names listed were Classical and Hellenistic Age statesmen, generals, and poets.

64. "Foreign News," *Portsmouth Journal of Literature and Politics*, December 15, 1821.

65. Percival, *Clio No. III*, 23.

66. Percival, *Poems by James G. Percival*, 33–34.

67. Percival, *Poems by James G. Percival*, 35.

68. Waldstreicher, *In the Midst of Perpetual Fetes*, 294–300; Travers, *Celebrating the Fourth*, 225.

69. *U.S. House Journal*, 1822, 17th Congress, 2nd sess., December 3, 1822, 16.

70. *Annals of Congress*, 17th Congress, 2nd sess., 458.

71. *Annals of Congress*, 17th Congress, 2nd sess., 459.

72. See Fitz, *Our Sister Republics*.

73. Quoted in St. Clair, *That Greece Might Still Be Free*, 152.

74. "Poets of England," *Boston Daily Advertiser*, June 16, 1823.

75. "Communication," *Richmond Enquirer*, October 28, 1823. This news report and various abbreviated versions of it were printed in newspapers in New York, Connecticut, New Hampshire, Virginia, and as far south as the Arkansas territory.

76. *Annals of Congress*, 18th Congress, 1st sess., 22.

77. As debate on the Greek question unfolded in January 1824, it quickly became clear that although a good number of philhellenes were in Congress, also present were many outspoken members who saw no clear benefits to American interests if they openly recognized or assisted the Greeks.

78. D. Webster, *Mr. Webster's Speech*, 37.

79. Samuel Breck to unknown recipient, January 22, 1824, box 316, folder 18, "Ferdinand J. Dreer Autograph Collection 0175," Historical Society of Pennsylvania.

80. Joel R. Poinsett to Joseph Johnson, January 7, 1823, in "Gilpin Family Papers, Joel R. Poinsett Correspondence," Historical Society of Pennsylvania.

81. Adams and Adams, *Memoirs of John Quincy Adams*, 173; Fitz, *Our Sister Republics*, 131; see also Branson, *These Fiery Frenchified Dames*.

82. "Present Condition and Future Prospects of the Greeks, December 31, 1823," *American State Papers: Foreign Relations*, 5:252.

83. "Official Documents: Condition and Prospects of the Greeks," *Baltimore Patriot and Mercantile Advertiser*, January 9, 1824.

84. "Patriot. Saturday, December 20, 1823. The Greeks," *Independent Chronicle and Boston Patriot*, December 20, 1823; "Connecticut Courant. Hartford, December 30. Greek Cause," *Connecticut Courant*, December 30, 1823.

85. "Greek Cause," *Columbian Centinel*, December 20, 1823.

86. This gesture was quashed by the more practical John Quincy Adams.

87. Repousis, "'Cause of the Greeks,'" 343; Bradsher, *Mathew Carey*, 64, 68–78; Burke, "Afterword"; Dolan, "Mathew Carey"; and J. Green, *Mathew Carey*.

88. Meredith Family Papers 1756–1964, series 3, box 6.

89. Dallas, "Philadelphia, Jan. 5, 1824."

90. Meredith Family Papers 1756–1964, box 37, folders 2–6.

91. "Aid of the Greeks," *American Federalist Columbian Centinel*, December 6, 1823.

92. Greek Committee of New York, *Circular*.

93. *Annals of Congress*, 18th Congress, 1st sess., 3106.

94. Grecian Ladies, *Grecian Wreath of Victory*, 5.

95. Grecian Ladies, 11; Byron, *Childe Harold's Pilgrimage*, 223, 273; see also Santelli, "'Depart from That Retired Circle.'"

96. Grecian Ladies, *Grecian Wreath of Victory*, 19.

97. Grecian Ladies, 4.

98. Grecian Ladies, 111.

99. "Periclean Society of Alexandria, Virginia, 1821–1824," Library of Alexandria. From the time the society was formed in September 1821 to the time the Grecian Society was organized, meetings largely consisted of writing and rewriting the organization's constitution. Attendance dwindled considerably and the meeting minutes repeatedly noted the lack of attendance of its members. This changed when the society directed its efforts toward aiding the Greeks.

100. *Periclean Society of Alexandria*, December 27, 1823.

101. *Periclean Society of Alexandria*, December 13, 1823.

102. "We Beg Leave to Call the Attention of Our Readers to an Advertisement of the Periclean Society," *Alexandria Gazette and Daily Advertiser*, January 13, 1824.

103. Pericles and Epaminondas were leading figures in Athens and Thebes during the classical age in Greece; "Hoffman & Johnson's Present Prices for Pork, Beef, & Offals," *Alexandria Gazette*

and Advertiser, January 29, 1824; and "Periclean Society," *Alexandria Gazette and Advertiser*, January 24, 1824.

104. Meeting minutes, January 31, 1824, in *Periclean Society of Alexandria*.

105. *Periclean Society of Alexandria*, March 8, 1824. Leonidas, Pericles, Miltiades, and Epaminondas were all generals during the classical age of Greece.

106. "Greek Celebration and Washington's Birth-Day," *Providence Patriot*, February 21, 1824. .

107. "Washington's Birth-Day Was Celebrated in Petersburg and Norfolk with Enthusiasm," *Richmond Enquirer*, February 26, 1824.

108. "The Greeks," *Richmond Enquirer,* January 15, 1824.

109. *Annals of Congress,* 18th Cong., 1st sess., 916.

110. I conducted a tally of newspaper articles published in forty-six newspapers throughout the North and the South from December 1823 to April 1824 on the subject of the Greek cause. Approximately 575 newspapers were in business in the United States in the early 1820s; thus, the sample constitutes about 8 percent of the total. For research on the growing number of printers in the early republic see Pasley, *"Tyranny of Printers,"* 403.

111. "The Greeks," *Salem Gazette,* December 23, 1823.

112. "Notice—It Is Proposed to Celebrate the Birthday of Washington," *Baltimore Patriot and Mercantile Advertiser*, January 14, 1824.

113. "Greek Benefit: Mr. James A. Zander, a Barber," *Baltimore Patriot and Mercantile Advertiser*, January 12, 1824.

114. "Washington Hose Company," *Baltimore Patriot and Mercantile Advertiser*, January 10, 1824.

115. "At a Meeting of the General Society of Mechanics of New-Haven," *Providence Gazette*, January 24, 1824; and "At One of the Methodist Churches in New York," *Baltimore Patriot and Mercantile Advertiser*, January 9, 1824.

116. Nord, "Benevolent Books," 221. David Paul Nord describes how Christian faith in early America "energized human action" and could be "transferred from religious conversion to social change." In particular, he discusses the role print played in this transfer.

117. Greek Committee of New York, *Circular.*

118. Committee for the Relief of the Greeks, *Address of the Committee.*

119. Bedell, *Cause of the Greeks*, 10.

120. Dwight, *Greek Revolution*, 4.

121. Dwight, 27–28.

122. Durbin, *Substance of a Sermon*, 4.

123. Drowne, *Oration, Delivered in the First Baptist Meeting-House*, 3.

124. "The Quakers in England," *New-Bedford Mercury*, March 14, 1823; "Lest the Fastidiousness of the Lovers of Peace Should Shrink from Aiding the Greeks in War," *Providence Gazette*, January 24, 1824.

125. "The Greeks," *Richmond Enquirer,* January 15, 1824.

126. "For the Centinel," *Columbian Centinel*, December 27, 1823.

3. Philhellenism Joins with American Benevolence

1. Cunningham and Cappel, *Circular Letters*, 1152, 1281, 1282.

2. Repousis, "'Cause of the Greeks.'"
   Repousis discusses the progression of philhellenic efforts toward humanitarian relief.

3. A klepht is an anti-Ottoman insurgent. Roessel, *In Byron's Shadow*, 68.

4. Bryant, "Song of the Greek Amazon," 253; Bryant and Ives, "Song of the Greek Amazon"; and Muller, *William Cullen Bryant*, 67–68.

5. Roessel, *In Byron's Shadow*, 68.

6. Ginzberg, *Untidy Origins*, 5–6, 83–85. Ginzberg's study of women in the antebellum era examines the ways in which the history of ideas can be understood through personal, local, and national experiences. Similarly, I believe that female involvement in the Greek war effort inspired and shaped women's roles in American reform movements. Boylan, *Origins of Women's Activism*, 135–37; Keetley and Pettegrew, *Public Women*, 120–22; Kelley, *Learning to Stand and Speak*; Kierner, *Beyond the Household*, 180; and Hewitt, *Women's Activism*.

7. St. Clair, *That Greece Might Still Be Free*, 170, 179–80.

8. "Death of Lord Byron," *Boston Commercial Gazette*, June 28, 1824.

9. "American Independence," *Saratoga Sentinel*, July 6, 1824.

10. "Public Dinner," *City Gazette and Commercial Daily Advertiser*, July 14, 1824. This article is an example of the detailed reports on Fourth of July celebrations in Washington, D.C., including information regarding formal dinners and toasts, which were reprinted in newspapers across the country.

11. "Independence," *Salem Gazette*, July 6, 1824.

12. "The Number of Celebrations of Our National Independence Were Never Greater," *Norwich Courier*, July 14, 1824.

13. "Lord Byron Is No More!" *Watch-Tower*, July 5, 1824.

14. Reported in newspapers in Massachusetts, New Hampshire, and New York and as far south as South Carolina in July and August 1824.

15. "Greek Deputation, London, June 12, 1824," *City Gazette and Commercial Daily Advertiser*, August 11, 1824; and "From the *New-York American*, Greek Cause: We Have Great Satisfaction . . . ," *Rochester Telegraph*, August 17, 1824. This article is a reprint from the *New-York American*, which means the article was more than likely printed in other New York newspapers as well. "Greek Fund," *Rhode-Island American*, August 31, 1824.

16. "From the *New-York American*, Greek Cause: We Have Great Satisfaction . . ."

17. Dakin, *British and American Philhellenes*, 5–6.

18. Larrabee, *Hellas Observed*, 96.

19. St. Clair, *That Greece Might Still Be Free*, 336.

20. St. Clair, 337; Larrabee, *Hellas Observed*, 113–14.

21. St. Clair, *That Greece Might Still Be Free*, 337.

22. "From the *Boston Daily Advertiser*: Greece," *American Mercury*, March 3, 1825.

23. "To the Greek Committee in Boston, Mass.," *Portsmouth Journal of Literature and Politics*, April 30, 1825.

24. George Bethune English to James Monroe, August 11, 1824, in Adams Family Papers, microfilm edition, reel 465. The timing of English's advice to both Monroe and Adams in addition to the desire to negotiate a treaty with the Sublime Porte suggests a joint effort to change the purpose of the American philhellenic movement toward humanitarian aid. The treaty negotiation side of this story is discussed in chapter 4.

25. "From the *Boston Daily Advertiser*: Greece."

26. "Interesting from Greece," *Independent Chronicle and Boston Patriot*, September 14, 1825.

27. "Salem: Interesting Letter from Greece," *Essex Register*, September 5, 1825.

28. "Interesting from Greece."

29. St. Clair, *That Greece Might Still Be Free*, 298.

30. Miller, *Letters from Greece*, 4; and Larrabee, *Hellas Observed*, 107–8.

31. Larrabee, *Hellas Observed*, 238; Repousis, "'Cause of the Greeks,'" 336; and St. Clair, *That Greece Might Still Be Free*, 134–35.

32. Stratford Canning to George Canning, May 17, 1826, FO 78/142, 157, British Foreign Office, Stratford Canning.

33. Larrabee, *Hellas Observed*, 128.

34. Miller, *Letters from Greece*, 16–17; Larrabee, *Hellas Observed*, 102; and Dakin, *British and American Philhellenes*, 245.

35. "Interesting from Greece."

36. "Interesting from Greece"; and Miller, *Condition of Greece*, 23–24; see also Miller, *Letters from Greece*.

37. Contostavlos, *Narrative of the Material Facts*, 4.

38. Several pamphlets were published by Greek and American officials outlining the facts and arguments made by those involved in the Greek frigate controversy. Selections from these pamphlets were also printed in newspapers. Contostavlos, *Narrative of the Material Facts*; Platt, Ogden, and De Rham, *Report of the Evidence*; Duer and Sedgwick, *Examination of the Controversy*; Sedgwick, *Refutation of the Reasons Assigned by the Arbitrators*. See also "Papers in Relation to the Greek Ship *Liberator*," in *American State Papers*, Naval Affairs, 2:746–48; and Larrabee, *Hellas Observed*, 84–84.

39. "The Concern of the People of the United States for the Greek Cause," *National Gazette and Literary Register*, October 19, 1826.

40. "Greek Ships," *City Gazette and Commercial Daily Advertiser*, September 14, 1826.

41. These two articles are both reprints of the *New-York Post* article: "From a paragraph in the *New-York Post*," *Republican Star*, October 24, 1826; "The ship *Liberator*," *City Gazette and Commercial Advertiser*, October 27, 1826.

42. "Greek Meeting," *New York Spectator*, October 31, 1826.

43. St. Clair, *That Greece Might Still Be Free*, 241–43.

44. "Boston, June 8—From Smyrna," *Essex Register*, June 8, 1826.

45. "The Following Is from the *Paris Etoile*," *Baltimore Patriot and Mercantile Advertiser*, June 8, 1826.

46. "Foreign Intelligence: The Ship Leeds at New-York," *Portsmouth Journal of Literature and Politics*, June 10, 1826.

47. "Missolonghi—The Defence of Missolonghi and the Final Catastrophe," *Essex Register*, July 3, 1826.

48. "Poetry: Fall of Missolonghi," *Essex Register*, July 6, 1826.

49. Snow, "Missolonghi," in *Eliza R. Snow: The Complete Poetry*, 10. This poem was originally printed in the *Western Courier*. Narcissa, "Missolonghi," *Western Courier*, July 22, 1826. Eliza R. Snow later married Joseph Smith and became a prominent female member of the Church of Jesus Christ of Latter-day Saints.

50. Contostavlos, *Narrative of the Material Facts*, 11.

51. St. Clair, *That Greece Might Still Be Free*, 339; and Newbold, "George Newbold Papers." Receipts collected by the Greek Committee of New York support this conclusion.

52. "A Meeting Was Held in Philadelphia," *Boston Commercial Gazette*, November 16, 1826.

53. "Greek Subscriptions," *American Mercury*, December 26, 1826.

54. "Greek Ships," *Essex Register*, August 14, 1826, originally printed in the *Columbian Centinel*; "Greek Loan," *Eastern Argus*, March, 31, 1826. American newspapers reported on and denounced the mismanagement of funds for the Greeks by London officials; See also St. Clair, *That Greece Might Still Be Free*, 298–99, 338.

55. Everett, "'Cause of the Greeks'"; also printed in *Philadelphia, March 27, 1827: Sir, We Respectfully Inform You*, 2.

56. Greek Committee of Philadelphia, *Philadelphia, March 27, 1827: Sir, Presuming That*, 1.

57. Greek Committee of Philadelphia, *Philadelphia, April 3, 1827*, 1.

58. Greek Committee of Philadelphia, *Philadelphia, April 3, 1827*, 3.

59. St. Clair, *That Greece Might Still Be Free*, 339; and Bass, *Freedom's Battle*.

60. "Meeting of the Greeks," *Richmond Enquirer*, January 16, 1827.

61. *U.S. House Journal*, 19th Cong., 2nd sess., January 11, 1827, 146–47.

62. "Greek Fund—The Ship Chancellor, Laden with Supplies for the Greeks," *Richmond Enquirer*, March 23, 1827.

63. Greek Committee of Philadelphia, *Cause of the Greeks*, 6.

64. Greek Committee of Philadelphia, *Philadelphia, March 27, 1827: Sir, We Respectfully Inform You*, 1. Additional shipments of supplies were sent to Greece in the year that followed.

65. Jonathan Peckham Miller, "The Present State of Greece Is Inconceivably Wretched," *Boston Commercial Gazette*, November 16, 1826.

66. Larrabee, *Hellas Observed*, 112.

67. Newbold, "George Newbold Papers."

68. William Meredith, box 37, in Meredith Family Papers 1756–1964. Receipts show wages paid and the amount the collector made for the committee.

69. Newbold, "George Newbold Papers."

70. Dexter, *Biographical Sketches*, 181.

71. Hezekiah Belden to Edward Everett, April 9, 1828, in Newbold, "George Newbold Papers."

72. Fitz, *Our Sister Republics*, 94. Fitz similarly describes how figures such as Henry Clay exhibited a disconnect between the domestic slave question and slavery abroad during the Missouri Crisis. Waldstreicher, *In the Midst of Perpetual Fetes*, 293. Waldstreicher's work details the different strategies by which local and national identities were forged through toasts and celebrations. Even though his study does not extend into the antebellum era, he argues that these strategies continued to be used after the Missouri Crisis. See also Mason, *Slavery and Politics*, 177–212; and Sinha, *Slave's Cause*, 195–227.

73. St. Clair, *That Greece Might Still Be Free*, 316–17, 331–33.

74. Dozens of articles were printed throughout the United States. In as much detail as was available, all reported on British, Russian, and French efforts to militarily support the Greeks in ending their conflict with the Turks. "European News," *Alexandria Gazette*, November 1, 1827; "Latest from England," *Farmer's Cabinet*, December 1, 1827; and "Latest from France," *Augusta Chronicle and Georgia Advertiser*, November 6, 1827.

75. *Philadelphia, April 2, 1827*, 1.

76. Greek Committee of New York, . *New-York, March 6, 1828*, 1.

77. "Greece: Massachusetts Donations," *Portsmouth Journal of Literature and Politics*, January 12, 1828.

78. Greek Committee of New York, *(Circular.) New-York, March 6, 1828*, 2–3.

79. Larrabee, *Hellas Observed*, 158; and St. Clair, *That Greece Might Still Be Free*, 342.

80. Mathew Carey to Mrs. William Meredith, 1826, box 28, folder 6, in Meredith Family Papers.

81. Boylan, *Origins of Women's Activism*, 51–52, 54; and Jeffrey, *Great Silent Army*, 18; see also Hansen, *Very Social Time*.

82. Boylan, *Origins of Women's Activism*, 16.

83. Kelley, *Learning to Stand and Speak*, 5–15; Santelli, "'Depart from That Retired Circle.'" This article expands specifically on the role women played in the Greek war effort and beyond.

84. Greek Committee of Philadelphia, *Philadelphia, April 3, 1827*.

85. Greek committee account books and receipts in New York and Philadelphia list donations made or collected by female groups. These groups were either officially recognized by the local Greek committee or by independently formed female groups. Newspapers and committee-published pamphlets throughout the United States also list female groups involved in the cause.

86. Larrabee, *Hellas Observed*, 70; and Winterer, *Culture of Classicism*, 64.

87. "3000 Well Made Garments for the Greeks," *Pittsfield Sun*, May 8, 1828.

88. "Relief of the Greeks," *American Mercury*, March 11, 1828.

89. "Ladies! Greek Meeting," *Baltimore Patriot and Mercantile Advertiser*, March 24, 1828.

90. "About 40 Ladies in Canandaigua . . . ," *New Bedford Mercury*, February 9, 1827.

91. "The *N.Y. Enquirer* Mentions a Ball . . . ," *Essex Gazette*, March 24, 1827.

92. "Relief of the Greeks."

93. "Ladies! Greek Meeting."

94. "The Greeks," *Hallowell Gazette*, May 9, 1827.

95. Greek Committee of Philadelphia, *Philadelphia, April 3, 1827*, 3.

96. Greek Committee of Philadelphia, *Philadelphia, April 3, 1827*, 3.

97. Greek Committee of Philadelphia, *Sir, the Annexed Resolution*, 4.

98. Newbold, "George Newbold Papers." There are a few receipts from married, single, and widowed women, but these are in the minority when compared to the numbers of donations received from female groups.

99. "From the *Richmond Compiler*: Relief of the Greeks," *Macon Telegraph*, April 21, 1828.

100. Petrino, "'Chain of Correspondence,'" 450–51.

101. "From the *Richmond Compiler*: Relief of the Greeks."

102. Hezekiah Belden to Edward Everett, April 9, 1828, in Newbold, "George Newbold Papers." Receipts written by the Greek Committee of New York as well as letters sent to philhellenic leaders reveal that Southerners did not have many local outlets for Greek aid and instead sent their donations north. Lockley, *Welfare and Charity*. Lockley also addresses charitable movements in the South.

103. "Copy of a Letter from Some Widows of Ipsara," *Norwich Courier*, January 28, 1829.

104. "Letter from Greece," *Baltimore Patriot and Mercantile Advertiser*, May 5, 1829.

105. American Home Missionary Society, *Home Missionary and American Pastor's Journal*, 98; for an analysis of King's influence as a missionary, see Heyrman, *American Apostles*.

106. "From Mr. King's Journal, Published in Greece," *New London Gazette*, July 22, 1829.

107. Castanis, *Greek Exile*, 135; and Trent, *Manliest Man*, 179.

108. Castanis, *Greek Exile*, iii.

109. Stephanini, *Personal Narrative*, i.

110. Stephanini, 129.

111. Castanis, *Greek Exile*, 212.

112. Greek Committee of Philadelphia, *Philadelphia, January 31, 1827: Sir, the Subscribers*, 1.

113. Greek Committee of Philadelphia, *Philadelphia, March 27, 1827: Sir, We respectfully inform you*, 1.

114. Meredith Family Papers 1756–1964, box 37, folder 6. At least one receipt was written in 1828 for the printing of one of the Greek Committee of Philadelphia's addresses in German.

115. Larrabee, *Hellas Observed*, 69.

116. Everett, "Edward Everett to the Greek Executive Committee," case 2, box 23.

117. Howe, *Historical Sketch*; Everett, "Greek Revolution," *North American Review*, (July 1829), 142.

118. Everett was very much involved in the preliminary conversations concerning whether an American agent should be sent to Greece. Several congressmen and advisers to the president sup-

ported Everett's appointment. John Quincy Adams, however, had already sent an American secret agent to the Ottoman Empire to negotiate improved commercial relations in the Levant.

119. St. Clair, *That Greece Might Still Be Free*, 334–35.

4. Philhellenes Clash with American Commerce

1. Strangford had managed to establish a relationship with Sadik Efendi such that Ottoman officials working under him more or less served the interests of the British embassy. Ilicak, "Radical Rethinking of Empire," 25; and Heraclides and Dialla, "Intervention in the Greek War," 111–12.

2. Viscount Strangford to George Canning, September 7, 1823, FO 78/116, 2–3, in British Foreign Office: Viscount Strangford.

3. See Field, *America and the Mediterranean World*, vii.

4. See Anderson, *History of the Missions*; American Board of Commissioners for Foreign Missions, *Annual Report*, 1821; Conroy-Krutz, *Christian Imperialism*; and Heyrman, *American Apostles*. Both Conroy-Krutz and Heyrman provide important studies on the ABCFM in the Mediterranean.

5. Wertheimer, "Commencement Ceremonies," 36. Wertheimer examines the emerging nationalist sentiments as espoused by the poem "The Rising Glory of America," first printed in 1772 and reprinted in 1786.

6. Bass, *Freedom's Battle*; Field, *America and the Mediterranean World*; and Finnie, *Pioneers East*.

7. Thomas Paine's *Common Sense* is one example.

8. Field, *America and the Mediterranean World*, 7–24. Field examines several facets of American interest in the Atlantic World, including the expansion of self-determination among foreign societies as well as Christianity.

9. Dearborn, *Memoir on the Commerce and Navigation*, xvi.

10. Lambert, *Barbary Wars*.

11. McNeal, "Joseph Allen Smith," 69–70.

12. Morison, "Forcing the Dardanelles," 218–19. Examples of American merchants sailing under their own colors in the Black Sea are exceptional before the commercial treaty of 1830, though in the few cases that exist Russia provided assistance. British Foreign Office papers written in the 1820s reveal that the relationship between the United States and Russia continued and that Britain had concern for Russia's support of American commerce in the Black Sea. British Foreign Office: Viscount Strangford.

13. United States Congress, *House Documents*, doc. 250, p. 3.

14. United States Congress, doc. 250, p. 8.

15. United States Congress, doc. 250, p. 9; Ilicak, "Radical Rethinking of Empire," 42.

16. United States Congress, *House Documents*, doc. 250, pp. 10–11; and "Luther Bradish, Esq; American: A Letter from Gibraltar," *Connecticut Gazette*, May 23, 1821.

17. United States Congress, *House Documents*, doc. 250, p. 9. Bradish noted a Turkish piaster was worth 1/35 of a pound sterling. Larrabee, *Hellas Observed*, 50–51; and Oren, *Power, Faith, and Fantasy*, 106–7.

18. United States Congress, *House Documents*, doc. 250, p. 12.

19. Aksan, *Ottoman Wars*, 288; Ilicak, "Radical Rethinking of Empire," 240–43; and Oren, *Power, Faith, and Fantasy*, 107.

20. Field, *America and the Mediterranean World*, 127.

21. Field, 133.

22. Wolff, *Travels and Adventures*, 115.

23. Larrabee, *Hellas Observed*, 68.

24. Harvard University, *Historical Register*, 70–71.

25. English, *The Grounds of Christianity Examined*, 175.

26. Everett, *Defence of Christianity*, vii, xii.

27. Larrabee, *Hellas Observed*, 29; and First Church Cambridge, *Records of the Church of Christ*, 394.

28. English, *Letter to the Reverend Mr. Cary*, 8. *Nolens volens* means "like it or not."

29. "George Bethune English Harvard University," in *Harvard University Biographical Files*.

30. George Bethune English to John Thornton Kirkland, May 25, 1825, in Harvard University, "Harvard College Papers," vol. 11, item 148; and English, *Narrative of the Expedition to Donogola*.

31. Larrabee, *Hellas Observed*, 45.

32. Luther Bradish to John Quincy Adams, December 20, 1820, in United States Congress, *House Documents*, doc. 250, p. 7.

33. Luther Bradish to John Quincy Adams, December 20, 1820, in United States Congress, *House Documents*, doc. 250, p. 7.

34. Adams and Adams, *Memoirs of John Quincy Adams*, 6:172–73.

35. George Bethune English to John Quincy Adams, December 30, 1825, in Adams Family Papers, reel 473.

36. George Bethune English to John Quincy Adams, March 26, 1823, in Adams Family Papers, reel 459.

37. George Bethune English to John Quincy Adams, March 26, 1823, in Adams Family Papers, reel 459.

38. United States Congress, *House Documents*, doc. 250, p. 13.

39. George Bethune English to John Quincy Adams, December 27, 1823, in Adams Family Papers, reel 463.

40. United States Congress, *House Documents*, doc. 250, p. 14.

41. United States Congress, doc. 250, pp. 15–16.

42. United States Congress, doc. 250, p. 15.

43. United States Congress, doc. 250, p. 42; and Oren, *Power, Faith, and Fantasy*, 111–12.

44. The European ambassador whom the kapudan pasha refused to name was most likely Lord Strangford of Britain. United States Congress, *House Documents*, doc. 250, p. 15.

45. United States Congress, doc. 250, p. 16.

46. George Bethune English to John Quincy Adams, May 14, 1824, in Adams Family Papers, reel 464.

47. Walther, *Sacred Interests*, 47.

48. Adams and Adams, *Memoirs of John Quincy Adams*, 6:227.

49. Field, *America and the Mediterranean World*, 147. Field notes this practice of marking letters as "secret and confidential." It does seem to have been isolated to letters on the subject of the treaty and was not used in regard to other matters of state.

50. George Bethune English to John Quincy Adams, August 31, 1824, in Adams Family Papers, reel 465.

51. George Bethune English to James Monroe, August 11, 1824, in Adams Family Papers, reel 465.

52. "Norfolk Herald," *City Gazette and Commercial Daily Advertiser*, August 17, 1826. This is one of many examples of newspaper reports of incidents of piracy committed by Greek vessels against European ships.

53. "Smyrna, 19th May, 1825," *City Gazette and Commercial Daily Advertiser*, September 3, 1825.

54. "Greek Pirates," *Columbian Centinel*, December 17, 1825.

55. Quoted in Field, *America and the Mediterranean World*, 127.

56. Stratford Canning to George Canning, April 28, 1826, FO 78/142, 20–21, in British Foreign Office, Stratford Canning.

57. John Quincy Adams, "Message, Fellow Citizens of the Senate, and of the House of Representatives," *Richmond Enquirer*, December 8, 1825.

58. American papers printed numerous reports on the role of Greek revolutionaries such as Bouboulina, a Greek naval commander, and General Odysseus, who led the Greeks to victory on several occasions and more than likely attracted philhellenic interest because of his name. Odysseus was of particular interest: regular reports and stories were printed about him in American newspapers beginning in November 1821 until several years after his death in 1825. "Miscellany: Bobolina," *Alexandria Gazette*, April 28, 1825; "Greek Proclamation," *Washington Gazette*, November 12, 1821; and "The Following Is a Portrait of the Famous Ulysses of Modern Greece," *Eastern Argus*, October 10, 1828; George Bethune English to John Quincy Adams, August 30, 1825, in Adams Family Papers, reel 471; see also Petropulos, "Revolutionary Period."

59. George Bethune English to John Quincy Adams, December 30, 1825, in Adams Family Papers, reel 473.

60. Field, *America and the Mediterranean World*, 68; see also Heyrman, *American Apostles*; Verney, "Eye for Prices."

61. American Board of Commissioners for Foreign Missions, *Missionary Herald*, vol. 16, 266.

62. Bond, *Memoir of the Rev. Pliny Fisk*, 150.

63. Bond, 155.

64. Quoted in Heyrman, *American Apostles*, 141–42.

65. Bond, *Memoir of the Rev. Pliny Fisk*, 168–83. Fisk's printed correspondence provides details of Parsons's health after his residence in Jerusalem.

66. Field, *America and the Mediterranean World*, 94; and Obenzinger, "Holy Land Narrative," 257.

67. Bond, *Memoir of the Rev. Pliny Fisk*, 412.

68. American Board of Commissioners for Foreign Missions, *Missionary Herald*, vol. 19, 114.

69. American Board of Commissioners for Foreign Missions, *Missionary Herald*, vol. 17, 2; see also Conroy-Krutz, *Christian Imperialism*, 37–38.

70. Fisk states this repeatedly in his letters and reports to the board. American Board of Commissioners for Foreign Missions, *Missionary Herald*, vol. 19, 113.

71. American Board of Commissioners for Foreign Missions, 112.

72. Hodge, *Photius Fisk*, 17.

73. Hodge, 21–22.

74. Hodge, *Photius Fisk*, 152.

75. American Board of Commissioners for Foreign Missions, *Missionary Herald*, vol. 19, 113.

76. Moskos, *Greek Americans*, 6; American Board of Commissioners for Foreign Missions, *Annual Report*, 1826, 99.

77. American Board of Commissioners for Foreign Missions, *Missionary Herald*, vol. 19, 114.

78. Castanis, *Greek Exile*, 109.

79. Castanis, 211.

80. Field, *America and the Mediterranean World*, 104.

81. Field, 113; and *General View of the Rise*, 399–401.

82. United States Congress, *House Documents*, vol. 6, doc. 250, pp. 19–20.

83. John Quincy Adams to George Bethune English, January 3, 1825, in Adams Family Papers, reel 467.

84. John H. Schroeder, *Commodore John Rodgers*.

85. George Bethune English to John Quincy Adams, August 30, 1825, in Adams Family Papers, reel 471.

86. Adams and Adams, *Memoirs of John Quincy Adams*, 482; Larrabee, *Hellas Observed*, 136; and P. Pappas, "United States and the Greek War," 177. Newspapers reported on Evans' travels and

association with the Greek Committee of Boston; see "We understand that Mr. Estwick Evans," *Salem Gazette*, April 1, 1825.

87. Quoted in Larrabee, *Hellas Observed*, 135; and "Estwick Evans, Esq; Portsmouth; Greece," *New Hampshire Patriot and State Gazette*, April 18, 1825.

88. Howe, *Letters and Journals*, 87.

89. "The U.S. ship *North-Carolina*," *New-Hampshire Gazette*, April 5, 1825.

90. Henry Clay to William C. Somerville, September 6, 1825, in Clay, *Papers of Henry Clay*, 624.

91. P. Pappas, "United States and the Greek War," 182.

92. George Bethune English to John Quincy Adams, August 30, 1825, in Adams Family Papers, reel 471.

93. Stratford Canning to George Canning, April 28, and June 10, 1826, FO 78/142, 20–21, 285–86, in British Foreign Office, Stratford Canning. These are a few examples of reports of the British Foreign Office on Greek piracy issues.

94. George Bethune English to John Quincy Adams, August 30, 1825, in Adams Family Papers, reel 471.

95. William Turner to George Canning, August 25, 1825, FO 78/132, 63–65, in British Foreign Office, William Turner.

96. Commodore Rodgers to Henry Clay, August 31, 1825, in United States Congress, *House Documents*, doc. 250, p. 41.

97. United States Congress, *House Documents*, doc. 250, p. 42.

98. United States Congress, doc. 250, p. 45.

99. Commodore John Rodgers to the Koca Husrev Mehemd Pasha, September 20, 1825, in United States Congress, *House Documents*, doc. 250, p. 43.

100. Commodore Rodgers to Henry Clay, July 19, 1826, in United States Congress, *House Documents*, doc. 250, p. 48.

101. Commodore Rodgers to Henry Clay, July 19, 1826, in United States Congress, *House Documents*, doc. 250, pp. 48, 49, 50. The term *grand seignor* was often used instead of *sultan*.

102. Extracts of a letter from Commodore Rodgers to Henry Clay, United States Congress, *House Documents*, doc. 250, pp. 50–51. The Greek frigate controversy dominated newspaper headlines, and several pamphlets were printed on the subject. "Papers in Relation to the Greek Ship *Liberator*," in *American State Papers*, Naval Affairs, 2:746–48; Contostavlos, *Narrative of the Material Facts*; Platt, Ogden, and De Rham, *Report of the Evidence*; Sedgwick, *Refutation of the Reasons*; "The Concern of the People of the United States for the Greek Cause," *National Gazette and Literary Register*, October 19, 1826; and "Greek Meeting," *New York Spectator*, October 31, 1826.

103. Quoted in Larrabee, *Hellas Observed*, 85.

104. Commodore Rodgers to Henry Clay, February 14, 1827, in United States Congress, *House Documents*, doc. 250, pp. 50–51.

105. Commodore Rodgers to Henry Clay, February 14, 1827, 51.

106. "Relief of the Greeks," *American Mercury*, March 11, 1828.

107. Larrabee, *Hellas Observed*, 149. A chart illustrates the extent of public interest in sending food and supplies to Greek civilians; eight ships left the United States for Greece.

108. Ilicak, "Radical Rethinking of Empire," 282; Philliou, *Biography of an Empire*, 99, 131.

109. Adams and Adams, *Memoirs of John Quincy Adams*, 463.

110. Post, *Visit to Greece*, 259; and Larrabee, *Hellas Observed*, 162–63.

111. Dispatch from William Shaler to Henry Clay, June 4, 1825, in Clay, *Papers of Henry Clay*, 415.

112. Henry Clay to William C. Somerville, September 6, 1825, in Clay, *Papers of Henry Clay*, 625.

113. British Foreign Office, *British and Foreign State Papers*, 365.

114. United States Congress, *House Documents*, doc. 250, Executive, p. 9.

115. Pertev was described as a hard-liner on Ottoman policy. According to Charles Rhind, he did not hold favorable feelings toward the United States. See United States Congress, *House Documents*, doc. 250, 82–83; Heraclides and Dialla, "Intervention in the Greek War," 115; and Richmond, *Voice of England*, 166.

116. United States Congress, *House Documents*, doc. 250, Executive, p. 13.

117. *Treaty between the United States of America and the Ottoman Empire*; British Foreign Office, *British and Foreign State Papers*, 374. Pertib is the name given by Charles Rhind in a letter to President Andrew Jackson, but the correct name is Pertev. Oren, *Power, Faith, and Fantasy*, 114–15; and Philliou, *Biography of an Empire*, 227–28n28.

118. Dearborn, *Memoir on the Commerce*, 1:xv–xvi.

5. Abolitionism, Reform, and Philhellenic Rhetoric

1. John Smith the Younger, "New York Correspondence: Power's [*sic*]Statue of the *Greek Slave*," *National Era*, September 2, 1847.

2. Marr, *Cultural Roots of American Islamicism*, 273. Reports in New Orleans alone estimate 100,000 paying viewers of the statue. Green, "Hiram Powers's 'Greek Slave'; see also Richard, *Golden Age of the Classics*, 167; and Winterer, *Mirror of Antiquity*, 165.

3. Sumner, *White Slavery*, 11.

4. See Repousis, "'Trojan Women.'"

5. Dallas, "Philadelphia, Jan. 5, 1824."

6. N. Webster, *Effects of Slavery*, 8.

7. See also Allison, *Crescent Obscured*, 57–58.

8. For additional analysis of captivity tales and Franklin's *Federal Gazette* article, see Egan, *Oriental Shadows*, 84; Allison, *Crescent Obscured*, 103–6; Baepler, *White Slaves*, 8–9; and Marr, *Cultural Roots of American Islamicism*, 142.

9. Egan, *Oriental Shadows*, 83–84; and Lambert, *Barbary Wars*, 120–22.

10. Historicus, "To the Editor of the Federal Gazette," *Federal Gazette*, March 25, 1790.

11. Egan, *Oriental Shadows*, 85.

12. Mason, *Slavery and Politics*, 204–6; Morgan, *American Slavery*, 381; Peskin, *Captives and Countrymen*, 73; and Rozbicki, *Culture and Liberty*, 34–35, 48–52.

13. Foss, *Journal, of the Captivity*, 55.

14. Peskin, *Captives and Countrymen*, 77; Carey's history of Algiers also prefaced the Maria Martin captivity story published in Philadelphia in 1806. Martin, *History of the Captivity*.

15. Carey, *Short History of Algiers*, 32.

16. See Shankman, "Capitalism, Slavery, and the New Epoch"; and Shankman, "Neither Infinite Wretchedness nor Positive Good."

17. Tyler, *Algerine Captive*, 1:193.

18. Quoted in Tyler, *Algerine Captive*, 2:62; see also Spellberg, *Thomas Jefferson's Qur'an*, 37–39; and Erdem, *Slavery in the Ottoman Empire*, 2–3.

19. Peskin provides useful analysis on Royall Tyler's comparison of slavery in the American South and the Barbary States. See especially Peskin, *Captives and Countrymen*, 72; and Tyler, *Algerine Captive*, 1:213.

20. See Allison, *Crescent Obscured*, 210; Marr, *Cultural Roots of American Islamicism*, 53; and Riley, *Authentic Narrative*.

21. Riley, *Authentic Narrative*, 588.

22. Reports of the loss of the brig *Commerce* and its captain, James Riley, can be found in newspapers throughout the United States, especially in New York, Massachusetts, and Maryland, and in towns near Washington, D.C.

23. "Whereas, a Certain Book, Bearing the Title An Authentic Narrative of the American Brig *Commerce*," *National Advocate*, November 19, 1817.

24. Riley, *Authentic Narrative*, 590; Allison devotes a chapter to an analysis of James Riley and his captivity tale. See especially Allison, *Crescent Obscured*, 222–24.

25. Jared Sparks, "Riley's Narrative," *North American Review and Miscellaneous Journal*, no. 15 (September 1817), 391; see also Allison, *Crescent Obscured*, 221.

26. American Home Missionary Society, *Home Missionary and American Pastor's Journal*, 98; Greek School Committee, *Plan for Promoting*; and New-Haven Ladies' Greek Association, *First Annual Report*.

27. Castanis, *Greek Exile*, 212.

28. For further reading on American education offered in Greece, see Repousis, "'Trojan Women'"; Winterer, *Mirror of Antiquity*, 168; and Field, *America and the Mediterranean World*, vii. Field uses the phrase "secularizing missionary spirit" to describe one category of increased American presence in the Mediterranean.

29. Fitz, *Our Sister Republics*, 94, 190–91. Fitz describes how slaveholders such as Henry Clay comfortably discussed emancipation in Spanish America even in the midst of the Missouri Crisis. She also notes that by 1822 proslavery advocates such as South Carolina senator William Smith refused to vote for diplomatic recognition of Spanish America partially on the grounds of racial prejudice. The Greek cause, however, enjoyed sustained support because the Greeks were viewed as white. Sellers, *Market Revolution*, 129–31, 396–428; Shankman, "Neither Infinite Wretchedness nor Positive Good," 247–49; and Howe, *What Hath God Wrought*.

30. Hinks, *To Awaken My Afflicted Brethren*; Jeffrey, *Great Silent Army*; McDaniel, *Problem of Democracy*; and Sinha, *Slave's Cause*.

31. Shankman, "Neither Infinite Wretchedness nor Positive Good," 247–49; and Shankman, "Capitalism, Slavery, and the New Epoch," 243–45.

32. Mason, *Apostle of Union*, 7–8, 25–26, 48, 97–100; Hinks, *To Awaken My Afflicted Brethren*, 112–13; McDaniel, *Problem of Democracy*, 4, 37–47; and Sinha, *Slave's Cause*, 195–227, 247–48.

33. "People of Colour," *Freedom's Journal*, April 6, 1827.

34. "Observations on the History of the Negro Race," *Freedom's Journal*, December 12, 1828.

35. Walker, *Appeal in Four Articles*, 15.

36. Walker, 45; Hinks, *To Awaken My Afflicted Brethren*, 29–30, 172.

37. Marr, *Cultural Roots of American Islamicism*, 135.

38. Garrison and Garrison, *William Lloyd Garrison*, 57.

39. Garrison and Garrison, 63–64; McDaniel, *Problem of Democracy*, 27–28, 40.

40. Garrison and Garrison, 96–97.

41. William Lloyd Garrison, "The Insurrection," *Liberator*, September 3, 1831; and Marr, *Cultural Roots of American Islamicism*, 148.

42. Garrison, *Abolitionist*, 143.

43. "Insurrection of Slaves," *Portsmouth Journal and Rockingham Gazette*, September 24, 1831.

44. "Insurrection of Slaves."

45. "An Ordinance Has Been Passed by the Corporation of Georgetown," *Alexandria Phenix Gazette*, October 12, 1831.

46. "General Miscellany," *American Federalist Columbian Centinel*, August 20, 1825

47. "For the Centinel: Notice of Remarks on a Letter to Mr. Webster," *Columbian Centinel American Federalist*, October 22, 1825.

48. "Slavery," *Portsmouth Journal of Literature and Politics*, August 27, 1825.

49. "For the Centinel: Notice of Remarks."

50. Worcester, *Essays on Slavery*, 22; American Board of Commissioners for Foreign Missions, *Missionary Herald*, vol. 18, 234. Worcester was a missionary particularly known for his work with local Native Americans.

51. Patterson, *Sermon on the Effects*, 22.

52. See Stephanini, *Personal Narrative*.

53. Stephanini, 128.

54. Stephanini, 118. Stephanini states specifically that when he arrived in New York he was completely ignorant of the English language.

55. "A Young Greek Called Joseph Stephanini," *Vermont Gazette*, April 7, 1829.

56. Grimké, "Weld-Grimké Family Papers 1740–1930"; and American Colonization Society, *Annual Report*, 51 and 55. Grimké is listed as having contributed money to the American Colonization Society and was made a Life Member.

57. Stephanini, *Personal Narrative*.

58. Stephanini's departure from the United States was reported in local newspapers, for example, "Sailed This Morning Ship Six Brothers," *Baltimore Patriot and Mercantile Advertiser*, October 27, 1829.

59. Hodge, *Photius Fisk*, 13.

60. Hodge, 56–57.

61. Hodge, 13.

62. Hodge, 116–17.

63. Burgess, *Greeks in America*, 198.

64. Burgess, 200.

65. Zachos would have been a household name throughout the 1850s and 1860s, as his readers were advertised everywhere from Connecticut to Texas to California.

66. Zachos, *Appeal to the Friends of Education*, 7; Butchart, *Schooling the Freed People*, 237n84.

67. "News from South Carolina: Negro Jubilee at Hilton Head," *New York Herald*, January 7, 1863.

68. Jeffrey, *Great Silent Army*, 18; see also Hansen, *Very Social Time*.

69. Kelley, *Learning to Stand and Speak*. Kelley's work specifically addresses this topic.

70. Nash, "Rethinking Republican Motherhood," 177–78.

71. Kelley, *Learning to Stand and Speak*, 47; and Wollstonecraft, *Vindication of the Rights*, 20.

72. Kelley, 28.

73. Kelley, 29.

74. Hewitt, *Women's Activism*, 34–35.

75. "Domestic," *Western Recorder*, February 20, 1827.

76. Santelli, "'Depart from That Retired Circle.'" This article more specifically addresses the role of benevolent societies, how they came to be involved in the philhellenic movement, and the ways in which female involvement marked a moment of brief unity in reform.

77. Willard, *Address to the Public*, 5 and 7.

78. Repousis, "'Trojan Women,'" 447.

79. Willard and Troy Society, *Advancement of Female Education*, 4.

80. Willard and Troy Society, 9.

81. Repousis, "'Trojan Women,'" 461. Repousis makes the interesting connection between Willard's advocacy of education and nineteenth-century foreign affairs and imperialism.

82. "Education in Greece," *Episcopal Recorder*, December 10, 1831, 146.

83. "Female Education in Greece," *Ladies' Magazine and Literary Gazette*, September 1833, 424.

84. Religious Intelligencer, "New Haven Ladies' Greek Association," *Philadelphia Recorder*, May 22, 1830, 32; American Board of Commissioners for Foreign Missions, *Missionary Herald*, vol. 91, 91–92.

85. "Education in Greece," 146.

86. Greek School Committee, *Plan for Promoting*, 6; and Makdisi, *Artillery of Heaven*, 3. Although Makdisi's analysis focuses on missionaries, in many cases attempts to build schools in Greece were joint efforts with missionaries. Both groups articulated the notion that the Greeks would only benefit from the superior presence of American educators. Walther, *Sacred Interests*, 23. Walther also argues that missionaries intended to reform the Ottoman Empire in America's image, just as missionaries and education reformers hoped to do in Greece.

87. "The Experiment," *American Ladies' Magazine*, October 1834, 460.

88. "The Experiment," *American Ladies' Magazine*, October 1834, 457; and Repousis, "'Trojan Women,'" 463–64.

89. Phelps, *Address on the Subject*, 18.

90. Phelps, *Address on the Subject*, 18–19.

91. Phelps, *Lectures to Young Ladies*, 39.

92. Phelps, 39.

93. Phelps and Troy Society, *Address on the Subject*, 7.

94. Willard and Troy Society, *Advancement of Female Education*, 9.

95. Kellogg, *Powers' Statue*, 4.

96. Powers subtly indicated the religious identity of his subject by including a cross and locket necklaces near the Greek maiden's manacled hands.

97. Various articles and their places of publication illustrate the national interest in Powers's statue: "The Greek Slave," *Milwaukee Daily Sentinel*, November 8, 1850; "Powers' Greek Slave," *Vermont Watchman*, August 15, 1850; and "Powers' Greek Slave," *Mississippi Free Trader and Natchez Gazette*, March 22, 1851.

98. Quoted in Green, "Hiram Powers's 'Greek Slave,'" 32; see also "The Abolitionists Disclaim the 'Greek Slave' as Too White for Their Philanthropy," *Liberator*, October 22, 1847.

99. Dewey, "Powers's Statues," *Alexandria Gazette*, October 6, 1847.

100. Green, "Hiram Powers's 'Greek Slave,'" 34.

101. "The Greek Slave," *North Star*, October 3, 1850.

102. "The Greek Slave," *Christian Inquirer*, October 9, 1847, 207.

103. Smith the Younger, "New York Correspondence," 3.

104. Erdem, *Slavery in the Ottoman Empire*, 94–112; and Ehud R. Toledano, "Late Ottoman Concepts."

105. *Eastport Sentinel* (August 23, 1848), quoted in Green, "Hiram Powers's 'Greek Slave,'" 38; see also Marr, *Cultural Roots of American Islamicism*, 279–80.

106. "Powers' Slave," *Georgia Telegraph*, October 12, 1847.

107. "Powers' Greek Slave," *Mississippi Free Trader and Natchez Gazette*, March 22, 1851.

108. News reports on fund-raising for the citizens of New Orleans were printed in both Northern and Southern papers. For example, "Mr. Kellogg, the Friend of Mr. Powers and Who Has Charge of That Gentleman's Noble Statue of the *Greek Slave* . . . ," *Morning News*, October 1, 1847; and "News of the Day . . . The Proceeds of the Exhibition of Powers' *Greek Slave*," *Alexandria Gazette*, September 29, 1847.

109. "Powers's Greek Slave in St. Louis," *National Era*, January 16, 1851.

110. Walther, *Sacred Interests*, 35–36; W. J. Cooper, *Liberty and Slavery*, 178–80; and Mason, *Slavery and Politics*, 172–73.

111. Green, "Hiram Powers's 'Greek Slave,'" 37; Culkin, *Harriet Hosmer*, 59–60; and Manganelli, *Transatlantic Spectacles of Race*, 71.

112. "Fugitive Negroes at World's Fair," *Alexandria Gazette*, July 30, 1851.

113. "British Anti Slavery Society," *New York Observer and Chronicle*, August 14, 1851.

114. Mason, *Slavery and Politics*, 222–23. Mason's chapter "Antebellum Legacies" examines how the slave question continued to dominate antebellum politics from its origins in the early republic.

115. Sanchez-Eppler, "Bodily Bonds," 374–76. Sanchez-Eppler describes the legal status of women of the nineteenth century as being predicated on contemporary understandings of biology: "Medical treatises of the period consistently assert that a woman's psyche and intellect are determined by her reproductive organs."

116. Sanchez-Eppler, 375–76.

117. Kerr, *Lucy Stone*, 51–52; and "Mrs. Lucy Stone Blackwell Dead," *New York Times*, October 19, 1893. Stone's obituary links her adoption of women's rights as part of her reform interests to her viewing of Powers's *Greek Slave*. McMillen, *Seneca Falls*, 81.

118. Kerr, *Lucy Stone*, 52.

119. Alicia Faxon, "Images of Women in the Sculpture of Harriet Hosmer," *Woman's Art Journal* 2, no. 1 (April 1, 1981): 26.

120. Lydia Maria Child to S. B. Shaw, 1852, in Whittier et al., *Letters of Lydia Maria Child*, 68.

121. Culkin, *Harriet Hosmer*, 55–82; and "Miss Harriet Hosmer," *Frank Leslie's Illustrated Newspaper*, November 7, 1857. This article is one of many examples referencing Lydia Maria Child as a close friend and supporter of Hosmer. Child, "Miss Harriet Hosmer," *Liberator*, November 20, 1857, is an example showing that Lydia Maria Child wrote articles in newspapers praising Hosmer as an artist.

122. Elizabeth Barrett Browning, *Poetical Works* (New York: Macmillan, 1897), 293. Prins, "Classics for Victorians," 52.

123. Culkin, *Harriet Hosmer*, 60.

124. Harriet Hosmer to Lydia Maria Child, August 26, 1859, quoted in Culkin, *Harriet Hosmer*, 58.

125. Lydia Maria Child, "Miss Hosmer's Zenobia," *Lady's Home Magazine*, December 1859, 294.

126. Gage, "'Masculine Women,'" *Liberator*, January 15, 1858, 12.

127. Culkin, *Harriet Hosmer*, 57. Culkin explains that portraying a woman in chains and begging for liberty was initially an abolitionist icon, but women's rights advocates endeavored to alter this image to portray women as confident and strong. Sanchez-Eppler, "Bodily Bonds," 377–78. Sanchez-Eppler describes the attempts of women's rights advocates to command a stronger sense of personhood.

128. Marr, *Cultural Roots of American Islamicism*, 282; and Jirousek, "Ottoman Influences in Western Dress," 243.

129. "The Bloomer Costume," *Hinds County Gazette*, June 19, 1851. Gaiters were protective coverings placed over the shoes.

130. Marr, *Cultural Roots of American Islamicism*, 282–83; Faroqhi and Neumann, *Ottoman Costumes*, 243; and Elizabeth C. Stanton, "The Bloomer Costume," *Liberator*, May 21, 1852.

131. Berman, *American Arabesque*, 200.

132. Kietzman, "Montagu's Turkish Embassy Letters," 539.

133. Jirousek, "Ottoman Influences in Western Dress," 243.

134. Child, *Juvenile Miscellany*, series three, vol. v., (1833): 310–12; and Marr, *Cultural Roots of American Islamicism*, 12–13.

135. Patient of the Water-Cure, "Springfield Bloomer Celebration," 83.

136. "Siftings from Exchanges, with Editorial Sprinklings," *Semi-Weekly Eagle*, June 12, 1851.

137. "In the Hartford (Conn.) Procession on the 4th of July There Were to Be Thirty-One Young Ladies in the Bloomer Costume, to Represent the Several States of the Union," *Boston Daily Atlas*, July 7, 1851.

138. Stanton, "Bloomer Costume."

139. Stanton et al., *History of Woman Suffrage*, 471.

140. Stanton et al., 470.

141. Stanton et al., 71.

Conclusion

1. Trent, *Manliest Man*, 207–9.

2. Howe, *Letters and Journals*, xi.

3. Post, *Visit to Greece*, 236–39.

4. Hall, "Emma Willard," 17–18; and Repousis, "'Trojan Women.'"

5. *Treaty between the United States of America and the Ottoman Empire*. The specifics of the treaty were finalized between the United States and the Sublime Porte in 1830. The treaty was ratified in the Senate in October 1831 and proclaimed by President Andrew Jackson in February 1832.

6. Sumner, *White Slavery*, 12.

7. Stanton et al., *History of Woman Suffrage*, 14.

Bibliography

Published and Archival Primary Sources

Adams Family Papers. Microfilm, Massachusetts Historical Society.

Adams, John Quincy, and Charles Francis Adams. *Memoirs of John Quincy Adams, Comprising Portions of His Diary from 1795 to 1848.* Vol. 6. Philadelphia: J. B. Lippincott and Co., 1874.

——. *Memoirs of John Quincy Adams, Comprising Portions of His Diary from 1795 to 1848.* Vol. 7. Philadelphia: J. B. Lippincott and Co., 1874.

American Board of Commissioners for Foreign Missions. *Annual Report: American Board of Commissioners for Foreign Missions,* 1826.

——. *Annual Report of the American Board of Commissioners for Foreign Missions.* 1821.

——. *The Missionary Herald.* Vol. 16. Boston: Crocker and Brewster, 1820.

——. *The Missionary Herald.* Vol. 18. Boston: Crocker and Brewster, 1821.

——. *The Missionary Herald.* Vol. 19. Boston: Crocker and Brewster, 1823.

——. *The Missionary Herald.* Vol. 91. Boston: Crocker and Brewster, 1895.

American Colonization Society. *Annual Report of the American Colonization Society.* 1845.

American Home Missionary Society. *Home Missionary and American Pastor's Journal.* Vol. 4, 1831.

American Plays Printed 1714–1830: A Bibliographical Record. Stanford, CA: Stanford University Press, 1934.

American State Papers: Foreign Relations. Vol. 5. Washington, D.C.: Gales and Seaton, 1823–1832.

American State Papers: Naval Affairs. Vol. 2. Washington, D.C.: Gales and Seaton, 1860.

Anderson, Rufus. *History of the Missions of the American Board of Commissioners for Foreign Missions to the Oriental Churches.* 1872.

Annals of Congress. 17th Congress, 2nd session. Vol. 40. Washington, D.C.: Gales and Seaton, 1855.

Annals of Congress. 18th Congress, 1st Session. Vol. 41. Washington, D.C.: Gales and Seaton, 1856.

The Arabian Nights' Entertainments. Vol. 2. Hartford, CT: Bowles and Francis printers, 1822.

Barker, Henry Aston, Robert Burford, et al., eds. *Description of the View of Athens, and Surrounding Country.* Boston: Press of W. W. Clapp, 1837.

Barrell, George. *Letters from Asia.* New York: A. T. Goodrich and Co., 1819.

Bedell, Gregory T. *The Cause of the Greeks: A Sermon Preached in St. Andrew's Church, Philadelphia, on the Occasion of a Collection for the Greek Fund: Jan. 18, 1824.* Philadelphia,1824.

Bickerstaff, Isaac. *The Sultan; or, A Peep into the Seraglio: A Comedy.* New York: D. Longworth, 1812.

Biddle, Nicholas. *Nicholas Biddle in Greece: The Journals and Letters of 1806.* Edited by R. A. McNeal. University Park: Pennsylvania State University Press, 2010.

Bingham, Caleb. *The Columbian Orator.* Hartford, CT: Lincoln and Gleason, 1807.

Bond, Alvan. *Memoir of the Rev. Pliny Fisk, A. M.: Late Missionary to Palestine, from the American Board of Missions.* Boston: Crocker and Brewster, 1829.

Brackenridge, Hugh Henry. *Modern Chivalry: Containing the Adventures of Captain John Farrago and Teague O'Reagan, His Servant.* Lanham, MD: Rowman and Littlefield, 2003.

British Foreign Office, Stratford Canning. FO 78/142. National Archives, Kew.

British Foreign Office, Viscount Strangford. FO 78/116. National Archives, Kew.

British Foreign Office, William Turner. FO 78/132. National Archives, Kew.

British Foreign Office. *British and Foreign State Papers.* Vol. 19. H. M. Stationery Office, 1834.

Browning, Elizabeth Barrett. *Poetical Works of Elizabeth Barrett Browning.* New York: Macmillan, 1897.

Bryant, William Cullen. "The Song of the Greek Amazon." *United States Literary Gazette,* 1824.

Bryant, William Cullen, and Elam Ives Jr. "Song of the Greek Amazon." Philadelphia: John F. Nunns. Library Company of Philadelphia.

Byron, George Gordon. *Childe Harold's Pilgrimage; a Romaunt and Other Poems.* London: Printed by T. Davison for J. Murray, 1812.

Carey, Mathew. *A Short History of Algiers, with a Concise View of the Origin of the Rupture between Algiers and the United States.* New York: Evert Duyckinck, 1805.

Castanis, Christophoros Plato. *The Greek Exile.* Philadelphia: Lippincott, Grambo, and Co., 1851.

Clay, Henry. *The Papers of Henry Clay: Secretary of State 1825.* Vol. 4. Lexington: University Press of Kentucky, 1972.

Committee for the Relief of the Greeks. *Address of the Committee Appointed at a Public Meeting Held in Boston, December 19, 1823, for the Relief of the Greeks, to Their Fellow Citizens.* Boston: Press of the North American Review, 1823.

Contostavlos, Alexander. *A Narrative of the Material Facts in Relation to the Building of the Two Greek Frigates*. New York: s.n., 1826.

Cunningham, Noble E., and Dorothy Hagberg Cappel, eds. *Circular Letters of Congressmen to Their Constituents, 1789–1829*. Vol. 3. Chapel Hill: Published for the Institute of Early American History and Culture, Williamsburg, Virginia., by the University of North Carolina Press, 1978.

Dallas, George Mifflin. "Philadelphia, Jan. 5, 1824: Madam,—We Take the Liberty, on Behalf of the Committee of the Greek Fund," January 5, 1824.

Dearborn, Henry A. S. *A Memoir on the Commerce and Navigation of the Black Sea: And the Trade and Maritime Geography of Turkey and Egypt: In Two Volumes: Illustrated with Charts*. 2 vols. Boston: Wells and Lilly, 1819.

Dexter, Franklin Bowditch. *Biographical Sketches of the Graduates of Yale College with Annals of the College History*. Vol. 5. New York: Henry Holt and Company, 1911.

Dreer, Ferdinand. "Ferdinand J. Dreer Autograph Collection 0175." Historical Society of Pennsylvania.

Drowne, Solomon. *An Oration, Delivered in the First Baptist Meeting-House, in Providence, at the Celebration, February 23, A.D. 1824, in Commemoration of the Birth-Day of Washington, and in Aid of the Cause of the Greeks*. Providence, RI: Brown and Danforth, printers, 1824. Duer, John, and Robert Sedgwick. *An Examination of the Controversy between the Greek Deputies and Two Mercantile Houses of New York: Together with a Review of the Publications on the Subject, by the Arbitrators, Messrs. Emmet and Ogden, and Mr. William Bayard*. New York: J. Seymour, 1826.

Durbin, John P. *The Substance of a Sermon in Favour of Aiding the Greeks in Their Present Contest with the Ottoman Power: Delivered in the Presbyterian Church at Lebanon, Ohio, February 22d, 1824, at the Special Request of a Committee*. Cincinnati: Looker and Reynolds, printers, 1824.

Dwight, Sereno Edwards. *The Greek Revolution: An Addresses, Delivered in Park Street Church, Boston, Thursday, April 1, and Repeated at the Request of the Greek Committee, in the Old South Church, on the Evening of April 14, 1824*. Boston: Crocker and Brewster, 1824.

Elliot, Jonathan. *The American Diplomatic Code, Embracing a Collection of Treaties and Conventions between the United States and Foreign Powers: From 1778 to 1834*. 2 vols. Washington, DC: Jonathan Elliot, Jr., 1834.

English, George Bethune. *A Letter to the Reverend Mr. Cary: Containing Remarks upon His Review of the Grounds of Christianity Examined, by Comparing the New Testament with the Old*. Boston: Printed for the author, 1813.

——. *A Narrative of the Expedition to Donogola and Sennaar, under the Command of His Excellence Ismael Pasha, Undertaken by Order of His Highness Mehemmed Ali Pasha, Viceroy of Egypt*. London: John Murray, 1822.

Everett, Edward. "The Cause of the Greeks." *Rhode-Island American and Providence Gazette*, December 15, 1826.

——. *A Defence of Christianity, against the Work of George B. English, A. M., Entitled The Grounds of Christianity Examined, by Comparing the New Testament with the Old*. Boston: Cummings and Hilliard, 1814.

——. "Edward Everett to the Greek Executive Committee of New York," February 4, 1827. Gratz Collection. Historical Society of Pennsylvania.

First Church Cambridge. *Records of the Church of Christ at Cambridge in New England: 1632–1830, Comprising the Ministerial Records of Baptisms, Marriages, Deaths, Admission to Covenant and Communion, Dismissals and Church Proceedings.* Boston: E. Putnam, 1906.

Foss, John. *A Journal, of the Captivity and Sufferings of John Foss; Several Years a Prisoner at Algiers.* Newburyport, MA: A. March, Middle-Street, 1798.

Garrison, Wendell Phillips, and Francis Jackson Garrison. *William Lloyd Garrison, 1805–1879: The Story of His Life Told by His Children.* Vol. 1. New York: Century Co., 1885.

Garrison, William Lloyd. *Abolitionist, or Record of the New England Anti-Slavery Society.* Boston: Garrison and Knapp, 1833.

A General View of the Rise, Progress, and Brilliant Achievements of the American Navy. Brooklyn, NY, 1828.

Goldsmith, Oliver. *The Grecian History.* 2 vols. London: G. Woodfall, 1800.

Grecian Ladies. *The Grecian Wreath of Victory.* New York: Printed and published by W. E. Dean, 1824.

Greek Committee of New York. *Circular—New-York, December 12, 1823.* New York: s.n., 1823.

——. *(Circular.) New-York, March 6, 1828. Rev. Sir, The Committee Lately Appointed by a Large and Respectable Meeting of Our Citizens to Raise Supplies for the Suffering Greek.* New York: s.n., 1828.

Greek Committee of Philadelphia. *The Cause of the Greeks.* Philadelphia: Mathew Carey, 1827.

——. *Philadelphia, January 31, 1827: Sir, The Subscribers . . .* Philadelphia, s.n., 1827.

——. *Philadelphia, April 2, 1827: Sir, Instructed by a Resolution of a Large and Respectable Meeting of the Citizens of the City and County of Philadelphia.* Philadelphia: s.n., 1827.

——. *Philadelphia, April 3, 1827: Address to the Humane and Charitable Citizens of the United States: Fellow Citizens, It Is Now Three Years since You Were Addressed on the Subject of the Sufferings of Your Brethren of Greece.* Philadelphia: s.n., 1827.

——. *Philadelphia, March 27, 1827: Sir, Presuming That, with the Great Mass of Citizens of the State, You Sympathize with the Oppressed Greek Nation.* Philadelphia: s.n., 1827.

——. *Philadelphia, March 27, 1827: Sir, We Respectfully Inform You, That an Excellent Brig . . . Has Actually Sailed . . . for Greece, with Provisions, Clothing, and Medicines.* Philadelphia: s.n., 1827.

——. *Sir, the Annexed Resolution and the Appended Papers . . .* Philadelphia: s.n., 1827.

Greek School Committee. *Plan for Promoting Common School Education in Greece: Adopted by the Greek School Committee, New-York, May, 1829.* New York: s.n., 1829.

Grimké. "Weld-Grimké Family Papers 1740–1930." William L. Clements Library, University of Michigan.

Harvard University. "Harvard College Papers, 1st Series, 1636–1825, 1831," Courtesy of the Harvard University Archives.

Harvard University. *Historical Register of Harvard University, 1636–1936.* Cambridge, MA: Harvard University, 1937.

Harvard University Biographical Files, ca. 1700–. Courtesy of the Harvard University Archives.

Hodge, Lyman F. *Photius Fisk: A Biography.* Boston, 1891.

Howe, Samuel Gridley. *An Historical Sketch of the Greek Revolution.* New York: White, Gallaher and White, 1828.

———. *Letters and Journals of Samuel Gridley Howe.* Edited by Franklin Benjamin Sanborn. Vol. 1. Boston: D. Estes and Company, 1906.

Humphreys, David. *Life of General Washington.* Edited by Rosemarie Zagarri. Reprint edition. Athens: University of Georgia Press, 2006.

Jefferson, Thomas. *Notes on the State of Virginia.* Chapel Hill, NC: Omohundro Institute and University of North Carolina Press, 1996.

———. *The Papers of Thomas Jefferson Digital Edition.* Charlottesville: University of Virginia Press, 2009.

Kellogg, Miner K. *Powers' Statue of the Greek Slave.* Boston: Eastburn's Press, 1848.

Lyman, Theodore. *The Diplomacy of the United States: Being an Account of the Foreign Relations of the Country, from the First Treaty with France, in 1778, to the Present Time.* Vol. 2. Boston: Wells and Lilly, 1828.

Madison, James. "Message from the President of the United States, Transmitting a Treaty of Peace between the United States and the Dey of Algiers." Washington, DC: William A. Davis, 1815.

Martin, Maria. *History of the Captivity and Sufferings of Mrs. Maria Martin Who Was Six Years a Slave in Algiers, Two of Which She Was Confined in a Dark and Dismal Dungeon, Loaded with Irons.* Boston: W. Crary, 1806.

Meredith Family Papers 1756–1964. Series 3. Historical Society of Pennsylvania, Philadelphia.

Miller, Jonathan Peckham. *The Condition of Greece, in 1827 and 1828; Being an Exposition of the Poverty, Distress, and Misery, to Which the Inhabitants Have Been Reduced by the Destruction of Their Towns and Villages and the Ravages of Their Country, by a Merciless Turkish Foe.* New York: J. and J. Harper, 1828.

———. *Letters from Greece.* Boston: Crocker and Brewster, 1825.

Newbold, George. "George Newbold Papers, 1801–1858. Greek Committee Records." New York Historical Society.

New-Haven Ladies' Greek Association. *First Annual Report of the New-Haven Ladies' Greek Association.* New Haven, CT: Printed by Nathan Whiting, 1831.

Nott, Josiah Clark, George R. Gliddon et al. *Types of Mankind.* Philadelphia: Lippincott, Grambo and Co., 1854.

Offley Family Papers, Special Collections Research Center, William & Mary Libraries.

Patient of the Water-Cure. "Springfield Bloomer Celebration." *Water-Cure Journal (1845–1861),* October 1851.

Patterson, James. *Sermon on the Effects of the Hebrew Slavery as Connected with Slavery in This Country: Preached in the 7th Presbyterian Church in the City of Philadelphia.* Philadelphia: S. Probasco, 1825.

Percival, James Gates. *Poems by James G. Percival.* New Haven, CT: A. H. Maltby and Co., printers, 1821.

——. *Clio No. III*. New York: G. and C. Carvill, 1827.

Periclean Society of Alexandria, Virginia, 1821–1824. Alexandria, VA: Library of Alexandria.

Phelps, Almira Lincoln. *Address on the Subject of Female Education in Greece, and General Extension of Christian Intercourse among Females*. Troy: Printed by Norman Tuttle, 1833.

——. *Lectures to Young Ladies, Comprising Outlines and Applications of the Different Branches of Female Education, for the Use of Female Schools, and Private Libraries*. Boston: Carter, Hendee and Co., 1833.

Philadelphia (PA) Papers, Greek Fund Committee, American Antiquarian Society.

Platt, Jonas, Abraham Ogden, and Henry C. De Rham. *Report of the Evidence and Reasons of the Award between Johannis Orlandos & Andreas Luriottis, Greek Deputies, of the One Part, and Le Roy, Bayard & Co., and G. G. & S. Howland, of the Other Part*. New York: Printed by W. E. Dean, 1826.

Poinsett, Joel Robert. Papers. Historical Society of Pennsylvania, Philadelphia.

Post, Henry A. V. *A Visit to Greece and Constantinople, in the Year 1827–8*. New York: Sleight and Robinson, 1830.

Proceedings and Debates of the Convention of North-Carolina. Edenton, NC: Hodge and Wills, 1789.

Riley, James. *An Authentic Narrative of the Loss of the American Brig Commerce, Wrecked on the Western Coast of Africa*. New York: T. and W. Mercein, 1817.

——. *Loss of the American Brig Commerce: Wrecked on the Western Coast of Africa*. London: John Murray, 1817.

Sedgwick, Henry D. *Refutation of the Reasons Assigned by the Arbitrators, for Their Award in the Case of the Two Greek Frigates*. New York: Printed by J. Seymour, John Street, 1826.

Snow, Eliza R., "Missolonghi." In *Eliza R. Snow: The Complete Poetry*, edited by Jill Mulvay Derr, 9–11. Provo, UT: Brigham Young University Press, 2009.

Stanton, Elizabeth Cady, Susan Brownell Anthony, Matilda Joslyn Gage, and Ida Husted Harper. *History of Woman Suffrage: 1848–1861*. 3 vols. New York: Fowler and Wells, 1889.

Stephanini, J. *The Personal Narrative of the Sufferings of J. Stephanini*. New York: Vanderpool and Cole, printers, 1829.

Sumner, Charles. *White Slavery in the Barbary States: A Lecture before the Boston Mercantile Library Association*. Boston: William D. Ticknor and Co., 1847.

Treaty between the United States of America and the Ottoman Empire: Commerce and Navigation. Washington, DC: s.n., 1832.

Tyler, Royall. *The Algerine Captive; or, The Life and Adventures of Doctor Updike Underhill, Six Years a Prisoner among the Algerines*. 2 vols. Walpole, NH: David Carlisle, Jr., 1797.

United States Congress. *House Documents, Otherwise Publ. as Executive Documents: 13th Congress, 2d Session–49th Congress, 1st Session*. 22nd Congress, Vol. 6. Washington, DC: Duff Green, 1832.

United States Senate. *Public Documents: Third Session of the Twenty-Fifth Congress*. Vol. 3. Government Printing Office, 1839.

U.S. House Journal. Seventeenth Congress, 2nd session. Washington, D.C.: Gales and Seaton, 1822.

U.S. House Journal. Nineteenth Congress, 2nd session. Washington, D.C.: Gales and Seaton, 1826.

Vaux Family Papers, Historical Society of Pennsylvania.

Walker, David. *Appeal in Four Articles Together with a Preamble, to the Coloured Citizens of the World*. Boston: David Walker, 1829.

Washington, George. *The Papers of George Washington*. Charlottesville: University Press of Virginia, 1987.

Webster, Daniel. *Mr. Webster's Speech on the Greek Revolution*. Washington City: J. S. Meehan, 1824.

Webster, Noah. *An American Selection of Lessons in Reading and Speaking*. New York: C and R Waite, 1802.

——. *Effects of Slavery, on Morals and Industry*. Hartford, CT: Hudson and Goodwin, 1793.

Whittier, John Greenleaf, Wendell Phillips, Harriet Sewall, and Lydia Maria Francis Child. *Letters of Lydia Maria Child*. Boston: Houghton, Mifflin, 1883.

Willard, Emma. *An Address to the Public; Particularly to the Members of the Legislature of New-York, Proposing a Plan for Improving Female Education*. 2nd ed. Middlebury, VT: Printed by J. W. Copeland, 1819.

Willard, Emma, and Troy Society for the Advancement of Female Education in Greece. *Advancement of Female Education: Or, A Series of Addresses, in Favor of Establishing at Athens, in Greece, a Female Seminary, Especially Designed to Instruct Female Teachers*. Troy: Printed by Norman Tuttle, 1833.

Wolff, Joseph. *Travels and Adventures of the Rev. Joseph Wolff*. London: Saunders, Otley, 1861.

Wollstonecraft, Mary. *Vindication of the Rights of Woman: With Strictures on Political and Moral Subjects*. Auckland, NZ: Floating Press, 2010.

Worcester, Samuel M. *Essays on Slavery: Re-Published from the Boston Recorder and Telegraph*. Amherst, MA: Carter and Adams, 1825.

Zachos, J. C. *An Appeal to the Friends of Education, for the Immigrant, and the Freed-People of the South*. Boston: Printed by John Wilson and Son, 1864.

Newspapers and Magazines

Albany (NY) Argus
Alexandria (DC) Daily Advertiser / *Alexandria (DC) Gazette and Daily Advertiser* / *Alexandria (DC) Phenix Gazette*
American Ladies' Magazine / *Ladies' Magazine and Literary Gazette* (Boston)
American Mercury (Hartford, CT)
Augusta (GA) Chronicle and Georgia Advertiser
Baltimore Patriot and Mercantile Advertiser
Boston Commercial Gazette
Boston Daily Advertiser
Boston Daily Atlas
Boston Intelligencer and Evening Gazette
Charleston (SC) Courier
Christian Inquirer (New York)
City Gazette and Commercial Daily Advertiser (Charleston, SC)

Columbian Centinel / Columbian Centinel American Federalist (Boston)
Connecticut Courant (Hartford)
Connecticut Gazette (New London)
Cosmopolitan Art Journal (New York)
Eastern Argus (Portland, ME)
Episcopal Recorder (Philadelphia)
Essex Register (Salem, MA)
Farmer's Cabinet (Amherst, NH)
Federal Gazette (Philadelphia)
Frank Leslie's Illustrated Newspaper (New York)
Freedom's Journal (New York)
Hallowell (ME) Gazette
Hinds County Gazette (Raymond, MS)
Independent Chronicle and Boston Patriot
The Juvenile Miscellany, Or, Friend of Youth (Boston)
Lady's Home Magazine (Philadelphia)
Liberator (Boston)
Macon (GA) Telegraph / Georgia Telegraph
Milwaukee Daily Sentinel
Mississippi Free Trader and Natchez Gazette (Natchez)
Morning News (New London, CT)
National Advocate (New York)
National Era (Washington, DC)
National Gazette and Literary Register (Philadelphia)
New-Bedford (MA) Mercury
New-Hampshire Gazette (Portsmouth)
New Hampshire Patriot and State Gazette (Concord)
New Hampshire Sentinel (Keene)
New-York Commercial Advertiser
New York Herald
New York Observer and Chronicle
New-York Post
New York Spectator
New York Times
North American Review and Miscellaneous Journal / North American Review (Boston)
North Star (Rochester, NY)
Norwich (CT) Courier
Philadelphia Recorder
Pittsfield (MA) Sun
Portsmouth (NH) Journal and Rockingham Gazette
Portsmouth (NH) Journal of Literature and Politics
Providence (RI) Gazette
Providence (RI) Patriot
Republican Star (Easton, MD)

Rhode-Island American (Providence)
Richmond (VA) Enquirer
Rochester (NY) Telegraph
Salem (MA) Gazette
Saratoga (NY) Sentinel
Semi-Weekly Eagle (Brattleboro, VT)
Shamrock (New York)
Times and Hartford (CT) Advertiser
Vermont Gazette (Bennington)
Vermont Watchman (Montpelier)
Washington (DC) Gazette
Watch-Tower (Cooperstown, NY)
Western Courier (Ravenna, OH)
Western Recorder (Utica, NY)

Secondary Sources

Akalin, Esin. "The Ottoman Seraglio on European Stages." In *Ottoman Empire and European Theatre*, vol. 1, *The Age of Mozart and Selim III (1756–1808)*, edited by Michael Hüttler and Hans Ernst Weidinger, 339–73. Vienna: Hollitzer, 2013.

Aksan, Virginia. *Ottoman Wars, 1700–1870: An Empire Besieged*. New York: Routledge, 2007.

Allison, Robert. *The Crescent Obscured: The United States and the Muslim World, 1776–1815*. Chicago: University of Chicago Press, 2000.

Anderson, Benedict. *Imagined Communities: Reflections on the Origin and Spread of Nationalism*. New York: Verso, 2006.

Baepler, Paul Michael. *White Slaves, African Masters: An Anthology of American Barbary Captivity Narratives*. Chicago: University of Chicago Press, 1999.

Bailyn, Bernard. *The Ideological Origins of the American Revolution*. Cambridge, MA: Belknap Press of Harvard University Press, 1967.

Baker, Paul R. "Lord Byron and the Americans in Italy." *Keats-Shelley Journal* 13 (1964): 61–75.

Baron, Hans. *The Crisis of the Early Italian Renaissance: Civic Humanism and Republican Liberty in an Age of Classicism and Tyranny*. Princeton, NJ: Princeton University Press, 1966.

Bass, Gary Jonathan. *Freedom's Battle: The Origins of Humanitarian Intervention*. New York: Vintage, 2009.

Berman, Jacob Rama. *American Arabesque: Arabs, Islam, and the 19th-Century Imaginary*. New York: New York University Press, 2012.

Boylan, Anne M. *Origins of Women's Activism: New York and Boston, 1797–1840*. Chapel Hill: University of North Carolina Press, 2002.

Bradsher, Earl Lockridge. *Mathew Carey, Editor, Author and Publisher: A Study in American Literary Development*. Columbia University Studies in English. New York: Columbia University Press, 1912.

Branson, Susan. *These Fiery Frenchified Dames: Women and Political Culture in Early National Philadelphia*. Philadelphia: University of Pennsylvania Press, 2001.

Brown, Richard D. *Knowledge Is Power: The Diffusion of Information in Early America, 1700–1865*. New York: Oxford University Press, 1989.

Burgess, Thomas. *Greeks in America: An Account of Their Coming, Progress, Customs, Living, and Aspirations; with an Historical Introduction and the Stories of Some Famous American-Greeks*. Boston: Sherman, French and Co., 1913.

Burke, Martin J. "Afterword: Why Should We Listen to Mathew Carey?" *Early American Studies* 11, no. 3 (2013): 583–89.

Bushman, Richard L. *The Refinement of America: Persons, Houses, Cities*. New York: Knopf, 1992.

Butchart, Ronald E. *Schooling the Freed People: Teaching, Learning, and the Struggle for Black Freedom, 1861–1876*. Chapel Hill: University of North Carolina Press, 2010.

Cain, Mary Cathryn. "The Art and Politics of Looking White: Beauty Practice among White Women in Antebellum America." *Winterthur Portfolio* 42, no. 1 (March 2008): 27–50.

Coleman, Arica L. "Notes on the State of Virginia: Jeffersonian Thought and the Rise of Racial Purity Ideology in the Eighteenth Century." In *That the Blood Stay Pure: African Americans, Native Americans, and the Predicament of Race and Identity in Virginia*, 42–63. Bloomington: Indiana University Press, 2013.

Conroy-Krutz, Emily. *Christian Imperialism: Converting the World in the Early American Republic*. Ithaca, NY: Cornell University Press, 2015.

Cooper, Wendy A. *Classical Taste in America 1800–1840*. Baltimore: Abbeville Press, 1993.

Cooper, William J., Jr. *Liberty and Slavery: Southern Politics to 1860*. Columbia: University of South Carolina Press, 2000.

Cornell, Saul. *The Other Founders: Anti-Federalism and the Dissenting Tradition in America, 1788–1828*. Chapel Hill: University of North Carolina Press, 1999.

Culkin, Kate. *Harriet Hosmer: A Cultural Biography*. Amherst: University of Massachusetts Press, 2010.

Dakin, Douglas. *British and American Philhellenes during the War of Greek Independence, 1821–1833*. Thessaloniki: Institute for Balkan Studies, 1955.

Davidson, Cathy N. *Revolution and the Word: The Rise of the Novel in America*. New York: Oxford University Press, 1986.

Davison, Roderic H. *Turkey: A Short History*. Walkington, UK: Eothen Press, 1981.

Dolan, Regina. "Mathew Carey, Citizen and Publisher." *Records of the American Catholic Historical Society of Philadelphia* 65, no. 2 (1954): 116–28.

Dragonas, Thalia G., and Faruk Birtek, eds. *Citizenship and the Nation-State in Greece and Turkey*. Social and Historical Studies on Greece and Turkey. London: Routledge, 2005.

Dunn, John P. "Americans in the Nineteenth Century Egyptian Army: A Selected Bibliography." *Journal of Military History* 70, no. 1 (January 1, 2006): 123–36.

Earle, Edward Mead. "American Interest in the Greek Cause, 1821–1827." *American Historical Review* 33, no. 1 (October 1, 1927): 44–63.

Educational Research Library and Alvina Treut Burrows Institute. *Early American Text-books, 1775–1900: A Catalog of the Titles Held by the Educational Research Library.* Washington, DC: U.S. Department of Education, 1985.

Egan, Jim. *Oriental Shadows: The Presence of the East in Early American Literature.* Columbus: Ohio State University Press, 2011.

Eicher, Peter, *Raising the Flag: America's First Envoys in Faraway Lands.* Lincoln, NE: Potomac Books, 2018.

Erdem, Y. Hakan. "'Do Not Think of the Greeks as Agricultural Labourers': Ottoman Responses to the Greek War of Independence." In Dragonas and Birtek, *Citizenship and the Nation-State,* 67–84.

——. *Slavery in the Ottoman Empire and Its Demise, 1800–1909.* New York: St. Martin's Press, 1996.

Erdem, Yusuf Hakan. "The Greek Revolt and the End of the Old Ottoman Order." In Pizanias, *Greek Revolution,* 257–264.

Faroqhi, Suraiya. *The Ottoman Empire: A Short History.* Translated by Shelley Frisch. Princeton, NJ: Marcus Weiner, 2009.

Faroqhi, Suraiya, and Christoph K. Neumann, eds. *Ottoman Costumes: From Textile to Identity.* Istanbul: Eren, 2004.

Faxon, Alicia. "Images of Women in the Sculpture of Harriet Hosmer." *Woman's Art Journal* 2, no. 1 (April 1, 1981): 25–29.

Field, James A. *America and the Mediterranean World, 1776–1882.* Princeton, NJ: Princeton University Press, 1969.

Finnie, David H. *Pioneers East: The Early American Experience in the Middle East.* Cambridge, MA: Harvard University Press, 1967.

Fitz, Caitlin. *Our Sister Republics: The United States in an Age of American Revolutions.* New York: W. W. Norton, 2016.

Fleming, K. E. "Historiography, Historical Context, Sources, and a Brief Biography." In *The Muslim Bonaparte: Diplomacy and Orientalism in Ali Pasha's Greece,* 18–35. Princeton, NJ: Princeton University Press, 1999.

Gallman, Robert E. "Changes in the Level of Literacy in a New Community of Early America." *Journal of Economic History* 48, no. 3 (September 1, 1988): 567–82.

Ginzberg, Lori D. *Untidy Origins: A Story of Woman's Rights in Antebellum New York.* Chapel Hill: University of North Carolina Press, 2005.

Goloboy, Jennifer L. "The Early American Middle Class" *Journal of the Early Republic* 25, no. 4 (2005): 537–545.

Gordon-Reed, Annette. *The Hemingses of Monticello: An American Family.* New York: W. W. Norton, 2008.

Green, James N. *Mathew Carey, Publisher and Patriot.* Philadelphia: Library Company of Philadelphia, 1985.

Green, Vivien M. "Hiram Powers's 'Greek Slave': Emblem of Freedom." *American Art Journal* 14, no. 4 (October 1, 1982): 31–39.

Hall, David D. *Cultures of Print: Essays in the History of the Book.* Amherst: University of Massachusetts Press, 1996.

Hall, Mark David. "Emma Willard on the Political Position of Women." *Hungarian Journal of English and American Studies (HJEAS)* 6, no. 2 (2000): 11–26.

Hamadeh, Shirine. "Ottoman Expressions of Early Modernity and the 'Inevitable' Question of Westernization." *Journal of the Society of Architectural Historians* 63, no. 1 (2004): 32–51.

Hansen, Karen V. *A Very Social Time: Crafting Community in Antebellum New England.* Berkeley: University of California Press, 1994.

Hatch, Nathan O. *The Democratization of American Christianity.* New Haven, CT: Yale University Press, 1989.

Heraclides, Alexis, and Ada Dialla. "Intervention in the Greek War of Independence, 1821–32." In *Humanitarian Intervention in the Long Nineteenth Century: Setting the Precedent,* 105–33. Manchester: Manchester University Press, 2015.

Herzfeld, Michael. *Ours Once More: Folklore, Ideology, and the Making of Modern Greece.* Austin: University of Texas Press, 1982.

Hewitt, Nancy A. *Women's Activism and Social Change: Rochester, New York, 1822–1872.* Ithaca, NY: Cornell University Press, 1984.

Heyrman, Christine Leigh. *American Apostles: When Evangelicals Entered the World of Islam.* New York: Hill and Wang, 2015.

Hinks, Peter P. *To Awaken My Afflicted Brethren: David Walker and the Problem of Antebellum Slave Resistance.* University Park: Pennsylvania State University Press, 2010.

Howe, Daniel Walker. *What Hath God Wrought: The Transformation of America, 1815–1848.* New York: Oxford University Press, 2007.

Ilicak, H. Sukru. "The Revolt of Alexandros Ipsilantis and the Fate of the Fanariots in Ottoman Documents." In Pizanias, *Greek Revolution,* 225–239.

Ilicak, Huseyin Sukru. "A Radical Rethinking of Empire: Ottoman State and Society during the Greek War of Independence." PhD diss., Harvard University, 2011.

Jeffrey, Julie Roy. *The Great Silent Army of Abolitionism: Ordinary Women in the Antislavery Movement.* Chapel Hill: University of North Carolina Press, 1998.

Jehlen, Myra, and Michael Warner. *The English Literatures of America, 1500–1800.* London: Routledge, 1997.

Jirousek, Charlotte. "Ottoman Influences in Western Dress." In Faroqhi and Neumann, *Ottoman Costumes,* 231–251.

Keetley, Dawn Elizabeth, and John Charles Pettegrew, eds. *Public Women, Public Words: A Documentary History of American Feminism.* Madison, WI: Madison House, 1997.

Kelley, Mary. *Learning to Stand and Speak: Women, Education, and Public Life in America's Republic.* Chapel Hill: University of North Carolina Press, 2006.

Kerber, Linda K. *Women of the Republic: Intellect and Ideology in Revolutionary America.* Chapel Hill: University of North Carolina Press, 1997.

Kerr, Andrea Moore. *Lucy Stone: Speaking Out for Equality.* New Brunswick, NJ: Rutgers University Press, 1992.

Kierner, Cynthia A. *Beyond the Household: Women's Place in the Early South, 1700–1835.* Ithaca, NY: Cornell University Press, 1998.

Kietzman, Mary Jo. "Montagu's Turkish Embassy Letters and Cultural Dislocation." *Studies in English Literature, 1500–1900* 38, no. 3 (July 1, 1998): 537–51.

Lambert, Frank. *The Barbary Wars: American Independence in the Atlantic World*. New York: Hill and Wang, 2005.

Larrabee, Stephen Addison. *Hellas Observed: The American Experience of Greece, 1775–1865*. New York: New York University Press, 1957.

Lockley, Timothy James. *Welfare and Charity in the Antebellum South*. New Perspectives on the History of the South. Gainesville: University Press of Florida, 2007.

Lockridge, Kenneth A. *Literacy in Colonial New England: An Enquiry into the Social Context of Literacy in the Early Modern West*. New York: W. W. Norton, 1979.

Macintyre, Ben. *The Man Who Would Be King: The First American in Afghanistan*. New York: Farrar, Straus and Giroux, 2004.

Makdisi, Ussama Samir. *Artillery of Heaven: American Missionaries and the Failed Conversion of the Middle East*. Ithaca, NY: Cornell University Press, 2008.

Manganelli, Kimberly Snyder. *Transatlantic Spectacles of Race: The Tragic Mulatta and the Tragic Muse*. New Brunswick, NJ: Rutgers University Press, 2012.

Marchand, Suzanne L. *Down from Olympus: Archaeology and Philhellenism in Germany, 1750–1970*. Princeton, NJ: Princeton University Press, 1996.

Marr, Timothy. *The Cultural Roots of American Islamicism*. Cambridge: Cambridge University Press, 2006.

Mason, Matthew. *Apostle of Union: A Political Biography of Edward Everett*. Chapel Hill: University of North Carolina Press, 2016.

——. *Slavery and Politics in the Early American Republic*. Chapel Hill: University of North Carolina Press, 2006.

McDaniel, W. Caleb. *The Problem of Democracy in the Age of Slavery: Garrisonian Abolitionists and Transatlantic Reform*. Baton Rouge: Louisiana State University Press, 2013.

McKivigan, John R. *Abolitionism and Issues of Race and Gender*. New York: Garland, 1999.

McMillen, Sally. *Seneca Falls and the Origins of the Women's Rights Movement*. New York: Oxford University Press, 2008.

McNeal, R. A. "Athens and Nineteenth-Century Panoramic Art." *International Journal of the Classical Tradition* 1, no. 3 (1995): 80–97.

——. "Joseph Allen Smith, American Grand Tourist." *International Journal of the Classical Tradition* 4, no. 1 (July 1, 1997): 64–91.

Morgan, Edmund Sears. *American Slavery, American Freedom: The Ordeal of Colonial Virginia*. New York: W. W. Norton, 1975.

Morison, S. E. "Forcing the Dardanelles in 1810: With Some Account of the Early Levant Trade of Massachusetts." *New England Quarterly* 1, no. 2 (1928): 208–25.

Moskos, Charles C. *Greek Americans: Struggle and Success*. New Brunswick, NJ: Transaction, 1989.

Muller, Gilbert H. *William Cullen Bryant: Author of America*. Albany: State University of New York Press, 2010.

Murray, John. *Thomas Hope: 1769–1831 and the Neo-Classical Idea*. London: William Clowes, 1968.

Nance, Susan. *How the Arabian Nights Inspired the American Dream, 1790–1935*. Chapel Hill: University of North Carolina Press, 2009.

Nash, Margaret A. "Rethinking Republican Motherhood: Benjamin Rush and the Young Ladies' Academy of Philadelphia." *Journal of the Early Republic* 17, no. 2 (July 1, 1997): 171–91.

Nord, David Paul. "Benevolent Books: Printing, Religion, and Reform." In *A History of the Book in America*, vol. 2, *An Extensive Republic: Print, Culture, and Society in the New Nation, 1790–1840*, edited by Robert A. Gross and Mary Kelley, 221–46. Chapel Hill: University of North Carolina Press, 2010.

Obenzinger, Hilton. "Holy Land Narrative and American Covenant: Levi Parsons, Pliny Fisk, and the Palestine Mission." *Religion and Literature* 35, no. 2/3 (July 1, 2003): 241–67.

Oren, Michael B. *Power, Faith, and Fantasy: America in the Middle East, 1776 to the Present*, New York: W. W. Norton, 2007.

Panagiotopoulos, Vasilis. "The Filiki Etaireia (Society of Friends) Organizational Preconditions of the National War of Independence." In Pizanias, *Greek Revolution*, 101–128.

Pappas, Alexandre. *Greek Revolution and the American Muse: A Collection of Philhellenic Poetry, 1821–1828*. Thessaloniki: Institute for Balkan Studies, 1972.

Pappas, Paul Constantine. "The United States and the Greek War for Independence, 1821–1828." PhD diss., West Virginia University, 1982.

Pasley, Jeffrey L. *"The Tyranny of Printers": Newspaper Politics in the Early American Republic*. Jeffersonian America. Charlottesville: University of Virginia Press, 2001.

Perlmann, Joel, and Dennis Shirley. "When Did New England Women Acquire Literacy?" *William and Mary Quarterly* 48, no. 1 (1991): 50–67.

Peskin, Lawrence A. *Captives and Countrymen: Barbary Slavery and the American Public, 1785–1816*. Baltimore: Johns Hopkins University Press, 2009.

Petrino, Elizabeth A. "'A Chain of Correspondence': Social Activism and Civic Values in the Letters of Lydia Sigourney." In *The Edinburgh Companion to Nineteenth-Century American Letters and Letter-Writing*, edited by Celeste-Marie Bernier, Judie Newman, and Matthew Pethers, 450–64. Edinburgh: Edinburgh University Press, 2016.

Petropulos, John Anthony. "The Revolutionary Period, 1821–27: The Origins of the Parties." In *Politics and Statecraft in the Kingdom of Greece, 1833–1843*, 53–106. Princeton, NJ: Princeton University Press, 1968.

Philliou, Christine M. *Biography of an Empire: Governing Ottomans in an Age of Revolution*. Berkeley: University of California Press, 2011.

Pizanias, Petros. "From Reaya to Greek Citizen: Enlightenment and Revolution, 1750–1832." In Pizanias, *Greek Revolution*, 11–84.

Pizanias, Petros, ed. *The Greek Revolution of 1821: A European Event*. Istanbul: Isis Press, 2011.

Pocock, J. G. A. *The Machiavellian Moment: Florentine Political Thought and the Atlantic Republican Tradition*. Princeton, NJ: Princeton University Press, 1975.

Prins, Yopie. "Classics for Victorians: Response." *Victorian Studies* 52, no. 1 (2009): 52–62.

Quataert, Donald. *The Ottoman Empire, 1700–1922*. New York: Cambridge University Press, 2005.

Rawes, Alan. "Lord Byron." In *The Edinburgh History of Scottish Literature: Enlightenment, Britain and Empire (1707–1918)*, edited by Susan Manning, Ian Brown, Thomas Owen Clancy, Murray Pittock, Ksenija Horvat, and Ashley Hales, 178–82. Edinburgh: Edinburgh University Press, 2007.

Reinhold, Meyer. *Classica Americana: The Greek and Roman Heritage in the United States.* Detroit: Wayne State University Press, 1984.

Repousis, Angelo. "'The Cause of the Greeks': Philadelphia and the Greek War for Independence, 1821–1828." *Pennsylvania Magazine of History and Biography* 123, no. 4 (October 1, 1999): 333–63.

——. *Greek-American Relations from Monroe to Truman.* Kent, OH: Kent State University Press, 2013.

——. "'The Trojan Women': Emma Hart Willard and the Troy Society for the Advancement of Female Education in Greece." *Journal of the Early Republic* 24, no. 3 (October 1, 2004): 445–76.

Richard, Carl J. *The Founders and the Classics: Greece, Rome, and the American Enlightenment.* Cambridge, MA: Harvard University Press, 1994.

——. *The Golden Age of the Classics in America: Greece, Rome, and the Antebellum United States.* Cambridge, MA: Harvard University Press, 2009.

Richmond, Steven. *The Voice of England in the East: Stratford Canning and Diplomacy with the Ottoman Empire.* London: Bloomsbury, 2014.

Richter, Daniel K. *Facing East from Indian Country: A Native History of Early America.* Cambridge, MA: Harvard University Press, 2001.

Rodogno, Davide. *Against Massacre: Humanitarian Interventions in the Ottoman Empire, 1815–1914.* Princeton, NJ: Princeton University Press, 2012.

Roessel, David Ernest. *In Byron's Shadow: Modern Greece in the English and American Imagination.* Oxford: Oxford University Press, 2002.

Roland, Alex. "Secrecy, Technology, and War: Greek Fire and the Defense of Byzantium, 678–1204." *Technology and Culture* 33, no. 4 (October 1, 1992): 655–79.

Rouleau, Brian. *With Sails Whitening Every Sea: Mariners and the Making of an American Maritime Empire.* Ithaca, NY: Cornell University Press, 2014.

Rozbicki, Michal Jan. *Culture and Liberty in the Age of the American Revolution.* Charlottesville: University of Virginia Press, 2011.

Said, Edward W. *Orientalism.* New York: Pantheon Books, 1978.

Salerno, Beth A. *Sister Societies: Women's Antislavery Organizations in Antebellum America.* DeKalb: Northern Illinois University Press, 2008.

Sanchez-Eppler, Karen. "Bodily Bonds: The Intersecting Rhetorics of Feminism and Abolition." In *Abolitionism and Issues of Race and Gender*, edited by John R. McKivigan. New York: Garland, 1999.

Santelli, Maureen Connors. "'Depart from That Retired Circle': Women's Support of the Greek War for Independence and Antebellum Reform." *Early American Studies: An Interdisciplinary Journal* 15, no. 1 (2017): 194–223.

Schroeder, John H. *Commodore John Rodgers: Paragon of the Early American Navy.* New Perspectives on Maritime History and Nautical Archaeology. Gainesville: University Press of Florida, 2006.

Schueller, Malini Johar. *U.S. Orientalisms: Race, Nation, and Gender in Literature, 1790–1890.* Ann Arbor: University of Michigan Press, 1998.

Schwartzberg, Steven. "The Lion and the Phoenix—1: British Policy toward the 'Greek Question,' 1831–32." *Middle Eastern Studies* 24, no. 2 (1988): 139–77.

Sellers, Charles. *The Market Revolution: Jacksonian America, 1815–1846.* Oxford: Oxford University Press, 1994.

Sellers, Mortimer. *American Republicanism: Roman Ideology in the United States Constitution.* New York: New York University Press, 1994.

Shalev, Eran. *Rome Reborn on Western Shores: Historical Imagination and the Creation of the American Republic.* Charlottesville: University Press of Virginia, 2009.

Shankman, Andrew. "Capitalism, Slavery, and the New Epoch: Mathew Carey's 1819." In *Slavery's Capitalism: A New History of American Economic Development*, edited by Sven Beckert and Seth Rockman, 243–61. Philadelphia: University of Pennsylvania Press, 2016.

———. "Neither Infinite Wretchedness nor Positive Good: Mathew Carey and Henry Clay on Political Economy and Slavery during the Long 1820s." In *Contesting Slavery: The Politics of Bondage and Freedom in the New American Nation*, edited by John Craig Hammond and Matthew Mason, 247–66. Charlottesville: University Press of Virginia, 2011.

Shoemaker, Nancy. "The Extraterritorial United States to 1860." *Diplomatic History* 42, no. 1 (January 1, 2018): 36–54.

Sinha, Manisha. *The Slave's Cause: A History of Abolition.* Reprint ed. New Haven, CT: Yale University Press, 2017.

Spellberg, Denise A. "Islam in America: Adventures in Neo-Orientalism." *Review of Middle East Studies* 43, no. 1 (2009): 25–35.

———. *Thomas Jefferson's Qur'an: Islam and the Founders.* 1st ed. New York: Alfred A. Knopf, 2013.

St. Clair, William. *Lord Elgin and the Marbles.* Oxford: Oxford University Press, 1998.

———. *That Greece Might Still Be Free: The Philhellenes in the War of Independence.* Cambridge: Open Book, 2008.

Stein, Melissa N. "'Races of Men': Ethnology in Antebellum America." In *Measuring Manhood: Race and the Science of Masculinity, 1830–1934*, 27–88. Minneapolis: University of Minnesota Press, 2015.

Toledano, Ehud R. "Late Ottoman Concepts of Slavery (1830s–1880s)." *Poetics Today* 14, no. 3 (1993): 477–506.

Travers, Len. *Celebrating the Fourth: Independence Day and the Rites of Nationalism in the Early Republic.* Rev. ed. Amherst: University of Massachusetts Press, 1999.

Trent, James W. *The Manliest Man: Samuel G. Howe and the Contours of Nineteenth-Century American Reform.* Boston: University of Massachusetts Press, 2012.

Umunç, Himmet. "In Search of Exoticism: Byron's Reveries of the Ottoman Orient." In *Ottoman Empire and European Theatre*, vol. 3, *Images of the Harem in Literature and Theatre*, edited by Michael Hüttler, Emily M. N. Kugler, and Hans Ernst Weidinger, 327–40. Vienna: Hollitzer, 2015.

Verney, Michael A. "An Eye for Prices, an Eye for Souls: Americans in the Indian Sub-continent, 1784–1838." *Journal of the Early Republic* 33, no. 3 (2013): 397–431.

Vivian, Cassandra. *Americans in Egypt, 1770–1915: Explorers, Consuls, Travelers, Soldiers, Missionaries, Writers, and Scientists.* Jefferson, NC: McFarland, 2012.

Waldstreicher, David. *In the Midst of Perpetual Fetes: The Making of American Nationalism, 1776–1820.* Chapel Hill: University of North Carolina Press, 1997.

Walther, Karine V. *Sacred Interests: The United States and the Islamic World, 1821–1921.* Chapel Hill: University of North Carolina Press, 2015.

Warner, Michael. *The Letters of the Republic: Publication and the Public Sphere in Eighteenth-Century America.* Cambridge, MA: Harvard University Press, 1990.

Wertheimer, Eric. "Commencement Ceremonies: History and Identity in 'The Rising Glory of America,' 1771 and 1786." *Early American Literature* 29, no. 1 (January 1, 1994): 35–58.

Winterer, Caroline. *The Culture of Classicism: Ancient Greece and Rome in American Intellectual Life, 1780–1910.* Baltimore: Johns Hopkins University Press, 2004.

——. *The Mirror of Antiquity: American Women and the Classical Tradition, 1750–1900.* Ithaca, NY: Cornell University Press, 2009.

Wood, Gordon S. *The Creation of the American Republic, 1776–1787.* Chapel Hill: University of North Carolina Press, 1998.

Yeazell, Ruth Bernard. *Harems of the Mind: Passages of Western Art and Literature.* New Haven, CT: Yale University Press, 2000.

Yothers, Brian. *The Romance of the Holy Land in American Travel Writing, 1790–1876.* Burlington, VT: Ashgate, 2013.

Zagarri, Rosemarie. *Revolutionary Backlash: Women and Politics in the Early American Republic.* Philadelphia: University of Pennsylvania Press, 2007.

——. "The Significance of the 'Global Turn' for the Early American Republic: Globalization in the Age of Nation-Building." *Journal of the Early Republic* 31, no. 1 (2011): 1–37.

Zarinebaf, Fariba. "Istanbul in the Tulip Age." In *Crime and Punishment in Istanbul: 1700–1800,* 11–34. Berkeley: University of California Press, 2010.

Zelinsky, Wilbur. "Classical Town Names in the United States: The Historical Geography of an American Idea." *Geographical Review* 57, no. 4 (October 1, 1967): 463–95.

Index

Women (*continued*)
  mothers, roles as, 38, 39, 85, 174–175, 177
  in Ottoman culture, Western perceptions of,
    14, 37–38, 39–40, 104, 144, 155, 156,
    177, 179–180 (*see also* harem)
  See also benevolence; education reform;
    women's rights
women's rights
  education (*see* education reform; Willard,
    Emma)
  as extending the domestic sphere, 9–10, 172,
    178, 196, 211n6
  and fashion, 189–192
  philhellenic influence on, 114, 155–156, 161,
    163, 172, 173, 178–179, 185, 189, 197,
    198

  and slavery, linked with, 178, 179, 185–186,
    223n115
  suffrage movement, 192, 197–198
  symbolized in art, 185–189, 223n127
Worcester, Samuel, 169, 221n50

Ypsilantis, Alexandros, 24
  proclamation of uprising, 61, 62
  Russia, assumed support from, 60
  See also Filiki Etaireia

Zachos, John, 105, 169, 170–171, 221n65
  as an abolitionist, 172
Zagarri, Rosemarie, 11
Zenobia in Chains, (Harriet Hosmer), 186–189,
  223n127

CPSIA information can be obtained
at www.ICGtesting.com
Printed in the USA
LVHW051802031120
670608LV00021B/276/J